ALL RISE

Tales of Human Rights & Wrongs

ROGER CHENNELLS

ISBN 978-0-6397-7042-0

First published 2023 by
Roger Chennells
5 van Zyl Street
Somerset West
South Africa
scarlin@iafrica.com

Editing and proofreading: Anne Haarhoff
Text and cover design: Dominic Haarhoff

Front cover: Photo 15163834 / Namib Desert © Agap13 | Dreamstime.com
San in the Kalahari, Rex Reynolds, 1966
Back cover: Photograph of author by Amanda de Klerk
Aboriginal D55466779 © Pominoz Dreamstime.com
Title page: Gavel 33581700 / Law Scales © Sadalaxmi Rawa Dreamstime.com

Typeset in Palatino Linotype

For Amanda

and my children

Rebecca, Guy, Oliver, Clara, Sebastian

Contents

Acknowledgements

As a jumble of stories emerged several friends provided early encouragement, in particular Chris James, John Shepstone, Doris Schroeder, Merle Levin and Grace Garland.

Dorian Haarhoff encouraged me to turn what was a casual hobby into a viable project, namely the sharing of my experiences with a wider audience. His midwifery was light and masterful.

Antony Osler, a lawyer-turned-wordsmith with a flair for anarchic alchemy, inspired me.

Throughout all this, my life-partner Amanda de Klerk provided incisive comments and motivation, together with pots of Earl Grey tea.

And lastly, I want to acknowledge my clients and friends – many in low places – who inhabit these stories, but will probably not read this book. I am grateful for having met and learned so much from them all.

Foreword

Roger Chennells and I have shared this universe for a number of decades, being in the same kind of business and enjoying the same absurdities. A teasingly affectionate friendship that kept us afloat in difficult times. A friendship grounded in the conviction that our work in this life was to speak for those who had no voice.

To outsiders, Roger appeared to stroll whistlingly through the last years of the Apartheid state in South Africa. But his laconic, self-deprecatory style hid a nature that felt deeply the unfairness in our midst. He was always a person first, a lawyer second, meaning that he was ever willing to take off his tie and jacket on behalf of others and get his hands dirty.

Although he would never say it himself, Roger's professional contribution to South Africa was a deeply significant one, a principled stand at a pivotal time and, perhaps inevitably, a contribution more honoured outside the borders of his own country than inside. He stood up for the underdog with courage and good humour, as these stories show. There is also a great deal of skill in his craft. As many learned to their cost, Roger's courtesy and likeableness led legal opponents to underestimate him at their peril – for he was a *skelm* at heart, a trickster.

I have been reading the drafts of Roger's stories with a mixture of laughter and tears, and with gratitude for the infectious enthusiasm of a life fully and chaotically lived. They are both a testimony to his humanity and a tribute to his work.

He doesn't often ask favours, so the request for a foreword to this book was done with much hand-wringing. I meant to get my revenge here but, however hard I try, I cannot find a way to write this with the proper degree of insult. On the contrary, I feel honoured. I don't know how I will get over it.

Antony Osler
Colesberg
2023

Introduction

The authentic individual is neither an end nor a beginning, but a link between ages, both memory and expectation —Rabbi Abraham

I love stories. Whether deep and poignant, or light and frivolous, they are the threads from which our lives are woven. From my mother's bedtime stories, later to camp fire, ghost, apocryphal, tall and mythical, they have always enriched my life. It was only after sitting around fires with the San and later discovering the songlines of the Australian Aborigines that I began to fathom the bigger picture. Each of our lives is stitched together out of these tales, including our own family stories and myths, which together create our own broader meaning and context.

After spending time in Australia in the early 1990s, I began to record and assemble stories from my own 'songlines'. No spilling of beans on precious family, siblings, children and past marriages for obvious reasons, although occasionally they make guest appearances. I also shied away from weaving life lessons into the text, mainly because my most significant learnings do not impart easily to the written word, plus out of a fear inculcated in me by Aboriginal mentors. "If you record words in writing, they can be captured, misinterpreted, and later regretted." I get that. The truths that have shown themselves to me have their roots in mystery and wonder, are 'carried on the wind', and should rather be inferred or guessed at than explained.

Despite my career being that of a lawyer – the San jokingly referred to me as their *looier*, a tanner, or more colloquially, confuser – most of the tales in this book focus on individuals and situations, rather than on only law. I do believe that the Law is an excellent foundation for a career involving service, however, our being referred to jokingly as sharks reflects a generally disparaging public assumption. Nor does the term human rights refer to any morally superior endeavour; in my experience those choosing to work for the weak or less privileged are in no way more noble or worthy.

I have enjoyed pulling these stories out of the dreamlike past. Many of them involve me in idiot mode, and so it would be nice to conclude by saying that I finally emerged somewhat enlightened. Unfortunately, I cannot confirm that at all. The nicknames given to me over my lifespan also conspire to show an erratic trajectory:

Kandawengulube (head of a pig, soon after birth), Stulumazambane (potato stew, early days on the farm), Rog Pog (family name, due to shape and appetite), Die Kat (the cat, in Cape townships), Legs (during Pietermaritzburg law clerk years), Trophy (given by youngsters in the Strand surf) and finally, amongst San communities, Rotman. All far from honourable, by any stretch of the imagination.

My purpose with this book is firstly to entertain but also to inspire, and encourage others to share their stories, however humble and innocuous or poignant and meaningful. All our stories are worthy of telling, and the feelings they evoke confirm our shared humanity.

EARLY DAYS

1

Potato Stew

Leaping to my feet without embarrassment and assuming the crouched stance of a Zulu warrior, I grabbed one of the fighting sticks and launched into a furious war-dance routine around the room. The dust flew, with me grunting brutally at the appropriate moments of victory over the enemy. The small audience hooted and cheered with loud exclamations of approval when the dance was over. "Haibabo, madoda! (Wow, men!), "What a man this boy is!" and "Yo! This guy can dance!" were uttered amidst claps and laughter.

From about the age of four or five, after the midday family meal, I would leave our cosy and ordered house and stroll up to the beckoning universe of the farmyard beyond. Here ducks and chickens scuffled for morsels on the stony gravel, the air laden with competing aromas of manures, produce, growth and decay. Calves nuzzled each other in a pen, fretfully awaiting their mothers who lowed mournfully from the nearby shed. Wild-eyed goats (destined to be sold to Zulus for sacrificial slaughter to appease the ancestors) scavenged for food oblivious to their less than rosy futures. An anarchic turkey flock hustled about like a gang of football yobbos on match day with mischief and mayhem in mind. Every so often a cacophony of gobbles signified a frenzied peck-fest when they would suddenly turn on one of their own and peck it to death. A mangled turkey corpse would be visible proof that the pecking order, atavistic and ruthless, was lived out daily in the farmyard.

Acrid wood smoke wisping out of a grubby room near the cowshed exerted an irresistible magnetism to a perpetually hungry red-headed boy. In the dark interior, three Zulu men, Jabulani the stock man, Ngema the 'domestic' and Ephraim the gardener, sometimes joined by one or two casual workers, squatted on their haunches in the smoky gloom around a three-legged cast iron cooking pot.

My entrance was always exciting and unfailingly marked with the jocular welcome, "Hayi, nantsi u Loger" (Hayi, here comes Roger). Jabulani, handsome and athletic – often with chickenshit squished between his splayed toes – wore a bright orange overall that denoted his high-status job as head of cows. Ngema, a sombre and muscled warrior, stoically suffered the gross indignity caused by his white cotton with red trim 'houseboy' outfit – de rigueur for domestic workers those days in Natal. Ephraim, the youngest, whose job as gardener denoted a lower social status, was the joker in the group and was teased mercilessly by the others about his seduction of the female gardeners who entered his leafy domain. With confidence and anticipation, I entered this twilight and enticing world.

The smell from the blackened three-legged pot was intoxicating; a thick bubbling stew containing treasures of chunky meat and potatoes, garnished with wild spinach, vegetables and herbs of the day. Gristle and bone floated between unknowable objects, surprise ingredients jostling with recognisable items. My agenda, namely to satisfy a perpetual hunger, was no secret, but first there would be preliminaries. Easy banter exchanged, while the men indulged and teased me as a curious diversion from their adult worlds.

Squatting on my haunches amongst them and chatting happily in response to their remarks, I shared in the important tasks such as re-arranging the burning logs, sniffing the delicious aromas and prodding at the ingredients when the lid was lifted for inspection. Glorious lumps of *nyama, amathambo, namafutha* (meat, bones and fat) floated in the mix. Large, round lumps, the *amazambani* (whole potatoes), got softer and softer as the stew bubbled, accompanied by the *amakaroti, ubontjhisi, nethanga, nomfino* (carrots, beans, pumpkin and wild spinach) that gave each day's stew its special character.

Soon the men reverted to grown-up repartee involving work, women and compound life. Stories and jokes of the bawdiest nature flew far over my head. Some I cottoned onto, such as the frequent references to women with *amathanga amahle* (lovely pumpkins), the word *thanga* (pumpkin) used as slang for buttocks. Warmly accepted in that masculine world, I did not need to understand the adult humour in the air. Luxuriant farts broke the murky silence, causing instant hilarity between us, as readily as on a junior school playground.

Soon the ripening smells and tastes would announce the readiness of the food. Time to move onto the next phase of business. Eating. It had become the expectation, eventually the rule, that if I had any hopes of sharing their feast, I would first need to perform. "Giya, Stulumazambane, giya!" (Dance, Potato Stew, dance!) would be my cue for action.

Leaping to my feet I assumed that crouched stance. And I danced those energetic high-kicking steps of the war dance until the dust flew. Before long the quid pro quo – a steaming ration of stew – was ladled out onto a chipped enamel plate, together with a generous helping of *putu* (dried mealie porridge). By now perspiring furiously in the hot room, with my performance obligations over, I settled onto my haunches to eat the feast using the fingers of my right hand.

On one memorable Sunday afternoon, some time after the routine had been firmly established, I opened the humble door to find the room filled with ten strangers (some of whom I recognised from the cane-cutting team) who'd been invited to enjoy the stew as well as the white boy's performance that was fast becoming farmyard lore. I pretended nonchalance as I entered the crowded room to the usual murmurs of welcome. This was going to be showtime! For better or worse, my performance was going to reach a wider audience.

When the invitation finally came to "Giya, Stulumazambane," I leaped to give it my all. I added extra touches to my vigorous routine and proceeded to annihilate the imaginary enemy with adrenaline-charged fury. By the time I finally fell backwards onto the ground in the semi-comical hero's demise that signals the end of the mock-battle, I was pouring with sweat. The applause echoed beyond the walls. Laughter, thigh-clapping and exclamations of awe were laced with wry humour at the spectacle of the boss's plump son dancing in exchange for a plate of potato stew. As the applause died down, I basked in the glow of approval as we ate stew together on the dusty floor.

Decades later I visited the farm, now owned by my brother Jono and wife Janey. It was 1992. Mandela had been freed, the National Peace Accord had been signed and South Africa was awakening from its long Apartheid nightmare. I now lived in the faraway Cape, uprooted. As leaders of political parties strove to negotiate at the forum named CODESA,[1] killings were taking place around the country instigated by an alleged 'third force' intent on destabilising progress. The Boipatong massacre had just taken place leaving forty-three people dead, and the Hope after Mandela's release in 1990 was fast giving way to Despair in many hearts.

Feeling down, I took a slow walk through the old banana patch where the turkeys used to squabble, past the old chicken run, up to the beloved old compound. As I strolled past a group of old men sitting on a log in the sun, from an old timer came the shout, "Hau madoda, nants' u Stulumazambane" (Hey men, here comes Potato Stew).

I recognised the man as Ngema, the former houseboy, now grey-haired and grizzled with age. To my surprise this greeting was then followed, somewhat cheekily, by the old invitation, "Giya, Stulumazambane!" As this call resonated in my memory, I found myself poised for a long second between shyness and recklessness.

Tossing off the blanket of self-consciousness that had long settled over decades of 'adulthood', I reverted to that innocent and ever-hungry boy and launched into the vigorous steps of the old potato stew war dance. Within the first few seconds I was puffing like a hog, whilst the men hooted and slapped their thighs. Afterwards we chatted briefly. Reminiscing about the old days, many of the men commented on how I had grown old like my father, clearly meant as a compliment. As I went on my way the men continued to joke, exclaiming excitedly until I was out of earshot.

Such nostalgia makes me lightheaded and, like the concoction in the cast iron pot, has a haunting array of ingredients. The feeling of being accepted, even loved, by those African men had bubbled and seeped into my very marrow, into my very stew, as the smells and sounds of that distant smoky room were evoked in a flash. A scatterling of Africa I am, journeying to the stars, with a burning hunger for my country as expressed by Johnny Clegg in that exuberant iconic song, "Scatterlings of Africa."

I knew in an instant I would dance again, anytime, and would give anything for another afternoon with that potato stew.

2

Judas Iscariot in the Playground

The journey of love is perilous. At the age of ten boys simply did not speak about girls, let alone to them. They were forbidden as a species and a topic, so naturally my life skills in that encounter were lacking.

Despite this taboo, I secretly ogled Alison Noelle every available moment. A pretty girl, clean and fresh, she was a small and cuter version of my own mum. Every move she made in class, every word she uttered was furtively observed, and simply confirmed her utter perfection. She could do no wrong. That cute nose, those dimpled knees and how she carelessly tossed those blond locks off her forehead were all growing proof that she was the most desirable girl in existence. This feeling grew steadily until it had become a version of that stomach-churning state that I would later identify as 'love'. Whenever she caught me gazing at her, I would turn away, heart thumping and blush rising, pretending to sharpen a pencil, or rearrange my stationery. Or check my shoelaces.

On the rare occasions I found her staring at me, she turned crimson and pretended to be fascinated by the contents of her own pencil box or fiddle with her pink watch strap. Or with the book on her desk. This tentative dance moved forward at a songololo's pace, but soon we were equally smitten, wallowing in swamplands of unexpressed attraction. But how to take such a secret, forbidden longing forward?

One day, during morning break, whilst she was outside playing with her friends, I summoned my courage and made a bold move. In the empty classroom, heart pounding, I placed a chocolate sweet in her desk with a note: *Dear Alison, I hope you like chocolate. Love from, Roger.* Ms Mumby's maths class followed the break. I watched Alison intently through slit eyes, like a cobra his intended prey. Finding the note, her cheeks flushed pink. Then she read it slowly, smiling coyly, and peeled the wrapper off ever so carefully. Next, she ate it nibble by teeny nibble as Ms Mumby's voice droned on in the distance.

Not one glance came in my direction, but I knew, with ineffable knowing, that every bite was a further confirmation of her love. My elation knew no bounds, my joy extreme. Her eating of my chocolate had symbolically sealed our fates. We would, of course, share the perfect marriage. A cute house in a leafy suburb, children plus dogs and live happily ever after. It was so clear, all just a matter of time. I was popping to share the news with somebody, but with whom? That night I slept happily, folding the delicious secret in my bulging heart.

Morning break in Eshowe Primary School was where everything happened. Boys and girls, being different species, played their various games intensely during the allotted twenty minutes in separate parts of the playground. The girls' section had benches and mown lawn under shady trees, while the boys occupied the open fields, cricket nets and swings. Open gates, stingers, tops, marbles, swings and occasionally fist fights occupied the boys, whilst softer pastimes unknown to our sex kept the girls engrossed.

The next day, after Alison's and my unspoken engagement by chocolate, my trusty gang had captured the much-prized playground swings for break. I was on the prized middle swing, surrounded by my loyal sidekicks: Skeens, Ob, Blake, Tick and Dick. A tight band of brothers, committed to our gang rules which included loyalty to one another, secret passwords, code words, and then the usual taboo, no girls.

I was showing off by swinging as high and dangerously as possible, when suddenly an unwelcome sight disturbed our playground harmony. A posse of girls marched determinedly in our direction, giggling, chattering loudly and nudging one another in that way girls sometimes do. What worried me most was Penny Prince, the feared girl bully of our form. She strode boldly at the front. One of eleven siblings, Penny was razor-tongued, abrasive and fearless. Many a boy had been known to run away crying after an encounter with her unbridled meanness. A girl to be avoided.

A hollow feeling rose from my stomach up to my neck as the column marched towards the swings. An unwanted confrontation was imminent. Far more horrific was that my pretty wife-to-be Alison was walking alongside Penny at the front, looking distinctly uncomfortable. Perhaps Penny was holding her arm, I could not tell. Adrenaline rushed into my veins and my breathing became shallow as I allowed my perilous swinging to subside. Penny marched straight towards me and flounced to a dramatic stop a mere two metres away, legs akimbo, hands on her skinny hips. Alison had dropped a few paces back. Oozing malicious self-assurance, Penny's dark eyes now bore into mine like a hungry ferret staring down a rabbit. Vainly I attempted nonchalance, whilst my trusty sidekicks Ob and Tick rose to my defence.

"So, what do you girls want here, hey?" came from Ob, whose swinging had come to a total halt.

"Bugger off, Penny, we didn't ask you to join us," pitched in Tick with an insecure-sounding falsetto. Fred and Skeens gazed on in silence.

My voice had not yet reported for duty. In the silence, whilst my swing alone squeaked rhythmically, Fred or was it Skeens, piped up with something like, "Yes, so just bugger off you girls, okay?" These brave attempts had little or no effect upon my new tormentors, while my voice still refused to appear. Unphased, Penny ignored my gang's efforts to put her off and shrilled for all to hear.

"So, Roger, tell us now and don't lie, okay! Do you love Alison, yes or no?"

Mesmerised by this direct attack on my new and vulnerable secret, embarrassing seconds ticked by. It had only been a day since Alison had eaten my chocolate, thereby cementing our future union. How could I protect this fragile love from this awful attack? Transfixed with fear, my mouth opened and closed like a dying fish. "Of course, he doesn't love her, Penny, you fool," blurted Ob loyally, glancing at me for approval and of course oblivious of my secret affair. Penny's sharp retort of, "Shut up, Ob, you know nothing. We are not talking to you, anyway!" stunned him into silence. Her slit-eyed attention remained unwavering on her helpless prey. "Tell us, Roger, is it true that you love Alison?"

No escape beckoned and there was no place to hide. If I were to admit to this crime of passion in front of my gang I was as good as dead; my brittle classroom credibility blown forever. But would I really stoop so low as to deny my first true love? As I giddily processed this Catch-22, the telltale blush that I inherited from my maternal granny rose up my neck until my cheeks were crimson. Alison was gazing at the ground now, her shoulders hunched painfully as if dreading blows yet to come, whilst the ghastly girls nudged one another and tittered happily. Anticipation was sky high and rising, with the climax of this playground drama located on my blushing self. Accumulated adrenaline finally activated my nervous system, enabling a clear response. Drawing a deep breath, I blurted out at the top of my voice, "No, Penny, of course I don't like Alison, you stupid fool!"

A stunned silence followed this desperate lie. Feeling the need to beef up my flimsy retort, I finally delivered a parting shot which would ring in my ears for decades.

"And anyway, I think Alison is a stupid bitch!"

Gasps of shock rippled through the spectators, while Alison recoiled and shrunk physically as if from a blow. I dared not look at her, having forfeited all my former rights as her future husband, and vainly attempted nonchalance by smirking at my now speechless gang. Far from achieving its purpose, my crude response bore the stamp of one who protests too much, a spineless Judas Iscariot committing the ultimate betrayal and exposing his utter cowardice. Totally delighted by this outcome, Penny now turned her attention to the wilting Alison and to her chattering followers. I was no longer relevant.

With dignity rapidly draining, my rallying call to the gang, "Hey c'mon guys, let's get out of here," emerged in a hoarse squeak as my friends followed me unenthusiastically, me swaggering off in the direction of the cricket nets. Some other distraction drew our attention for the rest of break. Not a word was ever said in our little group about what happened at the swings.

As that vision of our perfect future dissolved like a Scottish mist, the shame of betrayal settled deep in my bones. And Alison, unsurprisingly, never spoke to me again.

Were she to read this confession, might I be forgiven?

3

My Farmer-Warrior Father

"I'm off to Spelonk today, Rog. You coming?" Spelonk (cave) was a cattle farm that Dad owned beyond Melmoth, two hours from home. "Just the two of us," he added. Spelonk was remote, teeming with snakes and wild animals. Dad also mentioned that an old Zulu on the farm was a former mat-carrier for the Zulu King Cetewayo's army at the Battle of Isandlwana. This fired my imagination. A real Zulu warrior living on the farm? "Yeah, sure I'm coming, Dad," I replied, hurrying to fetch my penknife. These trips were always exciting, and one-on-one father-and-son time was rare.

A small hitch. Five goats were to be taken to the farm; the creatures already trussed up in the back of the bakkie, shitting and bleating pitifully. I was ordered to sit with them and ensure they didn't commit goat hari-kiri by jumping out onto the tarred road. The glamour of the farm trip idea was wearing off, but it was too late to pull out.

The goats rolled their yellow eyes at me, glaring, as if I were responsible for this indignity. They crapped all over until the smell became normal. In a burst of panic one of them loosened its ropes and tried to leap out of the truck. At full speed I tackled the smelly creature firmly and retied its ropes. Goat hair all over me, crap and urine everywhere. The trip lasted forever. Dad turned and waved encouragingly through the back window whilst smoking his pipe. I glowered back at him, both arms still tight around the would-be escapee.

We arrived at the farm around midday, hot and dusty, where the goats were off-loaded, and staggered into the bush. The cattle were already at the dipping kraal, jostling and bellowing in the mud underfoot. Dad strolled confidently amidst the large-horned Nguni, like a benign high priest, jabbing and prodding rumps with a crooked stick, inspecting left and right, while talking earnestly with the Zulu headman. The famous Prussian military theorist Carl von Clausewitz believed that courage was the first quality of a warrior, and this fearless WWII hero and tough farmer-warrior father of mine had it in spades.

Trying not to be squeamish, I trod delicately in the slosh, avoiding the biggest cowpats while not showing my fear as the cattle thundered past, whites of eyes under flashing Nguni horns. *Just like the real Wild West*, I thought, *if only the guys at school could see me now*. Imagination inflamed with thoughts of heroes, cattle rustlers and cowboy rodeos. I savoured the dusty commotion punctuated by the huge splosh as each cow plunged into the dipping tank and tried to copy the two-fingers-in-mouth whistles of the Zulu herdsman. Then Dad, while walking between and prodding the milling beasts, absentmindedly placed one hand on my shoulder. Buddies in manliness, we were. That rare display of casual affection soon passed, but forever archived in memory.

When the dipping was over Dad led me about two miles up a path towards two grass beehive huts on a slope, overlooking a stream. "You will now meet Mtenjwa, Cetewayo's mat-carrier at Isandlwana," Dad breathed, aware of my excitement. "Imagine the courage needed for a Zulu boy of fourteen or fifteen, carrying sleeping mats for an army marching to war? And then helping the warriors when they returned bleeding from the battlefield."

A wrinkled old man sat leaning against a wall of the first hut, eyes closed, soaking up the sun. The warrior. Ragged clothes, grizzled white hair, earrings the size of coins hanging down from each earlobe. Hard to imagine him as an athletic junior member of Cetewayo's famous Redcoat-conquering impi. As I took in the scene, a middle-aged woman, possibly his daughter, scurried into the hut carrying a pot. Probably shy and put out by our unannounced visit.

"Mnumzane Mtenjwa" (esteemed Mr Mtenjwa) was my father's greeting. The old warrior opened his eyes slowly, blinked and took a few seconds to gather his senses. Soon he recognised my dad and their handshake pumped for ages as they exchanged traditional greetings. After a while, their attention turned to me.

"Le yindodana yami, u Roger" (This is my son, Roger). He extended a hand, a bunch of dry twigs, which I held, carefully. Gazing at me through eyes cloudy with glaucoma, his twigs gripped my hand tightly while repeating, "Hau, umfana wa Guy. Ngiyajabule kakhulu" (Wow. Guy's son. I am so happy). Voice reedy and thin. Gazing around I was disappointed not to see spears, shields or any other signs of a warrior past. Just a humble grass home reflecting simple rural pride. As we left the kraal I figured that if he was a fifteen-year-old mat-carrier in 1879, he must have been well over ninety-five years old. Not long for this realm.

We headed home, me thankfully in the front seat, free of the goat-chaperone task. Tired, but happy. Dad suggested a quick stop at the Melmoth pub, which seemed to be a good idea. Real men taking a drink together after a day of manly work. Together we pushed through traditional batwing swing doors into the gloomy interior where six or eight sunburned farmers sat on stools nursing beers. "Hello, Guy." The collective greeting sounded jocular and friendly.

I felt proud to be in this grown-up male sanctuary with my strong father. I checked out the men, some of whom looked as if they'd been there awhile. "Had any more kids recently, hey, Guy?" cracked one wiseguy, with a smirk. "How's that pretty wife of yours bearing up, hey, Guy?" chipped in another, a scrawny man with bad skin and a leery expression. Sniggers and snorts of laughter followed these remarks. The scrawny one nudged his overweight buddy, "Has a beauty of a wife, does our friend Guy," he smirked, conspiratorially, from side of mouth. The word *friend* out of place. And my dad, no longer fearless like he'd been in the cattle pen, shifted uncomfortably.

These seemingly innocent jibes had pierced soft tissue, and my presence probably added to my dad's embarrassment. "Gentlemen, this is my second-oldest boy, Roger," he announced in a formal tone which seemed out of keeping with the tone of the banter. The word *gentlemen* too inapt. One old-timer murmured a greeting at me, and another stuck out a tough hand which I gratefully shook. The others ignored me, and an air of submerged tension hovered in the smoky room. I took large glugs from my Coke.

"So, tell us Guy, have you worked out what causes all these kids yet, hey? And is it, er, five or six at the latest count?" Overweight wiseguy number one was becoming bolder, fixing his victim with a cheeky grin. He had intuitively found a soft spot, and his buddies roared with laughter, slapping sides and hooting. For some reason, unknown to me, they found this line of humour, and especially Dad's embarrassment, hilarious. "Come off it, you guys," said Dad with a hollow laugh, but his attempts at deflection were lame and impotent. Gone was the courageous cattle-pen king; in his place a helpless, embarrassed victim. A vulnerable man.

In later years I realised that my dad's hardworking qualities were guaranteed to make lesser men jealous. Buoyed by alcohol and numbers, they gave vent to their goatish instincts, namely to diminish a man who seemed to have achieved success: farms, pretty wife and six kids. Downing our drinks, we scurried out of the dingy pub and drove home in silence.

Two years later, Dad pulled me aside after supper one evening. "Remember meeting Mtenjwa, the old Zulu warrior, Rog?"

"Of course, Dad," I replied. That embodiment of humility and courage. How could I forget?

"Well, he died. They buried him at Spelonk yesterday," Dad said, with a rare catch in his voice. Then, as an afterthought, he added, "Five people at his funeral." We sat in silence.

No words seemed appropriate.

4

A Cross between Ears and Eyes

Twice every month a Nguni ox was chosen to provide meat for the farmworkers. Jabulani, the stockman, a natural athlete who wore denim overalls and *patat* sandals made of car-tyre rubber, selected the beast. Then he and a few assistants wrestled the ox into submission and tied it up. Jabulani was the farmyard boss and the youngsters that he selected to capture the ox welcomed the opportunity to show their manhood. My father would be summoned and dispatched the animal with one shot from his Webley 45 revolver.

When Dad was away from home, Jabulani and team happily slaughtered the beast in the traditional manner, which I witnessed often, with heart in mouth. The chosen executioner first jumped on the bound ox's back and with dramatic posture and a loud "haaii!" plunged the assegai into the back of its neck. The weapon did not always hit the spot so would be squiggled around from side to side to the agonised bellows of the impaled beast until the spinal cord was finally and mercifully severed. When the animal at last collapsed in a moaning heap the jugular vein was slashed with a sharp penknife, emitting a gush of hot blood collected in a chipped enamel jug.

In dumb fascination I witnessed a number of ruthless farm executions, feeling desperate empathy for the ox, and shocked by the nonchalance as it was transformed from sentient creature into steaming piles of meat. The sickening smell of entrails, so difficult to describe and so impossible to forget, hung in the air for hours, invading my dreams with lurid scenes of death.

At age thirteen, my father pronounced me ready to kill the ox. There was no debate. He was due to be away one Saturday and carefully handed over his Webley army-issue revolver plus three ugly, snub-nosed bullets, with cryptic instructions. "Nothing to it my boy. Just be calm, aim at the cross between the eyes and the ears, and squeeze the trigger."

I wanted to ask why me? but instead asked, "Why the extra bullets, Dad?"

"If the first bullet does not do the job, take aim again and shoot in a different place. Just kill it!"

Nausea soon engulfed my pride at being chosen over my brothers to carry out this weighty task. The horror! Throughout that long morning I contemplated all avenues of escape. A sudden sickness, or injuring my right hand and claiming it was an accident might do the trick?

After I had weighed each avoidance plan, the honour associated with the job won the day. None of my siblings had been offered the gun duty, and there would be bragging rights at school. Like a man on death row, I paced up and down my parents' bedroom, opening the drawer every few minutes to gaze upon the weapon of death. I marvelled awhile at its malevolent beauty and delicious gun-oil smell. Its deadly confidence. Then panic set in all over again. By the time the allotted time came, I was exhausted by the stress and close to collapse.

Like a man destined for the gallows, some form of resignation set in. I drew deep breaths, feeling a core of stability seeping into my being. I loaded the three weighty bullets into the revolver and lined them up so that the first bullet would be struck by the first pull on the trigger. The weapon lay heavy in my hand as I left the house. I walked up towards the milkshed, gun pointing at the ground as I had been taught. Walking bravely towards my grim destiny, I felt like the tragic town marshal, Will Kane (Gary Cooper) in the movie *High Noon*, having to face a gang of killers and their outlawed leader, alone.

The youthful execution squad waiting with Jabulani appeared unsurprised at my arrival. As I faced the victim, a huge red Nguni ox with massive horns, they encouraged me with the words, "Dubula, Nkosana!" (Shoot, young boss). Gripping the heavy handgun in both hands, and from point blank range, I rapidly did the trigonometry (a virtual cross between ears and eyes), aimed at the spot and squeezed the trigger. The deafening shot made my ears ring, the gun bucked wickedly and the impact rocked the doomed beast backwards on its haunches. To my shock and horror, when the smoke cleared, the ox was far from dead. It had not even fallen, and was glaring accusingly at me with a thin stream of blood dripping down its snout.

"Pinda, Nkosana!" (Again, young boss). The youths laughed happily at this unusual turn of events, enjoying my discomfort and utterly unfazed by the agony of the ox. Gasping for breath, I struggled to calm my spinning head, then raised the weapon again for a second thunderous shot. This one crashed into the beast's skull right next to the first entry hole. Again, it rocked backwards as far as the ropes allowed, this time rolling its eyes and letting out a long and agonised moan. A rivulet of blood now flowed from nose and mouth as the execution team whooped again with delight. Clearly, I had missed the brain, simply the worst scenario imaginable.

Heart now pounding and with one bullet remaining, I was close to the point where panic would lead to failure, my own collapse, and lasting shame in farmyard folklore. "If it does not work, shoot in a different place," my father had said. With my last ounce of courage, I aimed two inches higher than the two oozing holes, squeezed the trigger, and kapow! This time the ox collapsed heavily into merciful and instantaneous death.

Its throat was slashed to release a crimson gush, and the rapid transformation from bellowing beast to piles of meat commenced. The execution crew worked like bloodied demons; their banter replete with jokes about my maiden performance. Traumatised, I staggered down the hill to my waiting home. No longer the hero of my own version of some Western movie, I had rapidly reverted to being a thirteen-year-old boy who had prematurely ventured into grown-up terrain. I had caused the ox an agonised departure from this world, and dreams of it moaning at me, crimson blood dripping from its snout, haunted me for years.

"So how many bullets did you use, Rog?" my father asked on his return that afternoon, thinking that that would be a good indicator of the success of the operation.

When I told him, "Three," he raised his eyebrows, perhaps aware of what he had put a young boy through.

"You learn anything, Rog?" he asked, his stock question after any incident.

"Of course, Dad."

"Good," he rumbled, satisfied with the response. "First class, my boy!"

What I didn't say was that the ox had become my teacher. I would never again take a creature's life.

There would be no fourth shot.

5

The Mamba Dragon-Beast

"Out, out, you silly snake," she hooted, her plump corseted body straining. My English granny, Victorian and short-sighted, once swept a massive black mamba out of her kitchen. Gripped by the whole drama, I asked her again and again to tell and re-tell the story. I could imagine her scolding it crossly in a falsetto Buckinghamshire tirade, oblivious of the danger, accelerating its departure with brisk broom sweeps. For a person who had her tonsils removed at the age of forty with nothing but half a bottle of brandy to dull the pain, she scored cult status in my early life for this and other equally eccentric exploits.

Back to snakes. Zululand is prime snake country, and of the countless tall stories involving killer snakes doing the rounds in Zululand by far the scariest were of the black mamba. *Dendroaspsis polyepsis* to the scientists, the fastest, most aggressive and dangerous of South African snakes. Growing into an athletic 4.5 metres, it ejects copious rapid-acting neurotoxin poison through front fangs, and is known to be one of the deadliest snakes in the world.

One tale of a mamba striking a man trying to escape a galloping horse stuck in my memory. Another is the mamba death in the Okavango swamps of a famous crocodile hunter named Wilmot, who should have known better. He broke his only syringe of antivenom due to the hand-shaking effects of the nerve poison, and wrote a wobbly farewell note to his family as asphyxiation closed down his breathing. And closer to home. My dad had imported a massive Sussex bull called Boswell II from the UK to inseminate his Nguni herd.

He typically failed to insure the precious animal. A large mamba bit it during its first week in Africa. Boswell II died within half an hour.

The mamba's mythical status grew and grew.

From the age of eleven I caught snakes, starting with easy varieties, and then graduating towards the dangerous. Before long, dozens of them slithered around in boxes on our veranda, earmarked for sale to the Durban Snake Park. I learned to negotiate, and the combination of species rarity, size, length and danger translated into steady pocket money. Snakes of all kinds inhabited that stoep, from spitting cobras, boomslang, vine snakes and puff adders, even to green mambas, the lesser relative of the black.

People asked why? Hard to answer, really. There was no affection shown for my troubles, and any indiscretion would be punished with a bite. Yet something about the inscrutable stare and unsentimental nature got to me. The rinkhals's contempt never abated, as much as I served it quivering sacrificial frogs. It greeted me every day with a squirt of poison aimed at my eyes. Once, a night adder turned cannibal overnight, overwhelmed by hunger and temptation I assume, devouring five smaller snakes that shared its cage. Pitiless killers, without exception. With deadpan expressions they would squeeze the life out of or poison their terrified prey and munch them down without a blink of remorse. I watched, fascinated as countless innocent mice, frogs and lizards were mercilessly consumed, empathising with the terror of their last moments.

Out of respect but perhaps also common sense, I avoided catching the black mambas that crossed my path. Their time would come. With a forked stick and a hessian sack, my confidence grew as I scooped up lesser reptiles. Stick placed confidently over the reptile's neck, quick grab firmly behind the head, pop it in the sack. Easy-peasy! Steadily I grew ready to face the ultimate snake challenge.

Elias Ngobese was the Zulu headman on my dad's bushveld farm in Nkwalini, twelve kilometres from Eshowe. Built like a Greek god and wearing only a duiker-skin loincloth on a sweltering Zululand day, he strode with my dad through the herd of Nguni cattle, prodding some and talking to others with an air of utter confidence. Single-handedly he wrestled to the ground any ox that needed medical attention (a task that usually required at least two, normally three men). Surprisingly gentle towards me despite his warrior exterior, at end of day he would quietly indulge my questions about wildlife on the farm.

According to Elias, the King, the biggest and most feared mamba of them all was no ordinary mamba, he explained, shaking his head and tapping his right temple, a gesture implying supernatural powers. "That snake is as big as this, Nkosana," indicating with a raised arm how it would tower over a man. "It is much cleverer than all other snakes," adding that it had killed three cattle in the past few years, including my dad's prize Sussex bull.

"Haibo, Nkosana. Basopha! inyoka leyo IMBI gabi" (Haibo, small boss. Be careful! That snake is really EVIL). As he walked with me to the kraal gate he muttered under his breath about its *mthakathi* (evil spirit). "Nkosana," he said, pointing out a distinctive koppie halfway up Mandawe hill, "lenyoka ihlala kulelo gquma" (the snake lives on that small hill).

The time had come. During the next September holidays I would climb Mandawe hill just to glimpse the fabled serpent. If things went wrong, I could always run like hell, and, of course, I carried my .22 gun. Worst scenario, the snake might not even show up. No advice was sought from grown ups, for obvious reasons. They would have said "Of course not, you must be crazy!" What an adventure that would be, and what a winner to tell my friends at school. Armed with .22 rifle, rucksack, peanut butter sandwiches and water, I left home before dawn and hitchhiked the twelve kilometres to the base of Mandawe hill.

The famous landmark loomed high and foreboding above the tarred road, with morning mists hanging over the rocky cliffs at the top. Despite overriding, nagging misgivings, I plunged into the thick acacia bushveld and began climbing, alert and with heart pounding. An hour's hard walking got me to the distinctive koppie half way up the hill. Where I stopped with shins bleeding from thorn cuts and sweating and tingling from excitement.

Massive granite boulders were strewn around, with large acacia and fig trees in between. Animal bones indicated predator activity; a leopard kill perhaps? Suddenly a rustling sound drew my attention towards a large boulder five metres away. To my utter thrill I noticed the tail of a mighty snake, disappearing around the right side. A black mamba for sure, massive, that slate shade a dead giveaway.

As I gazed at the retreating tail, to my amazement the head and long neck of another mamba, this one raised above my own head height, emerged around the left side of the same boulder. Two huge snakes at once? Moments later I clicked. It was the same snake circling the boulder, and by a quick estimate at least four metres long.

This *had* to be Elias's dreaded mthakathi, cow-killer. Clearly focused on me, it glided confidently towards where I stood transfixed, its trademark black mouth open in a half-gape, tongue flicking in and out. I stood enthralled, mesmerised, captivated, ready to sprint. At three metres away it slithered to a stop, its front body and head swaying left to right, unblinkingly holding my gaze.

The black mamba is the only snake to rise up to a third of its body at a forward angle, unlike the upright stance of the cobra. And its head was at least half a foot higher than mine. Stalemate? We each stared, waiting for the other to move. My head spun. An acute fear churned in my stomach, conscious that these moments might well be my last. Long seconds ticked by. Who would blink first?

Then I did one of those impetuous things. Hindsight confirms this is only done by a rare form of super idiot, that is those who tend to act first and think later. To break the deadlock, I deliberately shuffled my right boot sharply in the dry leaves.

Bad move. Instantly the mamba dropped its head and attacked, hurtling towards me like a whiplash, with dark mouth agape. I, wound as tight as a coiled spring, exploded into escape action, hurling myself backwards down the steep koppie slope. Rolling, tumbling headlong for about thirty metres in a cloud of dust, the gun, rucksack and contents flying out of my hands.

I came to a crumpled stop in a thick bush. Checked that I was no longer being pursued. No black killer slithering through the dusty murk. Heart pounding like a cowhide drum, I gathered bruised body and wits, senses awash with adrenaline and terror. I was dead lucky to have escaped the famous killer. One bite and I would have rapidly joined my ancestors.

But god, what a gorgeous, fantastic dragon-beast. As the dust settled, I recovered steadily, my heartbeat returning to normal.

Still no sign of the monster.

A wise person would have savoured the miraculous survival. Thanking ancestors and lucky stars profusely, he would have limped down the hill, safe and with a wondrous story to tell.

But no. An irresistible urge to see that beautiful brute again arose within me, closing down all debate. The African saying, "Muhle wena kona hamba, skati wena bona mamba, noko wena hayi tshetsha, wena ifa lapa stretsha" (It's advisable to run when you stumble on a mamba, for if you do not hurry, you'll expire on a stretcher) rang in my mind. Gathering rucksack and damaged rifle, I limped up the footpath towards the mamba koppie. Senses alert, eyes wide, breath shallow. About ten metres before the big boulder, the track led between two smaller rocks, where I needed to bend down to pass under an overhanging branch.

Nothing moved, the path looked clear. Two metres before I ducked forward to go under the branch an instinct within sensed danger. I stopped in my tracks. Something was wrong. Then I saw it. Draped on the overhanging branch, barely visible, the giant lay in wait, observing, poised for a perfect ambush. Black mouth partially agape in pre-strike hunting mode, slate-grey skin blending with the bark. My neck would have passed inches below him as I climbed between the two rocks. An easy victim. His dark eyes bore unblinkingly into mine as if to implore me to enter his ambush. Make my day, human, make my day.

Overcome with a sense of the snake's inherent evil, all boldness fled my body in a rush. I shook. Turned. Sprinted headlong down to the road far below as if pursued by the devil himself, oblivious to the thorny undergrowth, cuts and bruises. Breathless and gasping I reached the road, and waited for a passing car. Hours later I arrived home, still shocked, bleeding from countless wounds, and exhausted in body, mind and spirit.

The image of that malevolent killer lying in ambush lies coiled within me. When I go home and drive past Mandawe hill, I always feel a strong urge to return.

But not today.

6

Hannibal and the Mice

At Michaelhouse Jack Mudd was the acknowledged reptile king. He owned a python called Oubaas. A known eccentric, larger than life, overweight and of shambling gait, he was in a form two years ahead of me. His shock of straw-like hair and hanging-out shirt marked him as a sort of rebel showman, somewhat Boris Johnson-like, always the centre of attraction. Kids hung onto his tall stories, gawking at the reptiles slithering around his body. Jack regularly took his tame leguaan Lefty plus smaller snakes into chapel. Kids vied to sit near him because anything was likely to happen, such as one of his pets escaping and slithering down the church aisle causing mayhem.

One hot Sunday morning Jack brought a large cicada to the formal Sunday service. During a lull in old Reverend Sergeant's boring sermon he rubbed its hind leg against the abdomen, like a violin bow, making an unmistakeable penetrating trilling sound which the good reverend tried vainly to ignore. Soon Jack got the second leg going. A double-trilling now filled the air, and the entire school sniggered as four hundred and fifty heads craned in the direction of the obvious suspect. Jack looked around as innocent as pie, stopping the squeaks just long enough for calm to settle, with the poor old Reverend trying in vain to pick up his thread. At dramatically chosen moments the cicada would again punctuate the sermon until the entire congregation was buzzing like a hive of bees, and Jack's cicada achieved hero status. The Rev's sermon died a premature death.

After my Mandawe hill mamba story had done the rounds, Jack accepted me as a sort of up-and-coming snake guy, which I found oddly empowering. One day he invited me to see his snakes, a rare honour for a junior. Soon we were chatting our enthusiastic heads off, visiting a line of boxes containing Oubaas the python, a toad called Ponk (named after the bald maths teacher), the chapel hero leguaan Lefty, as well as a variety of venomous snakes. Not only was I invited into Jack's private den but I was treated like a snake buddy. We discussed each specimen whilst Jack casually smoked an unfiltered Texan. What a guy. I explained that my only snake at school was a smallish python which I fed with live field mice collected from traps set in the surrounding fields. Being particularly interested in the mice bit, Jack led me towards a large box standing on its own.

"Look here, Roger," he started, a thin stream of smoke sliding from his nostrils, "in this box is the largest puff adder you will ever see, *Bitis arietans*, thirty-nine inches long, only one inch off the world record." He paused meaningfully to emphasise this incredible statistic, and then opened the lid to reveal a puff adder curled up in the far corner of the box. "Only one inch to go, and a world record!" Jack breathed, misty-eyed and yearning.

I was impressed beyond words and gazed at the malevolent beast, mesmerised by its dangerous beauty. Thicker than my arm, at least five kilograms in weight, its spade-shaped head was as large as a prize fighter's fist. The epitome of deadly malice. Its Latin name *arietans* means rapid-striking. The puff adder kills more people in Africa than any other snake. A deadly creature indeed.

"Hannibal," announced Jack, pleased with my starstruck admiration. "I'll tell you what Roger, I am prepared to let you invest in Hannibal, if you like, and become a fifty percent shareholder."

It took a while for this offer to sink in. Imagine being part owner of this incredible snake, and then one day sharing in the glory with old Mudd when our 'pet' grew that final inch. My head spun with visions of glory. Mudd and Chennells. And Hannibal.

"Wow, Jack, amazing," I gushed. "I am so in. The cost of a half-share?"

The snake had cost Jack thirty rand plus another ten on food and the box. Forty rand was rock-bottom price, considering his champion potential. For a mere twenty (half a term's pocket money), plus provision of a steady stream of mice caught from traps I set, I could be co-owner of this fine specimen.

The deal was sealed with a self-conscious handshake. Jack drew up a one-page contract headed Hannibal the Puff Adder, and insisted on recording that the front half of the creature was to belong to him. So I was to be proud owner of . . . well . . . the rear half. A little like the back of a pantomime cow. Resisting all thoughts of renegotiation, I signed the contract, agreeing to make the capital payment of twenty rand the very next day. The deal done, I went to bed, proud owner of the rear half of a soon-to-be-famous puff adder, and world record holder!

During break the next day I furtively paid Jack in crisp notes, and agreed to bring Hannibal his first mouse feast on Friday evening. Being summer, a large puff adder could consume dozens of mice per week. On Friday, after supper, I took four large striped field mice caught in my favourite mousetrap in a brown paper bag to their final earthly destination. Jack's snake den.

We hurried straight to Hannibal's lair where the regal creature lay curled in a yellow and black display of contemptuous and treacherous beauty. Dark beady eyes, unwinking, only his flickering tongue proof of the reptilian life force lurking in the muscular frame. Already I felt that sickening feeling of betrayal, handing over the innocent Beatrix Potter field mice to their inevitable deaths.

I opened the paper bag and showed Jack Hannibal's dinner. His eyes gleamed with delight. "Chuck 'em in, Rog," he said breathlessly. "Just look at him man, our boytjie must be starved." Before I could be overcome with remorse, I spilled the squeaking contents of my bag into the cage. One clung to the bag while the others spilled out, a strong sense of self-preservation driving it to desperate acrobatic feats. Landing on the sandy floor, the unhappy few, this little band of brothers, scuttled to the furthest corner from their enemy and gathered in a circle, stealing fearful glances at the impassive monster, and squeaking pathetically.

What were they saying? Their obvious terror unsettled me. Were they praying, encouraging each other, perhaps saying goodbye? I never got used to feeding a frog or mouse to a snake, and always chose to look away as nature took its course. Hannibal seemed in no hurry for dinner, but his tongue flickered faster and faster in and out, indicating that the food delivery had been noted. Hannibal's massive head would soon be striking deadly fangs into the wee mice, and chugging them down that muscular throat.

"Let's leave him to it, hey Rog?" chirped Jack jauntily. "Bon appétit, Hannibal and enjoy those lekker mouseburgers, hey."

We turned out the lights and left.

Early the next morning we checked in to see how Hannibal had enjoyed his first meal. Jack was upbeat as we strode to the den. "I wish I could have watched him zapping those mice," he said enthusiastically. "Such killing machines, those puffies." I nodded, still ambivalent about my role as executioner.

Jack opened the lid.

Nothing, truly nothing, could have prepared us for the horror that awaited. Hannibal lay stretched out to his full magnificent thirty-nine inches, stone cold dead. A large chunk of his neck just behind that huge head had been eaten away, and four field mice gazed inquiringly up from their victory feast at two shocked human faces.

"Jesus flipping Christ!" exclaimed Jack, breathing heavily. "I can't believe it!" he muttered again and again. The mice lost interest in us and returned to their gruesome feast, nibbling off chunks of pink neck flesh, with gusto. From the marks on the sandy floor, it was clear that a fierce battle had raged. The four mouseketeers had plotted, strategised, and with sabres drawn, turned the tables on the mighty snake.

Perhaps one had acted as a decoy, whilst the others pounced on his vulnerable neck and delivered bites into his spine? We would never know. Perhaps a leader, with the charisma of a King Henry V at the Battle of Agincourt, or a Rassie Erasmus, coach of the Springbok World Cup rugby team, or a William Wallace from the movie *Braveheart* had risen to the occasion and inspired his mini warriors into desperate feats of bravery. Images of St Michael slaying the dragon, David toppling Goliath and other heroic odds-defeating tales came to mind. Yet it seemed impossible to believe that the field mice alone had conquered their giant opponent. For two stunned co-owners of a very dead not-quite-world-champion puff adder, it was game over.

Jack morosely undertook to bury Hannibal, including my half. Against his wishes to feed my heroic field mice to his other snakes, I insisted on setting them free. They deserved freedom after their epic victory, I figured, and a future in which they would regale rapt grandchildren with tales of how they had conquered the mighty Hannibal.

That afternoon, near the stream where they had been caught, I returned them to the freedom they deserved. "Well done, you guys, for your incredible feat," I murmured at the uncomprehending fellow creatures in the paper bag. In the idyllic glade I upended their bag reverently and invited them to return to their families, who by now must have feared the worst. Without a backward glance they scuttled off into the grass. I found myself fighting back tears. "I will never forget you, you brave, brave mice."

And Jack? Our new friendship never recovered. The world record for a puff adder still stands at thirty-nine inches.

7

Oubaas the Lucky Charm

Our dad had consulted a local sangoma to find out who was responsible for a deliberately started sugar cane fire on our farm.

"So, what spell did the sangoma cast, Dad?"

"Well, boys," he explained, "the sangoma cast a spell called *masende* (testicles). The balls of the firemonger will swell and if he does not confess, he will soon die."

We sniggered at the images evoked, gripped by the drama. Word of the spell spread like a fire throughout the rural community whose grass-hutted kraals adjoined the farm. A week later, Dad received a visit from two anxious Zulu men, asking him to call the ambulance. Their brother's swollen testicles needed the hospital urgently. The man was collected the same day, and he admitted to starting the fire. He had been disgruntled after being dismissed from the farm workforce. Charged, he pleaded guilty to arson. Case closed.

The power of the supernatural, entwined with superstition and sorcery, was never far from life on the farm. The goats that Dad sold to Zulus were for sacrificial purposes, destined to be killed very slowly so that their agonised cries would draw the attention of the ancestors. I tried to block out this knowledge, whilst retaining respect for the mystical unknown. So many questions hung in the air. Was the swollen-testicle victim brought down by his own psychosomatic guilt, or did the spell simply attach to his private parts with supernatural force?

A decade later. The school war cry echoes off the old buildings as I settle into the front row of a Michaelhouse school bus together with the first rugby team. "Sizo ba hlula; Yebo! Sizo ba hlula; Yebo! Sizo ba hlula, Yebo! Yeti yeti yeti ja, atizwi, atizwa, MICHAELHOUSE!" "We will conquer them, Yes!" repeated three times, ending with a roar of the school's name. A boisterous crowd of fans cheered as the old bus kicked into gear and rumbled down the drive.

That day's game was against Port Natal, the toughest Afrikaner school in the province, and a serious threat to our as yet unbeaten status over the year's first five matches. The first team mascot, a mighty teddy bear named Fred, wearing the red-and-white rugby jersey, was strapped in next to Willie Robinson, the team captain. As we were pulling off one of the fans shouted out cheekily, "Hey, Chennells. So, who you gonna maim today, hey?"

Ever since the previous Saturday's game against Greytown High, I had been teased as the meanest dude around. In the dying moments of the game, I'd dived desperately at their massive wing who was thundering down the touchline for a sure try. He fell hard, dropped the ball, and stayed down groaning. Try valiantly saved. As teammates whooped and helped me to my feet, two medics carried my victim off on a stretcher. Broken collarbone. We had won the game as a result of that last-ditch tackle. Chennells was hero of the day.

Being teased mercilessly was, of course, the highest form of schoolboy honour. Boys called out, "Hey, Rambo" and "Yo, Kamikaze" as I passed by, boosting my reputation as a destroyer of opponents. I pretended not to, but of course loved it.

The bus had no sooner turned out of the school gates when Bill Garland, sitting in the back seat where the raucous guys sat, started the first rugby song:

> If I was a marrying type, which thank the lord I'm not so,
> the kind of man that I would marry, would be a rugby scrum half.
> He'd put it in, and I'd put it in, we'd both put it in together,
> We'd be alright, in the middle of the night, putting it in together.

The last line shouted out at the tops of our voices, everybody grinning at the sheer naughtiness. Being the scrum half, my name was shouted as that first verse was belted outa, and I joined in merrily. Teammates bonding, building up spirit for the game. As the last line ended, a bucket of cold nastiness suddenly landed on my head. Oubaas! Oh my flipping god, Oubaas! I had forgotten my final ritual with Oubaas, the lucky charm that presided over my private study back at school.

The song continued noisily, but my jaw now hung open and breathing became shallow. This was bad. So very bad. Ever since I'd found the bleached dassie skull under a rock on my first weekend of that matric year at the base of Sarsden cliffs about five kilometres from Michaelhouse, Oubaas had become an integral part of my mental stability. With two front teeth missing between his incisors, I placed him at eye level on my study bookshelf, where he gazed at the world with a gritty knowing charisma.

I took to acknowledging Oubaas with a few words and a forehead rub before every important event such as a rugby game. Then, after each game, I would religiously repeat the ritual. "Oubaas, you have protected me again today. Helped me play well. Thank you so much. Thank you." His powers grew and grew and I could achieve nothing of importance without his support.

Back on the bus the next song, smuttier than the first, bounced off the windows. The belting out of these below-the-belt songs addressed our pre-game anxiety, with us dwelling on Port Natal's bulldozer Afrikaner forwards. Some of their team were said to be over nineteen years old, with the hardened beards of men. Mike Harris, my fly half and friend, approached my seat from the back of the bus, tapped me on the shoulder. "Hey, are you okay, man? You look like something's wrong?"

Of course I denied any problem. "Naah, Mike, thanks," I answered breezily, "just thinking about some of those moves." He and I had spent hours practising new moves, each prefaced with a code word we were going to try out. 'Scaramouche' was where I did a long skip pass straight to Dave at first centre. 'Whiplash' was where I would break and run past him for a dummy or scissors. 'Stevie' was the blind-side move, named after blind singer Stevie Wonder.

"I'm gonna make you look good today, Mike!" I tossed off. A private joke as to who would made the other look the best. With his sideways grin Mike slapped my shoulder and returned to his seat. How could I have told him the truth anyway, that my neglecting to rub my dassie-skull charm was giving me the *skriks*.

Despite the power of positive thinking, Oubaas trumped all my attempts to right-size the issue. Don't worry, Rog, I tried to reason, he is only a harmless skull that you have given special meaning and powers to. As you know he has zero actual powers. Nothing but the earthly remains of a dead dassie, for god's sake. Oubaas's grinning visage re-appeared in my mind like an unwanted ghost, sneering: *Okay, boy. Today I'll show you what happens when you fail to acknowledge me.*

The ongoing rugger songs now sounded as if in another universe, and the two-hour trip to Durban passed in a blur with me slumped in a damp blob of insecurity. How was I ever going to snap out? Joshing with my teammates in the changing rooms, the game now imminent, I steadily began to feel better. It might be okay. Perhaps old Oubaas would not take revenge for my unintended disrespect? The familiar pre-match actions, pulling on the famous red-and-white jersey, engaging in the nervous banter of much-loved teammates, that comforting smell of Wintergreen on legs. The old me stirred and returned. More teasing about my deadly tackle of last week led to gales of laughter and reminded me that I was the school's first choice for scrum half.

My skills were pretty damn alright. I should be fine today, why not? And who's scared of a bunch of hairy-back boere anyway? Hugging each other tightly in the final captain's huddle, we were a band of brothers. I felt good. Positive. To be sure, the Port Natal team in their scary red-and-black jerseys lining up on the other side of the field looked like giants, but we probably looked equally scary to them. *Let the games begin*, I thought. I am going to be fine. Me, not with swollen balls but with a swollen head.

That pause before the first whistle. Butterflies doing a final flutter, before dissipating under the focus of the arcing ball and the mayhem to follow. *Prrrt* went the whistle. Mike kicked the ball deep into their half and the game was on. As our red-and-white horde swarmed towards them, they passed the ball rapidly down the three-line to one of their famous bruisers, a massive wing called Andries Nel. A tough farmer's son from Vryheid, renowned as a Natal athlete and deadly finisher. He swerved inwards, past his opposite number, and next thing was heading directly towards me. Last week's encounter with the Greytown wing, now being replayed in slow motion. No time to think. Instinctively, I flung myself at his pounding legs, and his knee connected with my right temple. Lights out! The force of my head and body stopped him in his tracks and he lost the ball. I only heard about this much later.

In a crumpled heap I lay, much like my own Greytown victim, to be carried off unconscious on a stretcher. Minutes later I started returning to consciousness, a sugar cane fire burning in my head, with a doctor holding his finger before my eyes and asking how many fingers. Whilst trying to focus on his question, I slowly worked out what had happened. Within the first fifteen seconds of the opening whistle, I had been knocked unconscious. Oubaas had wasted no time to make his point.

Michaelhouse first fifteen lost the game 24-7, and the team returned in mourning. I was delivered to the school sick bay that evening in an ambulance, monitored for concussion, and released two days later. That brief aura of invincibility after the Greytown game was forever gone, replaced by me being the injured one, ruled out of all contact sports for four weeks. When I re-entered my small study, there was old Oubaas perched impassively on the shelf where I had left him, his gap-toothed grin more of a sneer. Suddenly menacing. *Now, will you ever ignore me again, hmm?* Could Oubaas really have exerted this power?

When I returned to the team weeks later, my confidence had shrunk, along with my swollen head. I showed Oubaas nothing but respect, rubbing his head and asking for his guidance before every game, and then before each matric exam. Like the man suffering from the *masende* spell back home, I had experienced the sharp end of occult power and was not about to question how it operated. Einstein once claimed that the height of stupidity is demonstrated by an individual who ridicules something he knows nothing about. However, after my last matric exam it was time to part with this scary talisman. I wrapped Oubaas carefully in soft paper and made my way to the Sarsden cliffs where I had found him. Placed him respectfully under that large rock. Still grinning.

8

Two on the Boko

15 June 1968. With shaven head and a duffel bag and brand-new kit, I joined over two thousand recruits reporting for military service at Valhalla Air Force training base, near Pretoria. Not knowing a single person, I had hoped to be assigned to a bungalow with a reasonable, maybe even friendly, group. Not to be. As I entered my allocated bungalow 28, I heard loud talk from a brute of a man who was acting like he was in charge.

Hans was older than us all, hard stubble darkening his jutting jaw, with the broad neck of a rugby prop. His pale blue eyes and thin lips greeted the world with an aggressive disapproval, while his alpha-male bark scattered fear wherever he went. Shortly after our arrival he assaulted one guy who tried to stand up to him after supper one evening. Gawie Blom was foolish enough to say what many of us were thinking. "Hou op met raas asseblief man, ons probeer slaap" (Please stop the noise, we are trying to sleep). Hans tipped him out of his bed onto his head leaving Gawie bleeding and slightly concussed. "Niemand praat so met my nie" (no one speaks to me like that) he shouted standing over the bleeding recruit. This cemented his status as the boss of the room. Within days he had gathered a couple of acolytes, headed by a tough, silent thug named Piet and wiry, shifty Japie, who acted as his sidekicks and followed him around loyally like pilot fish do a shark.

Hans and I disliked each other from the very first, and he quickly made me the object of his drive for dominance. "Wat de fok maak jy hier saam met ons boere, Soutie?" (What the fuck are you doing here with us Afrikaners, Soutie?) and "Manne, ek gaan nooit hierdie fokken Ingelsman vertrou nie" (Men, I am never going to be able to trust this fucking Englishman). Met with laughter from his sidekicks, as well as others. Nobody was going to stand up to Hans, least of all me. Avoidance the safest strategy.

"Hoekom is jy so 'n doos, soutpiel?" (Why are you such cunt, salt-dick?) shouted Hans on our third evening as I walked past his bed on the way to the showers. When I ignored him, he cracked his wet rolled-up towel across my naked back like a whip. I yelped and jumped away. Piet and Japie plus some nearby recruits sniggered at this diversion, whilst others averted their eyes, grateful perhaps that Hans's vindictive attention was fixed on me.

Wincing at the pain I ran for the door to escape another whiplash, while sycophantic laughter rippled behind me. I showered in trepidation, wondering how to avoid the ordeal on the way back to my bed. I was in no shape to challenge Hans. My physical defences were low, and Hans's targeted aggression against me became a daily encounter. During the months prior to my call-up, I had suffered a bout of jaundice, my weight dropping from 75kg to a scrawny 60kg, leaving my parents terrified to send me to the air force. The day before I was to board the train to Pretoria, I overheard them arguing heatedly in their bedroom, Mum in tears about my weak state, and Dad reassuring her that the air force would surely force me to recover.

Training is meant to be harsh, the daily programme of PT, drills and endurance exercises calculated to push recruits to breaking point and thereby turn them into soldiers. Surviving each day's ordeal was the easier part. Not a day went by without Hans assaulting and belittling me, his favourite ways being to flick me with his towel, messing up my bed just before inspection, throwing my boots out the window.

Desperation grew into a permanent stomach knot, whilst outwardly I tried to maintain a good-natured acceptance. Unbeknownst to my tormentor, something cosmic, which I might call ineffable, was brewing deep within. Long after lights out, while the entire bungalow slept, I would creep out of bed and tiptoe via the darkest shadows towards the concrete yard behind the dining mess. There, glinting in the security lights, were twenty or more metal bins that held the remains of the camp's evening meal. Each lid was lifted and the contents sniffed. Soon I would find the remains of beef stew, meat balls or cheap steaks and plunge my hands into the mush, grabbing the biggest chunks. Like a ravenous beast, I hunched over the bin wolfing down life-giving meat, throwing the fatty bits for the scrawny cats that gathered around. Every night we enjoyed this surreal carnivorous feast, purring cats and hunched scavenger illuminated by the dim security lights. Every day my weight and strength increased significantly.

Flashback. Ten years earlier and in my first year at school, I was bullied daily. Peter X, a large and much older boy who dominated the playground with his two sidekicks, scornfully punched me around during break and then made off with my peanut butter sandwiches. Retaliation never even crossed my mind as he was larger, stronger and scary. My humiliation grew and grew. I was too ashamed to admit the daily ordeal to my parents or teachers.

As for the white-cassocked German nuns in charge of the Eshowe Holy Childhood Convent School, they stood for a quaint universe of prayer and religion. How could *they* help me? Daily my self-esteem evaporated as my aversion to school grew. One day when Peter had taken the sandwiches and punched my shoulder harder than usual, I cried on the way home, finally admitting to my mother the daily fate of her son.

She told my dad when he returned from work. He became animated and pulled me aside, conspiratorially, in the passage behind the kitchen. "There is only one way to stop being bullied, Rog," he said grimly, checking that we were out of earshot of my mother. "You have to hit him as hard as you can, on the boko. Like this." At this he demonstrated a vicious roundhouse punch landing exactly on the end of my nose. (Boko is boxing slang for nose.) "Hit as hard as you can, but whatever you do, do NOT tell Mum, okay? Women simply don't understand these things." I got the message. This was men's stuff, between us two only. "And after you have hit him," he added as an afterthought, "if he comes for you, you better just run like hell!"

The next day I went to school strangely excited. At last I had a plan, despite the obvious danger. Nothing to lose. Dad had emphasised that success depended on the accuracy of that one surprise nose punch. "Remember, if you get it right, Rog," he had added, "he won't be in the mood for anything."

Soon into the tea break Peter and his two buddies sauntered over to where I was sitting, and one of them opened proceedings with a punch to my arm. "Hand 'em over, wimp!" said Peter, arrogant as ever, and reaching out to grab the sandwiches. The poor guy simply had no idea what was coming. I hit him so hard that his nose squished under my fist, and he fell like a sack of spuds, blood spurting. Pandemonium followed, with girls running around the playground screaming at the sight of all the blood. Sister Cecilia, who swooped to the rescue, cradled Peter's head in her lap, and within seconds her white cassock was stained crimson red. I was whisked away by a tut-tutting Mother Precopia, the principal nun, who phoned my mother. "Mrs Chennells, please come and collect your boy at vunce," she ordered, in her strong German accent, "he is assaulting ze boys on ze playground."

Driving home, my normally placid mum bit her lip, torn between protection of her small boy, and concern about the vicious monster that she had reared. "But why did you hit him, my darling?" she asked, again and again. I was, after all, her most gentle, nature-loving boy. I simply stuck to my story that when Peter punched me and took my sandwiches for the umpteenth time, I finally lost my temper and punched him.

When Dad got home and heard the news, wisely he feigned total surprise. Soon however he pulled me aside into the passage. "Well done, son, first class! First class indeed!" he whispered hoarsely. This was his favourite expression, which after his death ended up as a wine made in his honour. With great gravitas, as if awarding a medal to a war hero he reached into his pocket and placed a shilling into my palm, stating, "You have earned this reward, my boy. And if you ever need to use that punch to hit someone on the boko again, you will have another shilling and my full support." Bandage over his broken nose, Peter returned to school a week later, avoiding all eye contact with me. Neither Peter, nor anyone else, ever bullied me for the rest of my school days.

Back to Valhalla where with the nightly scavenged meat, the press-ups, sit-ups and hill-climbs with full pack got easier by the day. I was soon the fittest in our platoon. By the fifth week however, the bullying was close to intolerable. Hans had chosen me, the only soutie as his whipping boy, and a strategy with roots in that yesteryear playground drama was called for. A massive boko strike.

Another hot and difficult day ended with the order, "Battalion, dismiss!" We had started early with a route march before dawn, our fingers freezing around our .303 rifles which grew heavier and heavier over the fifteen-kilometre route. Hours of marching during the steaming morning and an obstacle course in the afternoon left us sweaty and exhausted. As I took off my sodden overalls and prepared to go to the showers, I saw Hans folding his wet green towel. In a flash, the knowing settled in me. The awaited moment was nigh.

Time slowed down and I witnessed myself as if from another perspective. Without any indication of the seismic shift within, I flung my towel casually over my shoulder and started walking down the wide passage between the beds. As I passed Hans's bed he let out a triumphant whoop and gave a towel-flick which connected despite my attempt to parry, leaving a red weal on my shoulder. Piet and Koos snickered as I winced at the blow, then stopped in my tracks.

Just as Hans was raising his arm for a second strike, I turned and walked towards him, eyes cast downwards, as if coming to plead for mercy. He paused with his hand raised, as this was odd behaviour. "Wat nou, soutie, wil jy met my praat of wat?" (What now, soutie, do you want to talk to me or what?) he said in a mocking tone. Two feet away, I stopped, body still strangely relaxed, and somehow suppressing the pent-up aggression inside.

As a look of concern began to form on Hans's face, the boko punch had already begun. With origins somewhere deep in my solar plexus, it arced into a wide roundhouse swing and ended with my clenched fist exploding on his not-small nose. The crack of bone and cartilage breaking preceded an agonised bellow as the big man collapsed backwards onto his bed, blood spurting. Cupping both hands around his nose, he screamed, "My neus, my neus, jy het my neus gebreek, jou fokken etter" (my nose you have broken my nose you fucking pus).

Piet and Koos, bewildered by the unexpected, fussed around him. Hans rose to a sitting position with hands around his swelling nose and eyes brimming with involuntary tears. "Jou fokken Engelsman, ek gaan jou moer," he screamed (You fucking Englishman, I am going to thrash you). Adrenaline racing and nursing a throbbing right hand, I awaited the fightback. His threats lacked conviction and his friends held him back, persuading him that his bloody mess of a nose needed medical treatment. As my dad had suggested years back, it is hard to fight after a good boko punch. The fight was over, and the awed throng moved respectfully out the way as I made my way to the showers. I knew that my days of being bullied at Valhalla were over.

Hans was taken to the sanatorium where his nose was pronounced broken and he was booked off for six days. When he returned with a plaster cast, he ignored me. And never messed with me again. My midnight visits to the bins stopped, and I was treated with a new respect far beyond my bungalow. Word of the big knock-down had spread fast. Gawie, who had tried to stand up to Hans many weeks earlier without success, became my ally and then a firm friend.

A week later, my first weekend pass. Still revelling in a lightness since the boko showdown, I hitched home to Eshowe. After hours on the road, I walked up the long driveway to a rapturous homecoming. Mum could not contain her joy, and gushed repeatedly how well and strong I looked compared to my sickly state a mere two months back. "It's wonderful what exercise and good food can do, isn't it dear?" chipped in my loving grandma Vivi. After the first bout of hugs and greetings I pulled my father to one side into the passage where we had first whispered boko-talk years back. Business time.

"Dad. Remember the shilling and the boko?" He nodded, smiling. "And you offered the same if I swung that punch again?"

"Of course, I remember."

"Well," I said, unable to hide the pride within, "you owe me another shilling."

Dad asked for the story, blow by blow. He was inexplicably moved by my tale and ill-equipped to express the emotions that welled up. As he rummaged in his pocket for the equivalent of a shilling, namely ten cents (South Africa had gone metric) he tried to wipe away the tears now rolling freely down his cheeks.

"First class, my boy," he said, again and again. "Right on the boko? First bloody class!"

An eye for an eye, and a nose for a nose. Felt good.

9

Bagging the Biggest Fish

Radio turned up high, fishing rod on the roof and new reel tucked in the boot, we scudded down the N2 highway southwards, each full of honeymoon hopes. For me, vivid images of that sweet reel casting irresistible bait far into the ocean, a heroic battle ensuing, and the groom emerging triumphant with a gasp-inducing catch.

To wind back. My not-yet father-in-law, Ken Shimwell, was what one might call an acquired taste. A ruggedly handsome Natal man with weathered features and a proud beer belly, Ken's manner in the world was forthright and, often, disconcerting. His robust sense of humour showed itself in odd ways, usually at the expense of others. While never sure where I stood, I certainly sought his approval. His role in my life would prove to be significant.

Asking the parent of one's beloved for their blessing to wed is rarely a stress-free undertaking. My trepidation on approaching Ken for the hand of his daughter Diane was met with, "Good god boy, are you out of your mind? She is worse than her mother!" I must have looked shocked, so he quickly tried to soften his response. "Of course you can marry her, boy, it's just that these Mindry women are totally impossible!" These words, spoken partially in jest, referred to their strong and no-nonsense ways in the world. My take on this was simply that Ken's wife Shirley was a spirited woman who refused to put up with Ken's nonsense, which led understandably to heated confrontations.

I was twenty-seven and firmly in love. Powering through this initial hurdle, I proposed to Diane (diplomatically omitting to share her dad's sentiments), and we plunged headlong into wedding preparations. I say we but in truth Diane and her mother planned the whole show. My duties were to show up sober, to produce the ring and, crucial to this tale, to plan the honeymoon. Since none of that required much forward-planning, Ken and I contributed by absconding on fishing trips up and down the steamy Natal coast. Naturally, on such men's excursions, the cool-bag beers were packed with as much care as the sardine bait; the banter lively, while the fishing stories became increasingly far-fetched with each passing beverage.

Central to all the teasing was the perpetual quest to be the Better Fisherman. The pressure to bag the finest, first or biggest fish was relentless; humility not an option. Not with Ken. He dangled the tantalising prospect of his everlasting respect in front of my nose, which bait I took to like a hungry shad. I could not wait for the day when I produced a massive fish, ending the competition once and for all. So as the wedding date approached, I was hooked in more ways than one.

When Ken approached me about a month before the big day, cradling a mysterious and bulky package in his hands, I perceived something unusual, even portentous, in his bearing. With a rare sense of occasion, he handed me the intriguing item wrapped carefully in newspaper. "For you, dear boy," he gruffed. "An advanced wedding present to assist with your meagre fishing skills! But only to be used once you are married, okay?" He was in a generous and almost sentimental mood.

Touched, I eagerly tore open the package. Before me the most glorious sight imaginable. Nestling in its special box, lay a wooden handcrafted Scarborough reel. As any fisherman knows, this was the king of reels, designed in an English town of the same name and used religiously by all authentic Natal beach fishermen. These reels – made of turned wood running on Rolls-Royce ball bearings – require serious skills, skills that separate the true fisherman from the amateur. I was smitten, mindful of the honour bestowed, and expressed my gratitude effusively. Somehow, thank goodness, I resisted the urge to hug him.

The big day came and the wedding passed in a blur of bonhomie and love. Given the fishing theme, one could say that Diane and I were finally 'hooked and landed'. After a first night in a local hotel, the freshly minted Mr and Mrs Chennells took to the road in my old Toyota Corolla, still clanking tin cans. Destination: Mazeppa Bay Hotel, Transkei, Wild Coast. With the honeymoon as part of my portfolio, I had sold the venue to Di on the merits of its beauty and isolation, and its promise of one-on-one time, beach swims and walks. The *romance* of Mazeppa was thus the chief of its attractions. Only as an apparent afterthought I added, casually, "Oh and I hear the fishing is good too."

And so, the honeymoon couple headed for fishing paradise. Through the green hills of the Transkei, past scrawny cows, bustling black pigs and waving locals we flew, my mind focused on the denizens of the deep lining up to be hauled on to shore. Silently I pledged to them that I was on my way.

Mazeppa Bay Hotel proved to be better than the brochures claimed: thatched and rustic, with views over coastal forest and cobalt-blue ocean, all bathed in the sound of breaking waves. Delighted, we unpacked, and after a lunch of freshly caught line-fish (a good sign) Di announced that she was heading to our honeymoon cottage for an afternoon nap. "Have a good rest, my dearest," I said solicitously, my own alternative ideas taking shape in the flash of a fin. "I think I'll try out that brand new reel your dad gave me. And don't worry, I will be back in time for dinner, I promise." To emphasise my serious commitment as a first-day New Husband, I repeated, "Really, I promise!"

And thus, the long-imagined scenario played out. Scarborough reel and rod firmly in hand, with a fresh packet of sardines emitting that glorious pong from my satchel, I scurried with indecent haste along the coastal forest path and across the white sand towards the 'island'. This famous fishing spot was a rocky promontory stretching far into deep water, separated from the mainland by a deep and dangerous gully, and crossed at one's peril via a rusty hanging bridge. A perfect setting for my imminent triumph over myself, nature, and – most importantly – my father-in-law.

I arrived at about three o'clock. Low tide. With pounding heart, I skipped across the swaying bridge where waves surged a metre below the wonky planks, hastening to a spot where the rocks cascaded down into deep green water. Inviting beyond description and not another soul in sight. Within seconds the first sardine of the day was hoicked from the box, beheaded, filleted and affixed to a sharp hook with stretchy cotton. Surveying my work, I beheld a seductive fishy temptation, deadly hook peeping out the side, and smiled. Sardines, the ubiquitous bait of choice for east coast fishermen, sacrificing their silver lives in the pursuit of the fisherman's dream.

I caressed the polished reel as I balanced on the edge, turned my back to the ocean and in the first sweeping cast launched the delectable offering deep into the sea. The reel whirred, the line sped out and as the bait and sinker landed sweetly on the water my pent-up breath escaped with a whoosh. I was in a fishing trance, that mystic fusion of calm yet latent excitement that erupts at any hint of quarry. The wind and swell were quickening, making it hard to tell whether occasional touches on the line were nibbling fish, or wave surges. The Rolls Royce reel purred. Twice, strong tugs had me striking furiously with heart in mouth, only to reel in sorry-looking bait that had been bitten without hooking the biter.

Ancestors were cajoled and cursed in turn as I cast again and again into the ocean. Ken Shimwell was my constant companion, his taunting spirit mocking me aloud, "Come on boy, is that the best you can do with my special reel?" On and on I laboured until suddenly it struck me that the sun had set. Waves crashed over the hanging bridge and the wind had picked up. But at the bottom of the box, a solitary silver sardine lay in wait. I stared at it, realising with a quiver of anxiety that around now-ish my New Wife would be donning her cocktail dress and starting to fret.

Di, unique in many ways, conformed to one stereotype: she was red-headed and feisty as a fox. I figured that a tropical storm was likely brewing within the four walls of our nuptial nest. Yet that last sardine bait could not be ignored. Destiny beckoned; surely that trophy monster was out there, waiting. I took the bait and prepared the hook.

Into the rich twilight air that sardine arced majestically, but this time, within seconds of its landing, chaos erupted. The rod bent double, the reel spun madly and the line hummed as a massive fish dived deep. Gasping with elation, I tried to inhibit the creature's escape; my fourth left finger, whose sole job it was to steady the line, was taking the brunt of the mad unspooling, while the whirring handles slammed into the digits remaining.

A Scarborough reel sports no gears, control is exercised by slowing the spinning reel with one's own fingers (soon lacerated) and hands (soon bruised and burning). Gritting teeth through the pain, I applied the fishing wisdom of ages: *Let the fish run and tire . . . Then pull her in slowly and steadily . . . time she runs, let her go, but apply brakes to tire her out . . . Repeat, keep going . . . Remember, if you give in now, you're the loser!*

The battle raged. I pleaded with gods known and unknown not to let my adversary, fighting for its life far below, escape our combined destiny. After some twenty-five minutes, the fish was finally close to the surface. My strategy, not having brought a gaff or a net, was to yank it onto the rocks with the help of a wave, grab it, and deliver the death blow. My body ached, but victory was surely nigh. I just needed to *land* the beast, then return to wife and hero's welcome.

At last, I caught a glimpse of my adversary. As I'd suspected, a massive kob, nearly five feet long, lolling in the water, exhausted. There was no time for congratulations, though I did indulge the thought of Ken's disbelieving face. Wave after wave surged onto the rocks. The timing had to be perfect to allow it to land on the ledge a metre below. After anxious moments, a perfect wave approached and I applied every ounce of strength left to lift the dead weight on the line. The rod bent double, and, as my prize swept onto the ledge, the extra tension ripped the hook (which was only snagged in the side of its mouth) right out.

The rod sprung upright like a whip, sending hook, sinker and bait flying dramatically backwards past my head. The scene before me froze in time. The massive beast lay for a moment gasping and stranded a metre below, still unaware of its last-minute reprieve. My mind blank but for one thought. Hurling rod and reel far behind me, I jumped down onto the ledge and threw my arms around the muscled body in a Siya Kolisi-type rugby tackle, crunching both knees and an elbow hard against sharp rocks. Wide, round fish eyes mere inches from my face, I tightened my embrace to heave it onto the upper ledge. Hugging a wet fish in the dark on the first night of my honeymoon, lifelong bragging rights over Ken were within my grasp.

Heartbeats later, a wave crashed over us. My fish, sensing freedom, thrust its powerful tail, propelled itself inexorably forwards, and, like a cake of fishy soap, slipped out of my agonised embrace. As my scream rent the air, the kob folded back into the ocean with a last pitying look, and, like Leonardo di Caprio in *Titanic*, slid oh so gently out of sight. In a daze, I crawled off the slippery, bloodstained rocks onto the ridge above. I had lost the game. I limped towards the hanging bridge, now disappearing and reappearing as each surge rolled over the boards. Any of those waves could have swept me away, forever. Somehow, I made it over in the dark and then hobbled like a wounded crab up the beach, through the forest towards the hotel's flickering lights.

As I staggered towards the group gathered on the hotel lawn, Di rushed forward, gasping with horror at my bloody appearance, all anger evaporated. From the wide eyes of the crowd I must have looked like a mutilated bomb survivor. Still numb with shock, I bathed, then had the numerous painful gashes cleaned and dressed. Hours later, covered in plasters, I attempted to re-enter the normal world represented by our first honeymoon dinner. Tough. Sitting with my new wife, with our holiday and life together stretching ahead, I kept returning to the image of that kob sliding forever into the deep. Fishermen will understand the agony of this. They know that 'there's nothing worse than the one that got away. It haunts you like a bad dream, eats away at your psyche like a termite on softened wood' (Bruce Littlefield).

The next morning I recovered the Scarborough reel and rod which lay unused for the rest of the honeymoon. On our return, Ken was naturally ready to milk the story mercilessly. "So, what did I hear about that tiddler that got away, hey boy?" he crowed over the phone, adding taunts about clumsy, inept fishermen. Normally these would have triggered a cheeky riposte and we would have bantered for weeks, but to Ken's disappointment I failed to rise to the bait.

Perhaps there was more to losing that one special fish than met the eye. Some years later, my marriage with Di entered troubled waters and I was in imminent danger of losing my entire family, washed off the precarious rock of marriage. I met with Ken. "To what do I owe this unusual pleasure, boy?" was Ken's jocular greeting as I entered the door of his municipality office, where he was manager of the local airfield. I blurted out the purpose of my visit, namely to inform him that I intended separating from his daughter.

After a long silence, during which he stared in disbelief, he suddenly burst out sobbing, body-shaking tears. This was unknown territory. Ken was not one for any display of weakness or emotion. Shaken, I walked around the large desk and tentatively put my hand on his shaking shoulders. "Don't be sad, Ken, I will keep in touch, I promise!" I murmured reassuringly. My words resulted in more intense sobbing. Slumped over the desk, with his head on his arms, he finally blurted out. "No man, I am not sad about *you*, you idiot! I am sad about myself. I never had the bloody courage to leave when I should have!"

As inexorably as did that massive fish, my marriage slipped away into the murky waters. And whilst I limped away and patched up the scars just as on Mazeppa island, the pain from that loss also went agonisingly deep. Many years later, and with Ken long departed to the heavenly fishing grounds, I am better able to reflect. Some losses, like that old kob at Mazeppa, simply cannot be fully recovered from. One can simply learn the lesson, and, occasionally, tell the story.

10

High Court, High Treason

In my final year at law school the Pietermaritzburg articled clerks arranged an 'international' rugby tour to Swaziland. As clerk secretary, my job was to book hotels, rugby fixtures and a bus for twenty-five enthusiasts, being the team plus hangers-on. This was to be our last outing as not-yet lawyers prior to the year-end final exams, and our lives beyond. I had also become engaged to Diane, who was on a six-month rotary exchange in the USA.

Former generations of Pietermaritzburg articled clerks included infamous characters such as Raka Randles, Snake Hedley, Spico Dickson, Jaws Vermaak and Grunter James who had developed a strong sub-culture stating, "Don't take law *too* seriously. Soon you will be a lawyer and will be stressed for the rest of your life!" During our law apprenticeships most of our bosses had served their own clerkship in Pietermaritzburg, and oft turned blind eyes when we deviated from the highest standards of the profession.

Worthy lawyers-to-be boarded the bus that winter's morning. Gasping-Gut Gemmel, Stroppy Boyes, Pump Larkan, Pinetree Scott, Superstud du Plessis, Murmer Migau, Harry Brown, Crime Bland, Beanbag Smith, Theory Reid, Smutty Smythe, and me, Legs Chennells. The journey to Swaziland via Zululand was spirited. Freedom and booze flowed down the bus aisle. Some jokers ostentatiously 'married' chosen partners on the bus, presumably to legalise their intended co-habitation, exchanging vows and making drunken speeches upfront next to the driver.

Superstud du Plessis professed undying love as he married a wild-eyed lass with the physique of a front row forward. Exuberant 'moonies' en route aimed bare bums out of windows at selected targets. I had earnestly reassured my fiancée that I would be responsible on the trip, but my blurred memory of the journey does raise concerns.

After winning three spirited games, we drew up at the Swazi Casino in Mbabane. This last night of the tour opened to a celebration. We descended on the casino like hungry locusts and the revelry quickly escalated into 'wheels off', namely that state of excess that one hides from parents. Stro Boyes performed his famous glass-eating trick, signalling that the evening was spiralling out of hand. In between swigs he bit large chunks from his beer glass, crunching and swallowing with a goofy smile. Onlookers egged him on and wondered when he would keel over and die. How I hated that trick, anticipating a midnight rush to hospital and his agonised death. Thankfully he munched up the entire glass, was rewarded with a fresh beer and the attention moved to the next drunken idiot. Some became more exuberant, others passed out.

At midnight the casino staff flickered the lights. Loud protests issued from revellers being herded into the darkness by the bouncers. Noisily, we streamed over the neat lawns in the direction of our nearby hotel, still clutching drinks. Three flagpoles adorned with fluttering flags suddenly appeared. It seemed an excellent idea to climb a four-metre pole and capture the most alluring flag. Shouts of encouragement egged me upwards. As I reached the flag the pole broke with a loud crack, tumbling me to the ground and striking the chief instigator, Stro, on the head. Unharmed by the fall, I loosened the flag, rolled it into a ball, passed it out to my fly half, Harry, sprinting past on the blind side. Into the darkness we careered, dodging imaginary opponents and diving to score a crowd-roaring try in a soft flowerbed. Then at our hotel, we fell into a deep slumber with the flag still wrapped around my body.

Before dawn the Swazi national police raided the hotel, hunting the miscreants who'd afronted the integrity of the Swazi State. I was shaken awake to find myself staring into two assault rifles. Barking commands, they yanked off my blankets, revealing the Swazi flag wound around me. Exhibit A. Evidence of a crime. In the Swazi flag, red is for past battles; blue for peace and stability; yellow for resources. A Nguni shield and two spears, the central focus, symbolises protection from the country's enemies. And we had insulted these symbols.

Triumphantly, the belligerent officer-in-charge, detective-sergeant Mbambo, manhandled me into the wire-caged police van, soon joined by equally dishevelled co-flag thieves, Stro and Harry. The van sped off with us jerking wildly from side to side. First stop the police headquarters where we were taken to the office of the Chief of Police, nattily dressed, very black, and urbane. He started the meeting politely and offered us tea in fancy cups. His polite questioning became irritated, when, in response to his question why, I suggested, "Chief, we were drunk and did not know it was the Swazi flag." An even bigger insult. The tea party ended.

"I am charging you with treason." The penalty was death. Detective-sergeant Mbambo smiled mirthlessly, his expression conveying something like 'Take that, you smug white boys!'

Curtly dismissed, we were then jostled back into the police van, disorientated. "Do you think they will come and release us?" asked a visibly pale Stro, no longer brave. Surely this crazy dream would end soon? An equally pallid Harry shrugged, in a vain attempt at nonchalance. Our plight sank in. Next stop was Mbabane police station where detective-sergeant Mbambo had a photo taken of himself with the stolen flag before shoving us into a pre-trial holding cell. Three by three metres, urine pot in one corner, walls grimy with graffiti, with one postage-stamp barred window, six feet high. Four surly black men sitting on the floor looked up suspiciously as we were pushed in. No option but to sit near the urine pot.

Communications were stilted. A gaunt man in ragged clothes spoke some English and introduced himself as a bicycle thief, whilst the others were less forthcoming. As we adapted to this scene-change, an elephant of hope began to stir in the room. Our tour bus had been scheduled to depart at midday for Pietermaritzburg. Surely our friends would not leave without us? Perhaps they could explain that the whole business was merely a student prank deserving of a sincere apology? Hours later we heard the diesel bus outside. Joy and elation. At last, the end was nigh, and we would be saved. Climbing onto a crouching Harry's back, I peered through the bars at our bus parked below. A delegation briskly crossed the courtyard. After a few minutes they returned to the bus, body language indicating defeat. As the bus growled away, I clambered down to face my dejected companions.

Night presented fresh challenges. To sleep in the tiny space we had to lie virtually on top of one another, whilst straining to keep heads as far from the piss pot as possible. One blanket each did little for warmth. The bicycle thief sang, "Way back then in sixty-three, oh what a night" from an old hit all night long. Our requests for him to shut up were met with manic laughter, and it seemed stupid to risk a fight. Another inmate warned that young men like us were prime targets in prison, where senior criminals vied to select 'wyfies' (mates) for sex. I fell into a fitful sleep and woke early with a black leg draped over my stomach, the owner snoring peacefully. Legs intertwined with strangers, bodies aching from the concrete floor, our nostrils had grown accustomed to the stench. Soon after dawn we were yanked out of the cell and hurled into Mbambo's familiar police van.

Next destination, the Swaziland High Security Prison. Personal details and fingerprints were recorded, followed by body searches involving removal of all personal items that might enable violence. While I was emptying my jeans pockets, a guard yanked at an object which resisted at first, and then snapped out, slapping his finger. The offending item that lay twitching on the floor was a pink rubber condom. Hilarity erupted amongst the guards who called others to look, danced around it as if it was a snake, one joker pretending to kill it with his truncheon. This levity at my expense resulted in sniggers from my mates and teasing over the next days. The clerk recorded the offending item: one open condom. Two muscled guards armed with handguns and handcuffs then hustled us to the maximum-security cell. Massive keys opened a double metal door, exposing a room some fifteen by five metres in size, with small windows above reach. Twenty black long-term convicts sitting in one corner looked up as one. Stro and Harry looked as pale as Sunlight soap, Stro muttering through the side of his mouth, "Fuck-sake, guys, this looks bad, hey?"

The head guard addressed us curtly: "One blanket each. Food twice a day. There are the toilets," he said, indicating the three holes in the cement floor on the far side of the room, where a man was casually defecating, as if to demonstrate. After a brief pause, he added, "See those buttons?" pointing to red knobs in the walls about six foot high at intervals around the room. "Just press one, and guards will come." *Phew, reassuring*, I thought.

Adrenaline flowing, we outwardly feigned nonchalance, as if checking into a high security jail was a daily occurrence, while masking inner terror. The inmates huddled in the far corner looked like hostile, mean-faced baddies in a cowboy movie. Mindful of wyfie-seekers, we placed our rough grey blankets against the wall as far from the group as possible, which meant close to the toilets.

As we were settling in an odd-looking inmate came loping on all fours in our direction, a messenger. "The king wants to speak to you," the young man whispered hoarsely in good English, crouched like a baboon. We discovered later that he was a wyfie of one of the senior gang leaders, and not allowed to walk upright. This privilege was only allowed for gang members. My first response was, "So why can't he just come and speak to us?" to which the wyfie's eyes widened in horror. Clearly refusal of a command was not an option. Submissively, we followed him towards the group in the corner, also shuffling on all fours and tightening our backsides. Surely Harry, as the youngest, would be first choice as a wyfie? We squatted at the perimeter of the gathering.

A bearded prison 'king' sat against the far wall. The cell was ruled by the feared 28 gang, where admissions and promotions take place via violence and death, and senior members are awarded titles such as Prosecutor, Enforcer and Judge. They checked us out. Most had tattoos, and some upper arms were marked with the dreaded number 28. A swarthy man sitting alongside the king spoke curtly to us in siSwati and our messenger-wyfie translated. "You people must know the rules. If you press a red button, you will die before the guards come. Nobody sleeps until the king sleeps. Nobody eats until they have offered their food to their seniors." Lesser rules emphasised our zero status.

SiSwati is much like isiZulu, so on impulse I spoke to the king, kicking off with a respectful greeting in isiZulu. He looked up in surprise. "Sinibingelela ngokuzithoba" (We greet you all humbly), "Siza ngenhlonipho" (We come with respect). "Eish, madoda, simoshile kabi"

(But eish, gentlemen, we have screwed up badly). The king smiled broadly at the last comment and his sidekicks followed his example.

The swarthy man said in siSwati, "Hau madoda! This white guy speaks our language." Encouraged, I continued. "iNkinga wethu, Numsana, sintshontshe ifulegi samaSwazi" (Our problem is, Sir, we stole the Swazi flag). "Bathi Inkosi uthukuthela kakhulu nathi" (They say the King is very angry with us). A burst of laughter followed the last reference to the Swazi King, shifting the mood in the cell. The Swazi King seemed to be held in low regard. The prison king's spokesman indicated with a dismissive hand that our audience was over, so we shuffled tight-bummed on all fours back to our blankets.

Another "Oh, what a night" lay ahead. In my exhaustion I fell asleep before the king, and started snoring. Rudely I was shaken awake by Stro who had been urgently alerted by our wyfie translator. Pointing wide-eyed at me he drew his finger across his neck. I lay awake for the rest of the night. Exhausted and hungry, the next day there was no escaping the call of nature. The so-called midday meal was another low point when we joined a line for pap (stiff porridge) and fatty gruel served on chipped enamel plates. We handed over the unappealing mixture to the gang. Not having eaten in two days, my hunger, with continuous adrenaline pumping, was now a dull stomachache.

That afternoon we were informed we had a visitor and were led down echoing passages to the meeting place. Friends back home had arranged legal assistance. Through metal bars we met our appointed attorney Mr X, who not only looked dishevelled and nervous, but also smelled of booze. One of the few white attorneys in Mbabane, known more for his fondness for alcohol than his prowess in court. Apologetically, as if responsible for our plight, he confirmed with a slight stutter that we had been formally charged with treason, and that the case had made headlines both in South Africa and Swaziland. Worse news was that the Swazi King was taking the insult personally, and insisted on making a public example. We were to be charged in the High Court the next day. Glumly, he added that the Swazi High Court still retained the tradition of a Sergeant-at-Arms, a man armed with a traditional bamboo rod for carrying out beatings in criminal matters. His, "S-s-see you in court, chaps," as he left the room evoked the opposite of confidence. How my loved ones would weep at my demise. What would they write on my tombstone, I pondered?

Trial day dawned. Stro and Harry looked and smelled terrible and confirmed that I was no different. We were hustled to a chaining room where Stro and Harry were shackled to each other with heavy iron leg clamps. I was roughly shackled to my own partner for the journey, a scary looking inmate who faced trial for armed robbery. The sorry procession shuffle-clanked into the street which led to the High Court. The shackles bit into our ankles, and as we passed groups of locals they gawked, sniggered and took photos. The three white South Africans were centre stage.

To metallic clanks, we shuffled into a large, panelled courtroom. I noticed the burly Sergeant-at-Arms at the entrance, brandishing *that* bamboo stick. Besides our lawyer, who was sitting meekly at the front, we three were the only whites in the court. The public gallery was jam-packed. The traditional call of "All rise" by a pompous orderly signalled the stately entrance of a grave and elderly black judge. An incongruous English-style wig perched on his head, relic of colonial days, lending him an avuncular and even comic air. The young prosecutor, wearing a traditional black cloak over his black suit, was similarly adorned with a smaller white wig.

The court orderly sang out, "The Kingdom of Swaziland v Chennells and two others." Now unshackled, we edged our way into the dock. The formal charges ended with the words, "You are hereby charged with the crime of treason against the Kingdom of Swaziland." Waves of nausea. We each had to plead to the charge. "Not guilty, Your Honour," I intoned, followed by the other two. An angry glare from the Sergeant-at-Arms hushed the buzzing at the back of the court. Our attorney, exuding submissiveness, first handed in a formal admission that we had indeed taken the Swazi flag, stating that would provide evidence in mitigation as to our intentions and state of mind. Detective-sergeant Mbambo then confidently related the facts, handing in as Exhibit A one Swazi flag, repeating that he had found it wrapped around my waist. He was clearly the star of this show.

As the flag was unfurled, the muttering from the audience grew. Truly their King had been insulted. If this had been a lynch mob, the ropes would be unfurled about now. Then it was my turn as the eldest of the accused to testify. Trying to strike a combination of humble and contrite together with firm and honest, I admitted that we had indeed wrongly taken the flag but were unfortunately drunk at the time. The audience murmured. This had clouded our judgement, I explained, for we did not know the Swazi flag, and had no intention of disrespecting the King. The judge listened respectfully, scribbling notes throughout.

Suddenly, the prosecutor approached the bench, delivering a note to the judge. Something strange was afoot. After reading it twice, the old judge announced a recess and returned to his chambers with a furrowed brow. Like three blind mice we whispered to each other in the dock while awaiting our fate.

Returning a long five minutes later, the judge creaked into his chair and then announced gravely, "Following an intervention from the King of Swaziland, the charge of treason is to be withdrawn" – he paused to give effect to his message – "and changed to theft of a flag." These words sank home. Only theft? No more treason, no more death penalty?

We shook hands with each other and with our equally bemused lawyer. The father of a friend back home had contacted the Swazi King directly, persuading him that it would be unwise to charge three white future South African lawyers with treason. Cheated of the drama, many in the court muttered their disappointment, whilst detective-sergeant Mbambo scowled; his chance of fame and glory had slipped through his fingers. Still nervous about the bamboo rod being included in our sentences, we pleaded guilty.

The judge confirmed the sentence, adding that we were to be banished from Swaziland as Lifelong Prohibited Immigrants. Gadoef! The bang of the gavel signalled the end of the trial. We were processed, thumb-printed, photographed, then driven handcuffed to the border in our favourite police van by the now-morose detective-sergeant Mbambo. Dazed and compliant, we watched the words *lifelong prohibited immigrant* stamped in each passport. Finally, we were pronounced free to go.

Unshaven, filthy and smelly, we entered South Africa and hiked to Pietermaritzburg, returning gratefully to our respective celebrations, explanations, and cover-ups. My own family's responses ranged from amused to embarrassed, whilst my fiancée Diane's relief had a certain thin-lipped quality. Future father-in-law Ken revelled in the dodgy exploits of his about-to-be son-in-law.

Early the next year, I lodged my attorney admission documents, briefing ex-yachtsman hero and advocate Bruce Dalling to guide my entry into the High Court. My proud parents drove three hours from Eshowe to attend the admission ceremony and to celebrate the first lawyer in the Chennells family. We rarely ate out as a family, but for this occasion we reserved lunch at an expensive restaurant.

When my case was called, I beamed at my parents from the dock, confident and proud. How far I had come. How special to be finally admitted to the hallowed ranks of the Side Bar. Judge-President Neville James shuffled through my papers, frowned, then leaned ominously over his desk with glasses on nose. Advocate Dalling blanched at this development, and I too stiffened, sensing an ill wind.

Gravely the judge pointed out to my now-perspiring advocate that his client's affidavit of good character was deficient. "Mr Chennells appears to have omitted a very public recent conviction, Mr Dalling." A titter ran through the court, and I clenched my knocking knees. Embarrassed by the oversight and shaking like an autumn leaf, Advocate Dalling adjourned my application *sine die*, thus withdrawing my admission. With cheeks burning, I returned to my seat in the court gallery, avoiding the eyes of my parents. The restaurant booking was cancelled and, after a stiff farewell during which we all muttered platitudes of recovery, my parents took off on the long journey home. English to the end, my humiliation in court that day was never discussed.

I formally apologised to the law society for my omission, and was then finally, and humbly, admitted as an attorney of the High Court, this time with no drama nor family. Detective-sergeant Mbambo and his dedicated men remained alive in my dreams. How could life ever be the same after I had experienced such profound humiliation? Being a white criminal in a black country had emphasised the privilege I had taken for granted, and increased my awareness of the black experience of apartheid. An intention to use the Law to challenge unfairness against the weak grew as the Swazi flag flew in memory attached to its pole. No lawyer could be proud of his criminal history, and I invited the waters of time to wash over all traces.

Not even my children knew the story, but I should have known that such a seismic event in my songlines could not stay hidden. Forty years later, as my career in law was in its dignified closing stages, the slumbering ghost of the Swazi High Security Prison awoke. My aunt needed a guarantor to enable her to secure admission to an old age home in Somerset West. I graciously offered to use my senior attorney status by signing as a guarantor for her lease contract. Days later, an embarrassed official informed me that that formal security clearance to confirm my status as a person of sound morals contained a terse comment: *Police clearance fails. Applicant has criminal record. Convicted of theft, Mbabane. Declared Lifelong Prohibited Immigrant to Swaziland.*

Detective-sergeant Mbambo, the last laugh was yours.

IN COURT

11

How to Tie up a Case

In his *Sketches By Boz*, Dickens writes that "Curiosity has occasionally led us into both Courts at the Old Bailey. Nothing is so likely to strike the person who enters them for the first time, as the calm indifference . . ." The Durban Magistrate's Court is such a place; an aesthetic atrocity, and was surely designed by a loveless bureaucrat. This squat human anthill daily absorbs myriad creatures that scurry from the concrete parking lots towards the four gaping entrances, only to be disgorged eight hours later onto the baking slab.

All need courage to approach the forbidding grey portals and to enter the maze of echoing passages that lead within. Every space teems with humans who are either prosecuting, witnessing or attempting to evade the clutch of justice. Bored policemen converse languidly, accused persons lean against walls, youthful offenders slouch alongside their long-suffering families, all breathing in the gloom.

The high priests of this nether world are the prosecutors, pallid and humourless, clutching khaki files underarm, whilst lawyers strut like gladiators, batman cloaks over-arm, towards their appointed battles. The overconfident idiot lawyer in the movie *My Cousin Vinny* would fit in well. Exuding self-importance, these officials of the court converse tersely with anxious clients who are fodder for the day's serving of justice. The apex species in this forbidding world were the magistrates, in those days mainly sombre white men in black cloaks, who held sway with unrivalled powers. Hardly a place to spend one's days.

I was a freshly-minted attorney recruited by the verbosely named firm Berkowitz Kirkel Cohen Moss-Morris and Greenberg (abbreviated to Berk-Jerk). After two weeks, I was still green out of law school, and overwhelmed by the tide of law practice on bustling Durban's shores. I was yet to make my first court appearance. I imagined that in the fullness of time I would prepare thoroughly for a first case and achieve a maiden performance.

Whilst visiting the court early one morning, carrying out routine clerical errands for Berk-Jerk, a jovial voice boomed in the passage making heads swing. "Hey, Chennells, ma boy, how are you t'day, you beauooty?" Seconds later, the suited body emitting the greeting came into view, followed by, "Hey, buddy, can you represent my good client Mr Moonsamy, today?"

Mick Goss, one of my Berk-Jerk bosses, was the source of this unwelcome challenge. Dapperly turned out in a grey tailored suit that vainly strove to elongate a stout frame, he strutted towards me. A bedraggled Indian man with drooping clothes and posture, presumably the good client, accompanied him. "Nothing to it at all, Roger, ma boy," he breezed as he came to a stop, puffing slightly and wasting no time on pleasantries. "All you have to do is just ask the old Mag for an adjournment so that you can take further instructions, alright? I would do it myself, but I have an important engagement." He glanced at a gold watch on his portly left wrist.

Mick was an impossibly buoyant character with the personality of a bulldozer, and a barely controlled obsession with racehorses, which I suspected might well be his 'important engagement'. "Umm, sure Mick," I stuttered, lost for a credible excuse, "umm, but I really have to say that I have not actually appeared in court yet, and, uh, perhaps Mr Moonsamy would prefer someone more . . ."

Mick cut me short with an expansive wave of his chubby arm. Freedom was within his grasp and he was going in for the finish. "Naaah, Rog, old chap, forget about all that stuff. You just jump up when his name is called, tell the Beak[2] who you are and go for it. Piece o' cake, boet, simplest thing in the world . . . nothing to it man." The bulldozer was unstoppable, the deal was struck and Mick beamed from ear to ear. "Okay then, cheerio, Mr Moonsamy," he concluded as my thoughts tumbled. "I am delighted to leave you in the capable hands of my trusted and brilliant colleague Attorney Roger Chennells."

Mick was a master of unsubtle manipulation, yet I found myself glowing involuntarily at his florid flattery. Beaming at his good fortune, the chubby maestro strode off purposefully down the passage, greeting people exuberantly, left and right, until his jaunty greet-fest faded into the ambient din. Reality flooded my senses together with a spurt of adrenaline. The die was cast; I was about to appear in court.

Moonsamy, somewhat crestfallen at the sudden departure of his confident lawyer, sniffed and blew his nose heartily into a crumpled brown-stained handkerchief. After a good long honk, he looked at me sideways as if determined to put a brave face on what lay ahead, whilst stuffing the awful rag back into his coat pocket. "Okay, boss, so what we-all doing now, huh?"

Decisive action was required. With my reluctant client shuffling alongside, I located Court C, a cavern jam-packed with humanity and bustling in anticipation of another day of melodrama. Moonsamy, charged with breaking the shad fishing laws, took his place shiftily at the back of the court, under my strict instructions to step firmly forward when his name was called, and not to sniff or blow his nose whilst in the witness box.

That fishery officials had found four oversized shad hidden in the back of his greatcoat did not indicate innocence. "I'm telling you boss, sum-udder-fellas dey-all plunted dose shads in my coat and-all!" he whined in explanation. I nodded, my mind conjuring up a spectacle of the shifty Moonsamy wearing a necklace of four large fish, and feigning indignant surprise on being arrested. With anxious heart I entered Court C.

Three lawyers at the front table hauled law books from briefcases, exuding a relaxed assurance. Trying to emulate their demeanour, I recognised Cedric Baldwin, an irritating and pompous know-it-all who had graduated a year ahead of me. Cedric nodded at me dismissively as I sat down next to him, continuing to regale his two colleagues with a tale which emphasised his legal virtuosity. Glancing around the room I noticed a pallid and dark-suited young man sitting at a table on the opposite side, paging through brown files whilst addressing two policemen. Aha, the prosecutor, I figured, getting into the swing. I was about to represent my first client, everything falling into place. As Mick had said, surely it was going to be just a piece o' cake.

"All rise." The court orderly's booming voice was pompous and well-practiced. Calling the bustling courtroom to order was probably the highlight of his otherwise tedious day, so the clerk squeezed every possible drop of drama from this precise task. Gazing imperiously around as the echo of his voice faded, as if daring any person to squeak, he basked in a brief glow of power. In strode Magistrate Max, the feared and infamously eccentric doyen of Court C.

Heavy footsteps and slouching shoulders evoked the aura of a retired and world-weary wrestler, persuaded against his will to return to the ring one more time. Under bushy eyebrows, he glowered peremptorily around the court and slumped into his chair, cue for the gathering to settle down respectfully on the creaking wooden pews. I gazed around the gallery, noting the smattering of whites amidst the predominantly African and Indian crowd. Moonsamy caught my eye, and with a cocky 'thumbs up' sign bared his stained teeth in a snarl-shaped smile of encouragement. In a sudden surge of anxiety, I turned to focus on my part in the play.

"State vs Mr Norman Naidoo," boomed the court orderly, and a nattily dressed young man strode casually forwards to take his place in the witness box. I wondered what crime he was being charged with, guessing some form of white-collar offence. The pallid prosecutor sprang to his feet. "The state asks for an adjournment for further investigation, Your Worship," he enunciated unctuously. "Does anybody represent this man?" were the first words to emanate from the bench, the surly magistrate vibrating like a hippo rumbling in a swamp. Up to his feet leaped Cedric, sleek as an otter. With jaunty demeanour he piped up, "I do, Your Worship, the name is Cedric Baldwin, attorney at X Attorneys."

Mag Max was not impressed. "Well, Mr Baldwun?" he growled at the smirking young lawyer, who had unwisely exchanged a wink with a pretty girl in the second row. Cedric was in exhibition mode, a side of him I knew all too well. "Um, the name is BaldWIN, Your Worship," he oozed, "not BaldWUN, and I have total equanimity with regard to the proposed adjournment." He placed a pretentious emphasis on the curious word 'equanimity', a mistake as he was about to discover.

"You have equa-WHAT?" thundered the magistrate, thumping both hands on the bench in front of him and leaning forward ferociously. He had found a target for the suppressed anger that roiled within. Cedric's eyes widened in terror; his confident hubris replaced instantly by the posture of a puppy awaiting discipline. The room held its breath as this flash storm erupted, whilst the temporarily forgotten Mr Naidoo gazed in alarm from the magistrate to his now-cringing lawyer.

I frowned at my notes in case Mag Max caught my eye and took umbrage. "Um, sir, I mean um, Your Worship, what I said was I have *equanimity* concerning the adjournment," he stumbled, trying to extricate himself. His female admirer in the second row was now wide-eyed, with hand in front of her mouth. I allowed myself a brief stab of empathy for the squirming Cedric.

"Who you trying to impress with your fancy language, Counsellor?" thundered the magistrate, his fearsome gaze matching the intemperate outburst. "I demand normal language in my court." He paused, as if waiting for an answer. "You trying to impress someone hey, boy?" Perhaps old Max had noted the simpering girl. "Umm, no sir, not at all, sir, what I meant was . . ." "I know what you meant, you idiot." Cedric's attempt to explain was abruptly squashed. "But don't ever use that poncy language in my court again, you understand? Case adjourned, Mr Naidoo, you may leave." And with a loud thump of his gavel on the desk he looked pointedly at the prosecutor, ignoring Cedric's ingratiating words of apology. Mr Naidoo scuttled gratefully out of the box as his lawyer sank to his seat in a puddle of insecurity.

The prosecutor stood up and announced the next case. "State vs Reginald Moonsamy." My surprise at discovering my client's first name jostled with the realisation that I was up next. I turned around and noted that Moonsamy was already shuffling purposefully towards the witness box as instructed, awful hanky out of sight. So far so good. Standing up as calmly as I could, I took a deep breath and spoke firmly towards the bench. "Your Worship, my name is Roger Chennells, from Berkowitz Kirkel Cohen Moss-Morris and Greenberg, and I represent the accused before the court."

To my surprise, Magistrate Max leaned forward over his desk and rumbled, "Mr Prosecutor. Does this man not have legal representation?" Odd, I thought. Surely, he must have heard me. Perhaps he had a blind spot? Slightly deaf maybe? In a firm and much louder voice, trying to mask quickening breath, I introduced myself in a manner that could not be ignored. "Your Worship, I am Roger Chennells, attorney of the firm Berkowitz Kirkel Cohen Moss-Morris and Greenberg, representing Mr Reginald Moonsamy today." Magistrate Max now became visibly annoyed. "Mr Prosecutor, if there is no representation for the accused, kindly read the charges." I simply did not exist.

I began to hyperventilate as a crimson blush, my ultimate display of deep embarrassment, rose rapidly up my neck. The three lawyers shuffled their papers. No help there. Moonsamy cast a miserable gaze in my direction, looking as if he was considering a dash for the door, whilst another titter of mirth rippled through the appreciative court audience. They were getting their money's worth, for sure, enjoying the refreshing sight of lawyers getting a roasting. I stood speechless with my cheeks burning as the prosecutor droned out the details of the shad regulations that had been breached by Moonsamy, as if I were invisible.

A lone fly buzzed noisily around the stifling court and after a few long seconds I sank into my seat, ignored and clueless. The lawyer sitting on my other side leaned over towards me and whispered, "Hey, Chennells, don't you get it man? The Mag cannot see you because you are not wearing a fucking tie!" Digging in his briefcase he yanked out a clip-on tie, and in a grateful flash I clipped on the tie, black as a Henry Ford car. After a deep breath, I stepped forward and ventured again into the dreaded impact zone of Court C. Third time lucky?

"Ahem! Your Worship, my name is Roger Chennells, and I am here to represent Mr Moonsamy." There was a pause as the court audience held its collective breath, anticipating the next explosion from the bench. Even the noisy fly stopped buzzing, probably landing on a wall to better take in the drama. The prosecutor was sitting with his head in hands, seemingly fearing the worst. He clearly had suffered the erratic rages of Magistrate Max of the Thunderdrome whose eyebrows and peptic glare now swung slowly like the head of a wounded buffalo towards the source of these words.

The silence in Court C throbbed. "Oh, good morning, Mr Chennells. How good of you to join us," he grumbled, leaning forward. I swayed dizzily, feeling faint with relief and totally blank as to what I should do next. As I recovered my breath and the blood drained from my cheeks, a glance at my client revealed that Moonsamy's brown teeth were optimistically exposed in a tentative smile. Trying to encourage me perhaps? His lawyer was back on his feet, and things were looking up. The faintest rumour of a smile softened the granite of the magistrate's visage as he leaned forward. "Well, Mr Chennells?" he rumbled. He had clearly enjoyed his game, as had the appreciative court audience.

The adjournment was duly granted without further mishap. Bowing deeply, I took leave of this scene of my humiliation, whilst Cedric remained slumped in his chair, the entire bubble of his florid persona now devoid of air. The pretty girl had vanished. Soon I was walking fast towards the exit, the jaunty Moonsamy bobbing beside me.

Tales of my open-necked blunder would spread like a rash in Durban legal circles; my strongest feeling was gratitude at having survived the bout in the ring. My client tugged at my sleeve and as his unfortunate teeth bared in a sly smile, my heart warmed involuntarily towards him.

"You did velly good today, boss."

"Really, Mr Moonsamy?" I was eager, needy even, to receive any wisp of a tribute, even from this ragged fisherman.

"For sure, boss." To my surprise Moonsamy's shoulders started shaking with suppressed mirth.

"Hey boss, you was hennyway betta dan dat damfool hudda white-fella lawya, he was da number one foolish today 'ey boss?"

"Thanks, Mr Moonsamy," I muttered grudgingly as I scurried out of the anthill. I fingered the clip-on.

On such a day, henny compliment was welcome.

12

Horse Sense and the Law

My first *real* job at the age of twenty-eight with the Berk-Jerk law firm tinkled a salary of R900 per month into the coffers. More than quadruple my articled clerk's salary, so a life of opulence in the fast lane of the Law beckoned. Partner Ken Cohen showed me to a posh fifteenth floor office with Roger Chennells on the door in gold letters. To further inflate my overloaded ego, I was then introduced to my own secretary, the voluptuous Zelda, who towered solicitously over me on heels that added to her looming height. She proffered a manicured hand. I glowed. For the past two years I had shared an office, had to beg my boss's secretary to type letters. A nagging thought registered that this opulent status would come with a price, but whatever it would be, I'd pay.

Ken led me to two filing cabinets containing six hundred files, named and numbered, each one representing a motor accident in or near Durban. Our firm acted for an insurance company, and my job would be to defend the insured party in every case. Three model Dinky cars stood on the leather top of my wooden desk – a red Chev Impala, a white Volvo sedan and a black Ford truck. All sand-pit specials from my Dinky-car loving youth.

"Ken, um . . . aren't these a bit odd?"

"On the contrary, Roger," explained Ken, "these toys will be your most valuable tools. You get the clients to re-enact the accident using them."

Clearly my law career was going to be built on a strong foundation of motor car accidents, with my desk the busy intersection. "An excellent grounding for law, my boy." Ken strode away, as if reading my mind.

Berk-Jerk was a serious firm. The partners worked hard, and conspicuously spent the money they earned. Experts in their fields, they had all been divorced at least once, regularly graced the Durban social pages, and drove flashy XJ6 Jaguars. On Fridays I joined them for lunch in the walnut-panelled boardroom. Erudite discussion of legal conundra would be evenly mixed with raunchy or teasing banter, one or other of the partners being the squirming recipient of juvenile taunts.

Reg Berkowitz was ragged about his weakness for the female sex, Ken Cohen for his obsession with marathon running, and Milton Kirkel for his dwarf-like stature. All the partners tucked heartily into ham sandwiches, mouthing fervent apologies in the direction of their Jewish faith. Mick Goss was the only non-Jewish partner, a debonair character with the good looks and confidence of a short if overweight Robert Redford. An emitter of a sunny bonhomie that warmed all around him.

Soon after my arrival I was invited to assist Mick present legal argument in a case set down for final argument in front of Magistrate Smith, infamous despot and destroyer of weak attorneys. A few weeks before, Mick had led the evidence in court – a complicated motor accident involving huge damages and legal intricacies. Now only the crucial and final legal argument remained.

Anxious to impress, I burned the midnight oil reading up a number of relevant cases, which I typed onto an expansive Heads of Argument. Mick would use this document to guide his argument and counter the onslaught from the opposing side. As arranged, I proudly delivered the document to Mick's desk the evening before the due date so that he could prepare overnight at leisure.

Early the next morning I knocked on Mick's door and entered, expecting him to be perusing the document in the final stages of honing his argument. To my surprise, the green file lay unopened on his desk.

And a debonair-looking Mick was lolling back in his massive armchair with a steaming mug of coffee in hand, feet on desk, avidly poring over racing fixtures.

Perhaps he had studied my Heads overnight, I fondly imagined, and was taking a short break? Ignoring my pointed glances at the waiting file, Mick launched into an enthusiastic summary of the racing prospects for the coming weekend. Best bet Starlight, the unknown gelding from the Barnabus stable, a shoo-in at 10 to 1 for a win in the third race. Such pearls were delivered conspiratorially, as if for my ears only.

Off to court we went, where Mick sauntered down the crowded passages, exuding the air of a portly gent off to a grand day at the Greyville races. Greeting every second passer-by with a wave and a smile and a typical, "Hey, Pete, howzit man, been meaning to phone you all week," leaving Pete gushing and beaming in the wake. We trotted into Court B in a cloud of bonhomie, five minutes before the starting gates opened.

"Let's go and meet the Mag, Rog," breezed Mick, making a beeline for a door marked Private, and entering without waiting for a response to his knock. I followed sheepishly, to find him already shaking the hand of a swarthy and thickset man, the feared Magistrate Smith himself. Grandly he introduced me as his trusted colleague, which brought an inward glow. Mick lost no time in sharing the Starlight and other hot tips with the feared legal maestro, who, to my great surprise, nodded, scribbling notes on a scrap of paper.

"Loves the nags, does old Smithy," was Mick's laconic comment later as he adjusted his batman cloak, settling down happily in the front row of court to await the hearing. I thought of Mark Twain's joke that whilst a good lawyer knows the law, a clever lawyer takes the judge to lunch. In this instance it would be the races.

Mick's opponent in the case, an elderly and respected Indian lawyer, Mr Paddayachee, had greeted him with a curt nod from his seat across the room, and unlike Mick, was restlessly paging over voluminous notes.

"So, what did you think of my Heads, Mick?" I could not resist asking at last. "To be honest, Rog, I haven't had a look yet," he said nonchalantly, flipping through my document in a vaguely appreciative way but with no focus. "I'm sure it's excellent stuff man, but I doubt that we'll need it," he whispered, oblivious to my dismay. "We are batting last, so we'll just let old Padda hang himself good and proper, and then I will wrap things up." I sank back defeated, concerned that with such nonchalance, if not pure laziness, our client's case was surely in trouble.

"All rise," preceded the haughty appearance of Mr Smith, who gave a curt nod at the full courtroom as the clerk announced the case. The two lawyers introduced themselves formally for the record, and Mick, rising confidently, introduced me as his learned assistant counsel for the defendant, which again left me glowing, although embarrassed at this insidious flattery.

"I will now hear legal argument," Mr Smith announced sternly, nodding in the direction of the elegant Mr Paddayachee. Impressively, counsel for the plaintiff then launched into a passionate and finely argued diatribe, criticising and demolishing each of the defendant's (our) witnesses in agonising detail. He then proceeded to construct an elaborate framework setting out the logical steps by which the plaintiff should surely succeed. Each laboured point was supported by a sombre tapping of the three piles of law report volumes, with frequent references to extracts read luxuriantly from selected texts. During a particularly erudite reading, elegantly punctuated with a manicured forefinger, the bored-looking magistrate cast a fleeting glance at Mick, as if sharing their impatience with all the words.

At last, during Mr Paddayachee's display of legal oratory, I was reassured to note that Mick was finally writing notes. *Thank god, I thought, he is at last taking this case seriously and planning the defence.* When I finally dared to peep at Mick's notes, there, in between a riot of loopy doodles, were primitive sketches of horses running at full tilt, as well as some other sketches that looked like winners' trophies.

Not one word had been written. Visions of himself raising racing trophies and rendering victory speeches, rather than thoughts of law, fuelled his artwork. My only glimmer of hope was that old Smithy was starting to sigh visibly at Paddayachee, bored more than impressed by the flow of eloquence. At one point, Mick looked up from his sketchpad at magistrate Smith, and gave him the tiniest wink, but I might have been mistaken.

Paddayachee ended his address with a verbal flourish. "And so, in closing, Your Worship, I trust that for all the many reasons I have submitted, you will award judgement to the plaintiff, with costs." He sank to his seat, mesmerised by the sheer magnificence of his articulacy. His client's extended family in the back of the court murmured in admiration and clapped respectfully.

I sank lower in my seat. Mick, unprepared as he was, could surely not match the powerful argument that had been delivered? He had not read my Heads, nor glanced once at the piles of law books that I had provided. Instead, he was putting finishing touches to the ears of a galloping racehorse. Wishing I were elsewhere, I steeled myself for the embarrassment that lay ahead.

Mick unfurled his stocky frame to a proud five foot six, jutting his jaw in the characteristic manner that I would later realise always preceded something dramatic. The slight grimace and neck-stretch was that of an earnest man, of portly mien and a just-too-tight collar, with an important message. "Your Worship," he began graciously, in a grave and respectful tone, "we have all listened at great length to the well-researched argument of my learned friend." At this point he bowed graciously towards Mr Paddayachee, who, unaware of the sting that lay in store, smiled indulgently in acknowledgement. Mick's stubby left hand now picked up my unread Heads of Argument and waved it around in the air. "We all know the facts of this case, Your Worship, and I will not attempt to insult your intelligence, as did my learned friend, by imagining for one second that you are not fully aware of all those facts."

At this point Mr Paddayachee stiffened, whiffing the odour of an unpleasant turn of events. But Mick was only warming up. "I have in my hand, Your Honour, our detailed Heads of Argument, in which we set out all the reasons and supporting cases showing why our client, the defendant, should succeed. However, Your Honour, you know these cases far better than we do, so I will merely hand this in without comment for your own later perusal."

Old Smith listened intently as Mick's flattery rose, and as he moved towards a respectful culmination. "There is in my view nothing I can add, Your Worship, being mindful of your own considerable knowledge." Mick's tone raised a few notches. "Indeed, Your Worship, I have no doubt at all that when considering your verdict, you will naturally conclude that the defendant must succeed, and I am not prepared to further waste the court's or even my learned friend's valuable time (at this point he bowed graciously towards the now glowering Mr Paddayachee) for one second further." Then the final unctuous *coup de grâce*, in a lower voice laden with earnest gravitas. "Your Worship, I fully anticipate that justice will be done, and entrust the result to your capable hands, sir."

Mick sat down. The plaintiff and supporters sat in stunned silence, aware of the sublime mastery with which their lawyer's case had just been eviscerated. Paddayachee had turned pale, staring ahead like a man who had seen a ghost.

Magistrate Smith shuffled his papers, trying not to glow from Mick's sycophantic words, and asked Mr Paddayachee politely if he had anything further to say. For once the great orator was stumped, and he shook his head heavily, his mouth pursed in a sulky pout. The magistrate then stated that judgement would be reserved due to the "complexities of the legal issues raised" and I began to pack the untouched volumes into two suitcases. Mick made a charismatic exit from Court B, after first shaking the deflated Paddayachee's reluctant hand and congratulating him sincerely on his excellent performance.

Judgement was duly delivered in our client's favour. How could it have been otherwise? Mick's masterclass showed that horse sense is a winner on the racecourse of the law.

13

Sonnyboy Sweetbreath and the Greatcoats

After completing a Master of Laws in London in 1980, I returned to Durban. My time with Berk-Jerk had given me confidence, so it seemed time to launch my own humble quest for justice; my very own law practice. An overworked phrase, but to make a difference.

I secured a humble second-floor suite of rooms in Denor House, corner of Field and Smith Streets, plus a bank overdraft facility which made me dizzy with financial power. Choosing typewriter desks, stationery, chairs, carpets, kettle, teacups and telephones was the fun part, plus an unnecessary brass plate that grandly announced, "R S Chennells & Co." There was no Co.

On 1 June 1981 I grandly opened my door to the eagerly awaiting world.

A lonely day. And then another crawled by, without a peep. Followed by two more. No client feet crossed the threshold that first week. Pencil triple-sharpened, desk re-tidied, pictures rehung, and all friends and relatives phoned. Where were all those needy people? During this lean period, I practised a variety of phone-answering styles, all designed to convey an impression of mature professionalism. The first version, "Good morning, Chennells speaking," murmured in a deep and sonorous tone. Then I tried the punchy and, in my mind, far more impressive version namely "Chennells?" spoken from the belly with a rising lilt, sort of indicating 'busy, but at your service, if you so wish?'

On Friday morning, my unemployed friend Dick Frost, proud inventor of Frosty's Floating Soap (a South African version of Soap on a Rope), who phoned to invite me for a beer after work, was greeted with the rendition of "Chennells?" Dick exploded in snorts of laughter which I found annoying. Recovering his composure, he was merciless. "Fuck Rog, who the hell are you trying to impress, man?" he wheezed, between shuddering gasps.

With pained dignity, I accepted that the greeting was perhaps, well, just a tad pompous. Over the next days I tried out more authentic answering styles in response to Dick's derision. On rare occasions, when the phone actually rang, I would first tense up over it, breathe deeply a few times, wait for another three rings so as not to seem too eager, then snatch it up and murmur, "Chennells and Company" in a controlled and reassuring voice. Somewhat detached, not too eager, available and at your service whoever the hell you might be. When the caller turned out to be my dear Mum, who phoned at least once a day to check if I had any clients yet, it was hard not to show my disappointment. After a year away I had no client base. My optimism dissolved like morning mist.

During the second week a dubious creature from the underworld sidled into my chambers. A Zulu man, well dressed despite being somewhat emaciated and sporting an erratic deck of bad teeth, slipped through the open door; unknowingly breaking my zero-clients duck and becoming my first case. He approached the reception desk in the wary manner of a hungry jackal approaching a lion kill. I ushered him into my office before he could retreat. My first real live client. I felt a gush of joy. Gazing over my new oak desk at this dodgy specimen, I savoured the significance. This was me, finally about to apply my years of training to bring justice into the world. I selected a viciously sharpened pencil, and assumed the position. "So how may I help you, Mr, um?"

A blast of halitosis accompanied his response, delivered in surprisingly good English. "Mr Mseleku," he stated firmly, "*wrongly* charged with dealing in dagga, and in need of an excellent lawyer." His watery eyes roved slyly around the room, darting back to me every few seconds, as if to check for danger. Prominent teeth yellow, and rotten, dominated an asymmetrical and pock-marked face set in a permanent humourless grimace. I marvelled at the fellow human, a perfect casting as a low-life hitman in a Coen brothers gangster movie. The expensive dark suit was grubby, confirming its owner's disinterest in hygiene. A further toxic blast that could peel paint off a wall followed his words over the desk.

Leaning backwards to escape the fumes did not help, so I opened a window. Taking short breaths through my mouth to lessen the discomfort, I prepared to get down to business. Gazing at the proffered identity document, I was astonished to see that his parents, in a fit of optimistic love but without foresight, had bestowed upon him the names Sonnyboy Sweetbreath Mseleku. Suppressing a recurring urge to giggle at this misnomer, I recorded his elaborate story of innocence, and prepared to defend him in court.

Sweetbreath's date with justice took place on a typical boiling Durban day. With my batman toga draped over my arm, I met my new client at the Umlazi Magistrate's Court, ready to do battle. With his sidling shuffle, bobbing limp, and dubious manner of gazing around with darting looks, my man looked every inch the shifty criminal I was trying to prove him not to be. As I gave him a full packet of XXX Mints designed to sweeten his 'aura', I was reminded of my elder brother Jono's favourite impersonation trick, namely the hoppy, limp-walk of Dustin Hoffman as the shifty Ratso in *Midnight Cowboy*. Destiny calling, walking and hop-limping, we made our way to Court C.

Sonnyboy paid no deposit, but had promised that his 'big boss' would attend the court case and sort out the finances. "Don' worry, Mr Roger, my boss, eishhhh, he a verrry reeeech man," he whispered with a conspiratorial leer-smirk meant to reassure. We took our positions near the front of the dark courtroom and rose to the traditional, "All rise in court." Mr Ntombela, heavy-jowled and sweating profusely in his black robes, shuffled in, bowed, and sat down with an audible sigh. Other than his discomfort, he seemed amiable enough. Gazing around the court, I noticed two massive black men with heavy greatcoats hulking in the back row, their felt hats and dark glasses adding an undercurrent of menace. One of them surely the boss.

Sonnyboy's case was next, and the magistrate raised a quizzical eyebrow at me as his unusual names were loudly called. I gave a sort of grin and eye-roll as if to say, 'Well, it takes all types doesn't it, My Worship?' My client sidled to the accused box looking for all the world like the shifty underworld dagga-dealer that we were trying to deny, flashing a smirk and a thumbs-up in the direction of the two men in the back row.

The court orderly read out the charge of dealing in marijuana, specifying that my client had been found in possession of no less than 2.5 kilograms of the illicit weed. This was a serious charge, and if found guilty, he would have a mandatory sentence of no less than two years in jail. "Not guilty, My Worship," stated Sonnyboy serenely and as planned.

I took a deep breath and gathered my wits. The very first case of R S Chennells & Co loomed like a mountain, and the shadow of the heavies in the back row loomed as large. After opening formalities, the first state witness was called to the stand, Constable JP van der Merwe. This heavy-set and serious young policeman had apprehended Sonnyboy at a road block with a car boot full of dagga, and had assumed from the large amount that he had to be a dealer. His evidence, that in light of the facts, it was fair to assume that my client, driver of the vehicle, was owner of the drugs. Drawing on street skills gleaned from my maestro-mentor Mick Goss, I smiled warmly at the sullen man who faced me uniformed and arms folded. "Be friendly, but brutal," Mick's rule 101. After some affable opening questions to make him relax, I ramped things up.

"So, Constable van der Merwe, I can understand you assumed that the marijuana belonged to my client."

"Yes, Your Worship."

"Was he the registered owner of the car, Constable?"

"No, he was not, My Worship."

"Has the registered owner of the car in fact ever been traced?"

"Um, no, My Worship, we have not been able to trace the owner."

"Did my client admit any knowledge of the marijuana?"

"Well, no, My Worship, he denied all knowledge of it, but I assumed that he was lying." (This line delivered with an ingratiating smirk aimed at the magistrate.)

"Did you ask him who the marijuana belonged to?"

"He said he knew nothing about it, that he was delivering the car as a favour to another person."

We were getting closer to the zone.

"Constable, have you any evidence whatsoever for this court, other than the fact that the marijuana was in the boot of the car, that my client knew about the marijuana and was thus dealing in the substance?"

"Well, um, no not as such, um, not actually, My Worship."

And then, the sting.

"I put it to you, Constable, that there is no *direct evidence* linking my client with the marijuana in the boot."

Mumbled answer, "Um, yes. I mean no, My Worship."

"And I put it to you, Constable van der Merwe, that the marijuana therefore might well belong to another person?"

"Well, I don't know, but I suppose it is possible, My Worship."

And then, my favourite part. These words seem unimportant, but if their timing is right, it indicates that I believe that the witness has nothing of value to offer.

"No further questions, Your Worship."

I demanded immediate dismissal of the State's case, reminding the worthy magistrate that my esteemed client was 'innocent until proven guilty', that the charges against him were purely circumstantial, and did not even make out a *prima facie* case. You can't *deal* in marijuana if it is not yours. The prosecutor knew he had no ammunition in the breech and handed in his deck. Folded. His only witness had been poorly prepared and could not sustain a conviction.

After some minutes of busy concentration during which he scribbled notes on a pad, Magistrate Ntombela pronounced that he was ready to deliver the verdict. "The police work has been shoddy," he pronounced gloomily, as he had probably said so many times before, "and the State evidence insufficient to prove the charges beyond reasonable doubt. No basis for guilt has been established." Solemnly, with a crash of his gavel, he concluded, "Mr Mseleku, the case against you is dismissed, you are free to go."

A grinning Sonnyboy lurched towards me for a beaming victory hug, and then Ratso-bobbed for the door doing an impromptu Kwaito jig as he went. The small crowd in court laughed at his unrestrained joy, a rare sight in this grim environment. Gathering my papers and books, I bowed towards the magistrate, then took the back door out of Court C into the bright summer's day.

Waiting for me on the tarmac were Sonnyboy and his two giant greatcoated friends. Those coats could hide a bunch of guns, for sure. The taller one, a blend of Mike Tyson and Laurence Fishburne, stuck out a ham to congratulate me, flashing a gold-toothed smile. In his other hand he held the largest wad of one-hundred-rand notes I had ever seen. Peeling them off he said in a hoarse rumble, "Mr Rogers, you very good lawyer, I want you to work for me!" A statement, no question involved. He then thrust the notes into my hand, which closed over them involuntarily like a clam. My first fees, like manna. To reject this payment would surely have been unwise.

Still enfolding my hand and the notes within, the Boss gave me the low-down. Intimately, with a subtle flavour of menace. He was in the dagga business, he said, as if talking about the laundry or restaurant trade. He employed about twenty drivers, including Sonnyboy. He 'kept' large numbers of policemen, even some magistrates, between Durban and Cape Town on his payroll. Sidekick nodded at me vigorously, as if encouraging me to believe every word, which I did. Boss was an underworld kingpin of note, for sure.

Was I now a brother, an insider, on Boss's mafia payroll? Mental gears ground and spun. By accepting his excess money and by hearing this incriminating information, had I now joined this immoral empire? Did I know too much? Would escape be followed by an unpleasant death? Shaking my money-stuffed hand warmly township style, the Boss ended our intimate *tete a tete* with a conspiratorial wink and a rumbled, "Okay, mister Rogers, I phone you soon."

With an escalating sense of unease, I forced a grimace as my new partners in crime climbed into their black Mercedes and sped off with squealing tyres. In a daze, I drove home. But what to tell Diane? How to explain such an excessive wad of notes? The answer came from a favourite mafia movie; the mafia boss, played by Al Pacino, guides the young gangster Donnie Brasco (Johnny Depp) how to respond when things get complicated and people ask questions. "You jus' look at them boy, and say, don' tok aboudit. And then you don' tok aboudit." I did so, and it worked.

Nor did I ever hear from the Boss or Sonnyboy again.

14

The Uitsig Squatters and the Magistrate

1988. Expectant eyes fixed on me. Johannes Pienaar, craggy-faced leader of the group, lit a pungent doobie, whilst a lanky youngster next to him idly scratched his crotch. Johannes's wife Katrina kept a gnarled hand on her man's knee, her wrinkled face corroborating San-Bushmen ancestry. The oldest by far, a man whom I later knew as Oom Andries, sat straight-backed and slightly apart, maintaining an air of refined dignity despite his tattered garb. At the far end of the pew a thin teenager hauled out a scrawny breast for her whimpering baby, whilst the girl next to her, possibly her sister, exuded a sexuality enhanced by the fake jewellery adorning her ragged dress. The smell of wood smoke, damp blankets and Boxer tobacco filled the reception area of the practice as the group slurped sweet tea served in tin mugs.

Chennells Albertyn was a young human rights law firm with one lawyer (me) and two long-haired articled clerks, David and Johan. We supported struggle organisations such as the Stellenbosch Advice Office, the Stellenbosch Housing Action Committee (SHAC), and anybody else on what we called the progressive or anti-apartheid side. The ragged group on our pew had that morning been forcibly evicted from Uitsig, a scattering of shacks on the outskirts of Cloetesville suburb. After eviction they had been criminally charged with trespassing on municipal land.

As I surveyed this assembly line, *The Dirty Dozen* sprang to mind. The heroes of that movie were a motley collection of desperate outcasts, dregs, misfits and losers who overcame adversity to achieve a miraculous victory. Back to my reality. All of the eleven characters on the pew, too, were a group of disparate, impoverished Coloured people. The acrid blend of wood smoke and stale alcohol accentuated precarious lifestyles on the edge of survival. Weathered faces contorted, bodies prematurely aged from sleeping rough, and ragged clothes all painting a picture of humble but resilient humanity.

The dirty dozen indeed. Most of them avoided my gaze, afflicted by shyness, and loathed to speak with the white lawyer. Regina, the activist from SHAC, who had brought them up the stairs looked at me trustingly. After a long slurp of tea, she said, "Roger, jy sal dan wiet wat om te doen, nê?" (Roger, you will of course know what to do, not so?) Patiently, I recorded personal details into a yellow case file. The heading read, "SHAC: State v Johannes Pienaar and ten others."

The brutalising of these homeless adults became the catalyst and rallying point for other unfortunates in town, who had been similarly mistreated. SHAC had been formed to assist the homeless in Stellenbosch and with the help of the advice office plus enthusiastic NUSAS students, the Uitsig evictions provided a potent focal point. By the time the first court appearance came around SHAC had grown into an energised activist organisation, fuelled by an eclectic membership of homeless, unemployed, unionists and vocal left-wing university students. Rousing speeches on housing and other rights were spouted forth at every opportunity, and the stirring singing of radical freedom songs like "Asimbonanga" became SHAC's powerful life blood. To the words "asimbonanga uMandela" (we have not seen Mandela) were added the names of struggle heroes like Neil Aggett, Steve Biko and others, sung in a mournful, moving dirge-like way.

Round One. A large mob of SHAC supporters gathered in town, toyi-toyied their way noisily down Alexander Street and streamed into Court B. Such aggressive support for a cause was uncommon in Stellenbosch. Police and court officials gazed on anxiously as the sombre, oak-panelled Court B filled with a murmuring sea of supporters. In my black suit and batman toga on this muggy February morning, I took my place in the front of the court, nodding curtly to my equally black-coated opponent, the chief prosecutor, Annette van Zyl. Her combined sniff and neck-twitch to my nod was as close to a greeting as one might hope for.

This humourless civil servant nurtured the belief that those entering her court were guilty as charged, and her mission was to get the court to confirm this fact. All those standing in the way of her quest for convictions, defence lawyers in particular, were obstacles standing in the way of justice. Magistrate van Niekerk, a surly career magistrate nearing retirement age, conservative of mind and belligerent of temperament, was already seated and glowering down at the court from his raised desk. We were ready to roll.

The court orderly, who had begun proceedings with the traditional "All rise," now announced the case, booming out, "State versus Johannes Pienaar and ten others," followed by the full names of all eleven accused. As my dirty dozen duly shuffled up towards the dock, the assembled faithful of SHAC immediately burst into a lusty, tumultuous rendition of the ANC freedom song "Nkosi Sikilel' iAfrika" (to become our national anthem) from the back of the court.

Van Niekerk erupted in magisterial fury, leaping to his feet, moustache and eyebrows bristling. "Stilte in my hof" (silence in my court) he bellowed, banging his gavel on the desk. Glowering at the now silent courtroom he snarled that if anybody uttered another syllable of that "blerrie Kommunistiese lied" (that bloody Communist song) they would be forcefully evicted and charged with contempt of court. His outburst had the desired effect. Mandela was not yet free, the Nationalist government was still firmly in charge, and all forms of open revolt were rapidly quashed. I rose to my feet in the hushed court and requested an adjournment in order to prepare the defence. Despite the prosecutor's objection, the magistrate grudgingly gave us two months.

A few weeks later Johannes Pienaar was injured and rushed to hospital. Possibly destabilised by cheap alcohol, he had fallen into a fire, suffering bad burns. He died within days, a shock to our preparations. SHAC ensured that he was buried with honour, the funeral becoming a barely-disguised anti-apartheid rally with rousing speeches of dissent and freedom songs. "Asimbonanga"[3] sung softly between the frequent shouts of the banned struggle war cry Amandla. Scores of surly police ensured law and order, and the upcoming court case against the squatters received wide publicity.

Round Two. By the time the trial date arrived, the SHAC support army had swelled, and exuberant singing of freedom songs in the street outside the courtroom had anxious officials peeping through windows. What revolution was taking place in peaceful Stellenbosch? The anticipation around the courtroom was at a high pitch, and scores of armed police stood by fidgeting and glaring. When the case was finally called a passionate rendition of "Nkosi Sikelel' iAfrika" erupted from those inside and outside the court. Magistrate van Niekerk became apoplectic, hammering his gavel on the desk, ordering the police to arrest any person who continued to sing.

The SHAC supporters quietened down and filed into court. As the trial started it was my task to address the still-fuming magistrate and inform him that the first accused, namely the late Johannes Pienaar had left the jurisdiction of the court. Ms van Zyl's irritated bearing as she reluctantly scratched Johannes Pienaar's name from the charge sheet seemed to imply that he had died deliberately to avoid the trial. The case name was then formally changed to "State vs Katrina Pienaar *and nine others.*"

I had pleaded with the SHAC supporters, whose ranks now filled the entire court, to curb the singing of freedom songs or any other disturbances during the hearing, as it would make my task more difficult. Plus, the magistrate was clearly dying for an excuse to have them locked up. To my surprise, Ms van Zyl now requested an adjournment as the State's key witness, the housing director in the Stellenbosch Municipality, had taken ill. Mr Cortina, a sensitive soul, had the unpopular task of dealing with the town's illegal homeless problem. He had been vilified by SHAC for his role in the squatter persecution, and at Johan Pienaar's funeral was repeatedly denounced in songs and speeches as an enemy of the people.

I resisted the temptation to attack Ms van Zyl for her chief witness's absence. Truth was that our case was not strong on the merits, and we were only too happy to enjoy the 'stay of execution'. The SHAC delegation filed out of the courtroom after the magistrate had departed, again singing "Nkosi Sikelel" whilst van Niekerk glared at them from the window of his office. He hated the entire SHAC movement, which seemed to embody what was happening in the country. Perhaps his loathing foresaw the ghastly prospect of a future ANC government.

The dirty dozen was to be further diminished. One cold night old Oom Andries, the frail and dignified old man whom I had warmed to on the first day, died following an asthma attack. I never found out how this refined man had fallen from grace, ending up living rough in an Uitsig shack. He would have smiled at the idea of becoming a struggle hero and was buried in Cloetesville with full honours and, like Johannes Pienaar, was lustily sung on his way by the SHAC faithful.

Round Three. When the next hearing came around and the court orderly read out the amended charge sheet, "Katrina Pienaar *and nine others,*" I again arose to inform Magistrate van Niekerk that sadly another member of the accused had involuntarily escaped from the court's earthly jurisdiction. The case renamed, "Katrina Pienaar *and eight others.*" A murmur ran through the crowd as the Beak glowered tetchily around the crowded courtroom, daring anybody to squeak. Without acknowledging the loss of another life, he barked at the remaining accused to rise, which they did with a creaking of prematurely aging limbs. Katrina on the far left, flanked by the eight remaining stalwarts. He lectured them on disrespect and wasting the court's time, implying a civic duty to stay alive when charged with a crime. To my horror, as he was in mid tirade, one of the eight survivors, a slight middle-aged grandma called Grieta, began to sway back and forth in the pew, eyes rolling. With a loud groan she suddenly keeled over backwards, crashing on the floor. She suffered from epileptic fits, but the timing could not have been more dramatic. Pandemonium erupted as the court officials rushed to assist, and the magistrate banged loudly with his gavel to curb the unfolding chaos.

Ms van Zyl's eyes rolled heavenwards in a theatrical display of pique, as if to say, "Typical! These people will do anything to escape justice." Key witness, Mr Cortina, was now ready, but it was clear after Grieta's collapse that the case could not proceed that day, so a final adjournment took place. An ambulance was called. Grieta died in hospital some days later, and then there were eight.

Round Four. 20 March 1990. Mandela's triumphant release from prison had taken place on 11 February 1990, mere weeks before. Reading out her much-amended charge sheet, Ms van Zyl announced the case as "Katrina Pienaar *and seven others.*" The cantankerous magistrate entered the court, and the members plus supporters of SHAC who filled the court to the brim, contrary to my strict instructions, hummed the forbidden "Nkosi Sikilel' iAfrika."

But the world we knew had shifted. As the melody of the forbidden tune rose in the wood-panelled courtroom, Ms van Zyl glared at the humming supporters, while we both awaited the predictable explosion from the magistrate. To my surprise, the big man stayed seated, shuffling his papers, scribbling notes until the song was over.

The case commenced. Mr Cortina nervously explained how his municipality had for years pleaded with the Uitsig squatters to leave, and repeatedly threatened them with eviction. Eventually the housing department prosecuted. When they did not leave by a certain date, they had evicted them physically, using the police to enforce the decision. Under cross-examination, I tried to expose weaknesses in their case following two lines of questioning.

Firstly, "Mr Cortina. Did the municipality ever explain to the unfortunate shack-dwellers where they could legally reside?"

"No sir, that was not our responsibility," was his uncomfortable answer.

"So where were they meant to go, Mr Cortina?" No answer, glum silence.

Secondly, "Mr Cortina. Why did you not deliver written notices of eviction to the eleven shacks?"

"Well sir, they did not have post boxes so we could not post them. In addition, we knew that none of them could read, so we felt that there was no point," was Cortina's timorous response.

These responses exposed two fatal errors on the part of the municipality. In closing argument, I claimed our clients' innocence, based upon Mr Cortina's incriminating answers. Case references confirmed firstly that those evicted for trespassing needed to have a place to move to, and secondly, that "legal notice" by an institution to tenants had to be delivered in writing. Ms van Zyl, deflated by her star witness's admissions, barely opposed the application for discharge. "As the court pleases," she uttered through white and compressed lips.

Without even calling for a recess to consider his verdict and with a curt glance at the sullen prosecutor, Magistrate van Niekerk rose to deliver his judgement. In habitual anxiety, I sat expecting some new version of apartheid treachery, as so often before. After a few sentences referring to the need to balance the rights of individuals and of the community, the magistrate stated that the municipality had failed to prove a *prima facie* case of trespassing. And then came the words, "En hiermee bevind ek hulle onskuldig" (And I hereby find them not guilty). The words landed like raindrops on parched earth. Down came his gavel. Case over. He sat down heavily, as if exhausted by the drama.

Joyful whoops and exclamations rang out. Hugs, handshakes, high fives throughout the buzzing court, while Katrina and her seven accused stalwarts hugged one another. I sat still, offering a silent prayer to gods and ancestors. The SHAC faithful joyfully ignored my instructions once again, and now launched into a full-blooded rendition of "Nkosi sSkilel iAfrika." Stirringly, the refrain rose to the rafters, the surviving squatter heroes joining in, while prosecutor van Zyl pursed her lips and awaited the magistrate's outburst. He would surely explode in fury and have them all locked up? But a sight met my eyes, never to be forgotten. Magistrate van Niekerk rose to stand at full attention, looking impassively ahead with his hand over his heart as the great song filled the room.

For me, the new South Africa began that day.

15

The Teaspoon Trial

At the height of the state of emergency during the late eighties revolutionary fever raged amongst the Left. Employers were filthy capitalists in cahoots with apartheid. As union lawyers, our clients expected us to share this simplistic view, and sometimes we did. One morning a delegation of shop stewards and workers filed up the rickety stairs to Chennells Albertyn. My secretary Elize scuttled through to my office with an anxious face, whispering, "Roger, SACCAWU (South African Catering and Commercial Workers' Union); they are angry and want to see you *now!*" I duly greeted and invited all eight into my small office to take instructions. All wore red T-shirts, with clenched fist prominently in front and 'An injury to one is injury to all' on the back.

Agitated, body language aggressive, they settled in chairs and on stools. One ardent comrade shouted, "Amandla" in an unsure voice and the others responded with "Awethu", clenched fists aloft. This struggle war cry was repeated three times, at first thin, reedy and unimpressive, but each time with growing confidence, and all the while I wondered what the conservative Eikestadnuus staff downstairs would be making of these rebellious noises. Daniel, a large man whose T-shirt stretched over a pronounced belly, rose to his feet, exuding self-importance. I knew him to be a regional organiser in the union and prone to bask in drama. Still short of breath from our steep stairs, he explained, between puffs, that the union's chief shop steward in Stellenbosch, Cynthia Cegu, had been arrested half an hour ago at Mike's Kitchen, for (and he paused for effect) theft of a teaspoon. I waited for a burst of laughter to signal that this was a joke, but eight glum stares signalled the opposite. With growing amazement, I established the facts.

The manager of Mike's Kitchen, a restaurant employing about ten staff, had called the Stellenbosch police at eleven o' clock that morning. Three armed white policemen had barged into the restaurant, roughly handcuffed the accused, namely Cynthia, and bundled her into a police van. Enquiries later confirmed that she had been charged with the theft of a teaspoon. I commiserated with the delegation on this evidence of the conspiracy between capitalists and apartheid. Comrade Cynthia was still in the police cells, pending a bail application. I knew her as an impressive person, a fiery and uncompromising natural union leader whose sneering disdain for management ensured that she was regarded with fear, if not dislike, by all employers in her path. An injury to her was an injury to all, and decisive action was called for.

Inspired by the assembled comrades' passion, I committed myself to challenging this injustice, to strike a blow on behalf of the working classes. Bail was set at the then large sum of five hundred rand. When Cynthia emerged from the cells, blinking in the sunlight, she was afforded a heroine's welcome by a raucous crowd. Loud shouts of Amandla and responses of Awethu had the police fingering their weapons. She raised her clenched fist and punched the air, looking every bit a revolutionary in the mould of Winnie Mandela. With perfect timing she played to her adoring audience, strutting a few steps of a mini toyi-toyi, evoking fresh shouts of approval.

When the fervour abated, I arranged a consultation with the incident fresh in her mind. Private consultations were taboo in the collective ethos of the day, so the entire perspiring red-shirted entourage trooped back up the narrow stairways with Cynthia at the fore. I wiped my brow, overpowered by the aroma of human sweat.

"So, Cynthia," I began. "This teaspoon allegation. Did you perhaps take one?"

Her indignant response was what I might have expected if my question had been 'so when did you last torture your children?'

"Never!" she snorted, with disdain. "They are lying, the capitalist scum. They hate me and want me dismissed!" As the chorus of affirmation rippled through the assembled reds, an inner voice acknowledged that Cynthia might well be a difficult person to employ.

Laboriously, I took her through her statement. She denied vehemently that she would ever steal anything. Persuaded of her innocence and relieved that the injustice was patently clear, I undertook to defend her in court. Another stirring round of Amandlas, then Cynthia and her faithful troops swirled noisily down the stairs. As they toyi-toyied across the Braak, the grassed town centre below my office, the African struggle songs echoed off the old Dutch buildings of Stellenbosch.

State vs Cynthia Cegu. The company had agreed that if Cynthia was found innocent, she would be reinstated immediately with full back pay. If guilty she would remain dismissed. The much-vilified restaurant manager Mr Terreblanche would give evidence first. A classic test of credibility, with his evidence weighed up against that of Cynthia's. My task? Challenge and destroy his version. Outside Court B, the anti-apartheid population of Stellenbosch had gathered to support their heroine, chanting and toyi-toying.

"All rise in court." Magistrate van Vuuren, peering suspiciously at the crowded court through steel-rimmed glasses, shuffled up the wooden steps and assumed his place. Van Vuuren, nearing retirement, exuded an air of tired boredom. The prosecutor was an old enemy, the prickly redhead Annette van Zyl, still pursuing her passion for convicting all lawbreakers of Stellenbosch.

I watched the magistrate closely for signs of collusion with Annette. He first glanced crossly through his thick glasses at the murmuring crowd of red T-shirted supporters at the back of the court, heavy eyebrows bobbing up and down with concentration, and then at the two of us standing at attention behind the front desk. Annette's smirking expression was an annoying reminder that these two shared the same tea room and political beliefs, if not a hatred of the working classes. The wooden pews creaked as we sat down and prepared to engage in that archaic form of warfare that is the Law. The teaspoon trial had begun.

Cynthia's case was called and she walked firmly to the dock accompanied by a murmur of approval from her supporters. The resulting glare from the magistrate silenced the court.

"Do you, Ms Cynthia Cegu, plead guilty or not guilty?" asked Annette in her shrill and heavily accented English.

"Not guilty, Your Worship," was Cynthia's assertive reply, gazing fiercely at the magistrate. Her defiant response led to another admiring murmur from the back rows. I breathed a sigh of relief, as I had fully expected her to disobey my instructions and to ring out a loud Amandla to conclude her plea.

First witness for the prosecution, Mr Terreblanche. Dressed in a plum-coloured suit with a trendy pair of glasses hanging from his neck, somewhat overweight for his mid-thirties. He swaggered up to the witness box, taking the oath with the air of a man in control. He recounted firmly, in Afrikaans, how he had long suspected Cynthia of theft of cutlery from his steakhouse. On the morning in question, he had entered the kitchen unannounced, to see Cynthia slipping a teaspoon into her handbag. When he ordered her to open her bag, she had refused, furious at the accusation and claiming her constitutional right to handbag privacy. Two of his loyal workers who had also witnessed the theft, he added smugly, were outside waiting to give evidence.

"So just to be clear, Mr Terreblanche," Annette concluded, "please tell the court again, what exactly did you see the accused place in her handbag?"

"A teaspoon belonging to Mike's Kitchen, Your Worship."

My head spun. Mr Terreblanche's testimony bore the ring of truth, and if two further witnesses were going to corroborate his version, we were sunk. My turn to cross-examine. I rose to my feet slowly, trying to disguise the doubt that had crept in. After asking a series of standard questions aimed at testing his evidence, I was getting nowhere. He had been thoroughly prepared by the prosecutor, was reciting his prepared script perfectly, and was not going to change one word. In one of my long pauses, which I hoped conveyed a methodical calmness rather than growing anxiety, I noticed that the glasses which hung around his neck during his evidence were now on his nose. Why did he not wear them whilst answering the prosecutor's questions? The only explanation, I figured, was that he was short-sighted. Breaking the first rule of cross-examination (never ask a question if you do not know the answer), I fired a shot in the dark.

"Mr Terreblanche, were you wearing your glasses when you came into the kitchen that morning?" To my amazement, he appeared flummoxed, gulped, flushed lightly. He then answered, "Um, I am not totally sure, Your Worship, I wear them sometimes when I need to, but not all the time."

My heart raced. Annette had clearly failed to prep him on this point. Instinctively, I slowed right down to allay his concerns and prepare the trap. "So, Mr Terreblanche, let me just understand this better. How far were you standing from the accused when you witnessed her taking the teaspoon?" A gamble. With permission from the magistrate, I walked down the centre aisle towards the back of the court, stopping about five metres away from the big man. "Were you about this far from the accused, Mr Terreblanche?" He seemed relieved at the change of tack from the glasses question and relaxed visibly. "Net 'n bietjie verder, meneer" (just a little bit further, sir).

I gratefully took another two steps further away. "About this far, Mr Terreblanche?" He nodded his head firmly, glancing anxiously at the prosecutor for approval. Annette sat thin-lipped and impassive, knowing that I would pounce like a tiger on any attempt to communicate with her star witness. The atmosphere in the courtroom bristled, and Magistrate van Vuuren leaned forwards in a rare display of interest.

"Mr Terreblanche, haal asseblief u bril nou af" (please take your glasses off now) I said firmly. He looked anxiously at the magistrate to see if it was necessary, and Annette rose to her feet, about to launch into one of her trademark sarcastic objections. Van Vuuren's impatient nod showed his interest in my questions, and she sank reluctantly into her seat.

"So this is about how far you were from the accused?" I confirmed. His nervous nod was not enough. "Please answer my question, Mr Terreblanche."

"Ja, meneer."

With a flourish I pulled a brown pencil out of my pocket and held it in the air between thumb and digit finger for all to see. "Mr Terreblanche, please tell the court what you see in my hand."

My heart stopped as he half-closed his eyes, squinting like a confused mole. Clearly, he was not sure. "Kom, Mnr Terreblanche, wat sien u in my hand?" (Come, Mr Terreblanche, what do you see in my hand?) The silence crackled. The prosecutor sat stiff as a rod, the magistrate leaning even further forward.

"Dis 'n teelepel, Edelagbaar" (It's a teaspoon, Your Worship) he blurted out, choosing confidence over caution. The exclamations of excited disbelief from the back rows were immediate. "Silence in court." The magistrate thumped the table with his gavel. Conscious of how wobbly my knees had become with this risky interchange, I now moved to slide in the knife.

"So, to sum up Mr Terreblanche. You were this far from the accused. You tell us that you do not know if you were wearing your glasses, and without your glasses you cannot tell the difference between a teaspoon and this pencil? With a dash of theatre, I handed the pencil to the magistrate as Exhibit A, stating, "I have no further questions for this witness, Your Worship." Interrupting his stammering attempt to correct his error, I walked back to my seat.

Annette was not able to repair the damage and Terreblanche left the court with shoulders sagging. The two company witnesses due to testify against Cynthia had mysteriously disappeared. Ms van Zyl called for an urgent recess to search for the missing witnesses. I wondered idly whether they might have received a persuasive visit from comrades the previous night. Sadly, our country is known for such tactics.

Annette finally returned with ashen face, announcing that her witnesses had absconded. She asked for an adjournment, but now it was my turn for an indignant objection. "Your Worship. My client has come here today prepared to face the case against her. The State has had ample time to prepare. Any adjournment will prejudice my client harshly, who is without work because of these trumped-up charges."

Magistrate van Vuuren, imbued with a rare spell of decisiveness, refused the adjournment. Annette slumped in her chair. I rose to apply for discharge of the State case on the basis that the evidence presented did not present a *prima facie* case. The main witness's version of what he saw could not be trusted, and there were no other witnesses in court.

The magistrate delivered his verdict immediately. "Ms Cynthia Cegu. The case against you is dismissed! You may leave the court," he boomed, and banged his gavel. The courtroom erupted in joyful shouts as the words sank in. My cross-examination risk had paid off. It felt good, oh so good, to know that justice had been done. An innocent person, wrongly charged by nasty bosses, had escaped conviction. This was what human rights law was all about. The sun shone, the birds announcing a sweet victory for justice. Cynthia ran up to me and gave me a pneumatic hug.

Then she and her noisy supporters gyrated and sang noisily all the way from court to my office, causing the Eikestadnuus staff downstairs to lock their doors as the unfamiliar refrain of the freedom song "Senzeni na" (what have we done?) echoed through the old building. Big Daniel, the shop steward, had purchased two-litre Cokes, decanted into styrofoam cups with a half-jack of brandy to spice things up. Happy cries of "Viva," "Amandla," filled the air and boisterous toasts were drunk to me, to Cynthia, to Nelson Mandela, to the struggle. As I floated on the sea of contentment for this victory for righteousness, Cynthia beckoned me aside with a conspiratorial whisper. "Comrade Roger, I want to show you something." I followed her, smiling. She opened her leather handbag and gleefully pointed to a clump of shiny teaspoons nestling in the bottom. Oblivious of my horror, she gave me a wink as if to say, 'Yo, comrade! We fooled those stupid bosses, didn't we!' Waves of nausea battered my shores as the room spun around me. Used, betrayed and a comrade idiot. No way to correct the injustice.

I'd have to take my medicine like a man from one of Cynthia's spoons.

16

Stellenbosch's Sophia Loren & the Crown Jewels

"No offence to all of you," said my son Guy at my sixtieth birthday party, "but that's my dad. He mostly has friends in low places, and rushes around in a mysterious way, spending time with them." Mostly my friends got the joke and laughed indulgently. Old Rog marched to an unusual drum, he went on, and his law practice had not brought wealth and status. Yet assisting the less fortunate had provided treasures of a different measure. During the eighties, an array of characters from what one might refer to as the lower echelons of Stellenbosch scaled the ancient staircase up to Chennells Albertyn. People who judge the success of a law firm by the quality (wealth) of its clientèle concluded that we were doing spectacularly badly.

My mother paid a visit one day, passing the two church pews that jostled with poor black and coloured clients and where aromas of tobacco, wood smoke and alcohol mingled. "We do worry about you so, Rog," she murmured, "if only you could just attract a better class of clientèle." Our clients, officially described as unemployed, faced criminal charges for deeds ranging from dagga dealing to car theft to robbery. Yet many were resourceful people seeking creative ways, not always legal, to survive between the cracks of proper society.

Sophie Lourens was such a creature of this intertidal zone. A busty woman of middle years, with few teeth surviving in her brightly lipsticked mouth, she sought my help for a problem encountered "relating to her work". She had been charged with theft for the sum of R330 from a certain Mr Samuels, a respected local builder. In her original statement to the police, she denied having stolen any money at all, which did not make sense. Why would a businessman waste his time and accuse her of theft if she had not taken the money?

After cross-examination in my office, she finally gave an eye-rolling sigh that denoted 'well alright then, I might as well spit it all out.' Yes, it was true, she had taken R330 from Mr Samuels' wallet because he owed her money for a past debt. Right, so now we were getting somewhere. I then asked her the obvious question. "Presies watter skuld praat jy van, Mevrou Lourens?" (Exactly what kind of a debt are you talking about, Mrs Lourens?) Again, she squirmed, gazed at the floor, and shifted heavily on the chair from one generous bum-cheek to the other. "Meneer, ek is 'n besigheidsvrou, sien, en Mnr Samuels het nie vir my dienste betaal nie" (Sir, I am a businesswoman, see, and Mr Samuels failed to pay me for services). When I still looked quizzically at her, she finally blurted out the truth, speaking faster to get it all over. "Jammer om te sê, meneer, maar om die warreyd te vertel. Meneer, my eintlike dienste was ek het met hom geseks" (Sorry to say this, sir, but to tell the truth, sir, my actual services were that I sexed him).

I looked up at her in surprise and with a tinge of respect. Way overweight, dour of demeanour and certainly not blessed in the attractiveness department, I wondered why Sophie had chosen that profession. She was surely a grandmother by now? And more to the point, how on earth did this ponderous belle attract her clientèle? Before my imagination could meander further down that dark alley, she explained that Mr Samuels had been a satisfied customer for many years. The previous month he had failed to pay and therefore, after their most recent transaction she had taken the overdue money from his wallet whilst he was taking a post-business snooze. Intrigued by her authenticity and by the inherent justice of her cause, I agreed to take her case. We duly prepared for trial.

When the court orderly announced, "All rise. State vs Sophie Lourens," my new favourite client waddled up to the dock in the confident manner

107

of one who had done this more than once before. Dressed to the nines in a red Pep Stores crimplene outfit, Sophie reeked of cheap perfume and had applied far too much matching red lipstick which more than amplified her thinnish lips. She presented a garish sight indeed, and I regretted not insisting that she dressed for court. To my surprise, from the wooden dock she flashed a bold smile in the direction of Magistrate Smit – dour, bald, in his fifties, and known for his grumpy disposition. The learned man shuffled earnestly through the files in front of him without looking directly at her again, pretending not to notice Sophie's charm offensive.

Shortly before the trial, I had informed the prosecutor of the nature of the so-called 'theft' that Mrs Lourens would reveal in her defence. The state's chief witness, I pointed out, was seeking recovery of an illegal prostitution payment. Ms Broeksma, a humourless brunette in her crisply ironed black batman cloak, was clearly surprised at this information, and she rose in court to ask for a quick recess to confer with the complainant.

The magistrate left the room and Ms Broeksma summoned Mr Samuels, a burly and well-dressed man, to check his response to the allegation. Samuels became visibly upset as she explained what Sophie was going to say. He had assumed that she would not dare to expose the nature of the illegal services. His quick and angry glance in Sophie's direction conveyed a 'how dare you break our agreement not to kiss and tell.'

The businesswoman, impervious to his outrage, sat peacefully in the dock examining her pink fingernails and exuding supreme confidence. When the trial resumed Ms Broeksma announced tautly to the magistrate that the complainant had inexplicably withdrawn his complaint, leaving the state unable to proceed with the case. We had called Mr Samuels' bluff. Obviously, he was not prepared to be exposed for enjoying Mrs Lourens' services for the past decade. What most surprised me however was Sophie's response to the announcement, namely, to grin cheekily at the magistrate.

"This case against you is withdrawn, Mrs Lourens. You may now leave the court," grunted Magistrate Smit through compressed lips, rapping his gavel unconvincingly, and gazing somewhere slightly above the distinctly jaunty woman in the dock. Sophie flashed a victorious smile round the court, then flounced out like a Hollywood star leaving the stage after a triumphant performance. We walked the short distance to my office, Sophie clumping alongside in her ill-fitting stilettos, still flushed with her victory.

"Meneer Roger," she whispered conspiratorially, tugging at my sleeve, the cheap perfume mingling with stale cigarette breath. "Het jy gesien hoe Landros Smit nie vir my in die oë kon kyk nie?" (Did you notice how Magistrate Smit could not look me in the eye?) I nodded. I had certainly noticed his odd behaviour. "Weet djy, Meneer Roger," she said in a low whisper, "hy is een van my oudste kliente?" (Do you know, Mr Roger, he is one of my oldest clients?) I gulped in surprise. Could it be so? How embarrassing for a white magistrate, responsible for daily enforcing apartheid laws. Sophie had never lied to me. I saw no reason for her to be lying now.

Jerome Alexander. A scrawny local gangster in his early forties, charged with sexually molesting or rather exposing himself to a young boy in a public toilet; precisely the kind of client that my mother hoped I could avoid. Wearing a grey hoodie tracksuit, floppy pants and shiny black shoes, he walked in with a pronounced gangster-pimp gait looking the epitome of trouble. As I glanced through the charge sheet and bail slips that he had handed over, I pondered why such nasty cases kept coming my way, and how I was going to get rid of him as soon as humanly possible. "Ek is Dzerome, meneer," he informed me, in his classic street vernacular. As I was about to inform him regretfully that I no longer took on this kind of case, he flashed me a brilliant, game-changer smile. Each of his front teeth was adorned with a magnificent jewel, two massive diamonds in the middle, flanked by a red ruby and green sapphire on left and right. God knows how and why he chose to display his wealth in this outlandish manner, but the effect was extraordinary.

As the moment for me to refuse to assist him slipped by, he went on to confess that he was short of cash to cover my request for a deposit and was in dire need of assistance. "Kesh flow, mista Tzennells." It was also clear that whilst he claimed to be 'unemployed', like Sophie Lourens, he was evidently quite busily employed in activities of a less salubrious kind. He became cagey when I asked him about his business which I could only conclude had to involve drugs, car theft and similar dealings of the deep shade. I needed a deposit, and he had no cash. We were stuck. After some quick thinking I agreed to assist, but on two strict conditions. Firstly, he needed to be truthful about his indiscretion, and ask for the court's forgiveness; secondly, he had to leave his bejewelled front teeth with me as a deposit. Deal, and we shook hands. Crestfallen and toothless he left my office, his gangster swagger muted, mouth firmly shut to disguise his indignity. Gingerly, my secretary Elize placed the valuable teeth in an envelope marked, Mr Alexander: Crown Jewels, and stored it in our wall safe.

Over the next weeks as we prepared for trial, Mr Alexander faced his demons, acknowledging the wrongfulness of his abuse of the young boy. A nucleus of self-awareness developed as he looked honestly at his life and assumed responsibility for his actions. From time to time, we shared lighter moments. My shock at the five teaspoons of sugar he ladled into his tea amused him, and he would tease me for being a larney (local slang for a wealthy white man). I teased him in turn about his alleged 'business', and his skollie ways. We grew to like one another, despite the power imbalance between lawyer and client. At our last meeting before trial I offered to give his teeth back for the court appearance, which he accepted with a gummy smile.

I walked the short distance to Stellenbosch Magistrate's Court with my smartly dressed, fully toothed and anxious client. Even his gangster strut was muted. As we had prepared, he swore on the Bible to tell the "whole truth and nothing but the truth", and then confirmed his plea of guilty. In order to mitigate the sentence to be pronounced on him, he explained humbly to the court how he had taken drugs and had succumbed to the devil on that day. Hand over heart, he swore fervently that he acknowledged the wrongness of his act, and would never again lose his way. Finally, and speaking in a hoarse whisper, he expressed deep remorse, apologising sincerely to the boy and his parents who sat quietly at the back of the court.

A psychologist then testified to confirm Mr Alexander's genuine state of shame, by now clear to all. To both his and my joy he was finally given the remarkably light jail sentence of two years, suspended for as long as he remained clean. He could walk free from the court that very day.

Avoiding jail was a massive victory, though he seemed even more overjoyed to be reunited with his beloved crown jewels.

Shaking my hand for a last time, and with a quivering lower lip, he said, "Mista Tzennels, dankie, djy het my nooit gejudge nie; ek sal djou nooit vergietie" (Mr Chennells, thank you, you never judged me; I will never forget you). Before he turned the corner at the end of the street, he looked back and flashed me that first-and-fifth-finger rapper gansta gesture that denotes homeboy brotherhood, a gesture of belonging. By the time I had worked out how to respond, he had limped out of sight.

Months later, after surfing at the Strand beach, I emerged from the water and gazed with a sinking heart at the empty space where I'd parked my red Toyota van. Containing briefcase, computer, cellphone and wallet. I reported the theft at the Strand police station, where locals gawped at the angry white man still in dripping wetsuit. I accepted that my van was a gonner, car theft being a sadly common occurrence, and began the tedious insurance process to obtain a replacement vehicle.

Three days later I received an accusatory phone call from a Stellenbosch policeman. "Mr Chennells, do you own a red Venture Toyota CL 15372?" I answered saying that I *used* to own such a car, but it had been stolen in Strand three days back. "Well, Mr Chennells, it is very strange, but there is such a vehicle parked outside your Stellenbosch office!"

I rushed to meet the police at the spot, and sure enough there was my car complete with cellphone, briefcase, wallet and suit as I had left them. The contents of the wallet had not been touched, and the keys were placed above the front right wheel. The policeman kept shaking his head. "Daar's iets fout. Daar's iets fout" (there's something wrong) he repeated. In all his years he had never heard of a stolen car being returned in this way. Something fishy was going on.

I drove off gratefully and tried to work out the story. After dismissing many theories, only one made sense. Jerome Alexander. His gang must have stolen the car, as part of 'business as usual', and then discovered after looking through the briefcase, the owner. My imagination fired to picture an agitated Dzerome berating some poor junior. "Djou fokken idioot! Hierdie kar is Meneer Tzennells s'n. Ons moet dit terugvat" (You fucking idiot. This car belongs to Mr Tzennells. We must return it). A

111

glow stayed with me for weeks as the police processed this suspicious case, the first ever where a stolen vehicle had been returned, unscathed, to its owner.

Friends in low places, occupying different worlds.

About a year later, I was walking down a street in Stellenbosch and noticed a familiar figure, pimp-swaggering in my direction, with hoody-adorned men on either side. Surely my old client Jerome would not risk the uncoolness of greeting a larney in front of his buddies? To my surprise, he leaned forwards as we crossed, and flashed that incredible crown jewels smile. Throwing that one-handed gangsta gesture, he then shouted over his shoulder as he walked away, "Heita, Meneer Tzennells" (Hi, Mr Tzennells). Flushed with happiness, I walked on, wondering how I could ever thank him for the return of my stolen car.

Months later word arrived that my favourite gangster had died mysteriously on the mean streets of Cloetesville. I hoped that they had allowed him to be buried with his beloved crown jewels.

OUT OF COURT

17

Mrs Baartjies and the Medical Mafia

Late winter. 1993. Sunday morning, alone in my office overlooking the Stellenbosch Braak. At breaking point. Career in danger of being ruined, insolvency imminent, wife about to leave. No way out. Darkly, I was pondering bleak options, suicide being one of the more attractive. And then the telephone rang . . .

One year earlier, an attractive lady with a neat hairdo had limped painfully on wooden crutches up our steep steps and sat puffing on the pew, asking to see a lawyer. Mrs Baartjies was impressive, Coloured, with a proud posture and a body that must have recently been athletic. In my office she laid her crutches carefully on the floor, leaned forwards and calmly told her story.

Before the loss of her leg, just over two years back, she had lived a full life as a teacher as well as a passionate netball coach at school and provincial levels. Troubled by painful bunions on both feet, she was admitted to the Stellenbosch Hospital for a routine bunionectomy. The operation performed by a reputable orthopaedic surgeon on that Friday morning was to trigger a living nightmare. Waking up from the operation later that day, the bandaged left foot felt fine, but her right foot throbbed. She alerted the nurse, who responded by raising her dose of painkillers and also giving her some sleeping pills.

When she awoke late the next morning, the pain in the right foot had become unbearable. She demanded to see the doctor. Again, she was reassured by a new nurse that post-operative pain was normal, and that she was probably overreacting.

Against Mrs Baartjies's wishes the nurse applied a drip with a further dose of painkillers. When she came around late on Saturday afternoon, she was delirious with pain. The surgeon had not yet visited. Still crying, she was again sedated. When she awoke early on Sunday morning the pain was so severe, she lost all restraint and screamed hysterically. Reluctantly, the sister removed the dressings to find that the foot was oozing pus and had turned black. Gangrene, the deadliest of all infections, had set in. The too-tight dressing had cut off the flow of blood. The surgeon came in haste and amputated the foot without delay. Despite efforts to contain the infection over the next ten days, the gangrene spread up her leg, which then had to be amputated above the knee to save her life. In two weeks, Mrs B had gone from being a healthy woman with two bunions to a one-legged cripple in intensive care.

Further complications set in, with two more months in hospital fighting the infection. When she finally returned home in a wheelchair she began a painful rehabilitation that included the fitting of a prosthetic leg together with physiotherapy, whilst a process to have her medically boarded from work was set in motion. Adding to her misery, lack of mobility forced her to relinquish her netball coaching. Her life altered forever. Friends had encouraged her to seek legal advice. She asked gravely, "Mnr Chennells, ek het min geld. Kan jy my help?" (I have little money. Can you help me?)

Medical negligence is notoriously difficult to prove in court. Not only does society have sympathy with the plight of doctors doing their best under trying conditions, but in most cases the act of negligence is not clear and can be defended. The biggest hurdle involves persuading a qualified doctor to testify in court against one of his or her peers. This case was in my view different. The doctor's inexplicable failure to visit or follow up on Mrs Baartjies's complaints until two full days later was an act of negligence which simply could not be defended.

The left foot had healed so well, a compelling example of what should have happened. Her plight cried out for justice and she would make an unshakeable witness. Doctor X, together with hospital and nursing staff, were together guilty for her misery, and I was determined to obtain justice. "Mevrou Baartjies, ek gaan jou saak opneem, en jy sal nie 'n sent moet betaal nie" (Mrs Baartjies, I will take your case, and you will not have to pay a cent).

Mrs Baartjies visited every two weeks to check on progress, accompanied by her husband who helped her up the stairs and then waited outside. In waiving all costs and fees, I bet on a sure victory; then we could take a fee. Legally, the main challenge was firstly to prove the doctor's negligence, which required access to the hospital files plus a doctor's evidence, and secondly to calculate the quantum or financial extent of the damages we would claim.

Prescription remains a lawyer's ultimate fear, being the period before a claim must be lodged. Failing which it falls away. In civil claims, such as this one, the prescription deadline was three years from cause of claim, which meant we had less than twelve months to issue summons.

The hospital was naturally hostile, and it took months of letters that started civilly and ended in threats to obtain the hospital's voluminous records. The file grew steadily fatter, filled with reports and documents in often illegible handwriting, and formed a foundation for our case. The documentary evidence was solid and simply required evidence from Mrs Baartjies plus a specialist doctor to complete the case.

After many rejections I found a physician prepared to examine the file and to provide us with a report on the medical negligence. He received the file and assured me of his positive intention. Weeks went by with no word or response, so I went to his offices. After shifting papers and straightening the pencils on his desk, he finally held my gaze. "Mr Chennells, the negligence that took place is beyond dispute. I am sorry, but I am no longer prepared to get involved." Clearly, the prospect of giving evidence against Dr X, an established local surgeon, was too dire. Four months to deadline. This was getting tricky.

New problems bubbled up. Mrs B's husband stopped bringing her for her meetings, and it fell upon me to assist her increasingly cumbersome frame up our narrow stairs. She was seeing a psychologist for depression and, along with her file, was gaining weight by the week. One day after I'd heaved her up the stairs and onto the wooden pew, her bravery buckled and she burst into tears. Through her sobs she blurted out, "Mr Chennells. I am in such trouble. My husband has left me, and I don't have money for rent and food."

Breaking a lawyer's cardinal rule, I lent her R5000. A month later I lent her money again, noting mentally that the stakes for winning this case were as high as could be, and climbing. Now just over one month before prescription, and final preparations commenced. A formal letter was dispatched to the doctor and hospital demanding damages to the sum of R300 000, being the estimated *quantum* of pain and suffering, plus 'loss of amenities of life'.

All we needed prior to issue of summons was confirmation from a reputable surgeon of the key components of the negligence, which he or she would need to back up in trial as an 'expert'. Giving up on local medics, I discovered a surgeon in the city of George, known to be independently minded and who agreed to examine the documents plus provide the crucial report. Relief.

Meanwhile, I had received a prestigious human rights award by the US Government to visit organisations in America for the month of August, and so needed to arrange to meet the prescription deadline prior to departure. The summons needed to be completed with doctor's report, plus being issued on or before 20 August 1992. My articled clerk D had strict instructions to receive the surgeon's report, to complete the particulars of the summons, and have it issued and served with two days to spare. My parting phone call to the surgeon was met with a breezy, "Don't worry, Mr Chennells. My report will be sent shortly."

I departed for the US with a spring in my step, knowing that Mrs Baartjies's case was in the bag, ready to fly. Justice would surely follow. Whilst gazing out over the Grand Canyon, ten days into my trip, I received a panicked call from D. With two days to go before prescription and after many reminders, the doctor had phoned to state that he could no longer provide the report. Clearly the medical mafia had got to him. It was not ethical to issue a summons without medical backing, and there was now no way to meet the prescription deadline. The ball had been dropped and no try could be scored. In the words of that famous poem by Sir Henry Newbolt, the gatling was truly jammed, the regiment blind with dust and smoke.

On the long flight home, I fretted about how I was going to break the news to my sad, sad client. Somewhere between London and Cape Town, inspiration struck. All lawyers were at the time insured up to the sum of R350 000 by the Attorneys Fidelity Fund. I would advise Mrs Baartjies to sue *me* for negligence for having failed to meet the deadline with her case, and then my insurance company would pay the damages to her. Simple. The solution creative, albeit daring. I would hand the entire file to a trustworthy lawyer who would then take Mrs Baartjies as a client and sue me. I would formally admit my own negligence in failing to meet the prescription deadline, which would make the case against me unlosable. And I, in turn, hoped the Fidelity Fund would bail me out.

Every person I spoke to, including my wife, said the plan was crazy, so I stopped asking for advice. When I told Mrs Baartjies she was shocked that we had missed the deadline, but even more confused at my solution. "Mnr Chennells, wat jy nou sê is, ek sal vir *jou* moet dagvaar?" (Mr Chennells, you are now telling me that I must sue *you*?) I reassured her that I would be fine, I was covered by insurance, and she should trust that this was the only way to recover her damages. Mr Baartjies phoned as well, full of questions. He was an interested party in his estranged wife's financial prospects, and loved the proposal. I now needed a trustworthy lawyer to do the job.

I phoned Tasmin Brown, a new lawyer in town, and explained my plan. She was grateful to be offered such a juicy case, whilst obviously surprised that I would provide a written admission of my own negligence. Still under the influence of a strange notion of honour, I called them both to my office where I handed over my entire file to Tasmin and took formal leave of Mrs Baartjies as a client. "In jou eie belang, Mevrou Baartjies, Tasmin Brown is nou jou prokureur," I told her firmly at our final meeting. "Sy sal jou saak hiervanaf bestuur." (In your own interests Mrs Baartjies, Tasmin Brown is now your lawyer. She will handle your case from now.) I assisted the perspiring Mrs B down the steps for the last time and, as she limped heavily across the Braak with her new lawyer, marvelled at how well they were getting on.

For some months I admired the agility of my solution, whilst immersed in other matters. My unhappiest client was soon to receive justice, and I would, hopefully, suffer no more than mild inconvenience. What could possibly go wrong? But Murphy's law was plotting a unique game changer which first peeped out when I phoned Mrs Baartjies for a chat. "Jammer, meneer Roger, maar Tasmin sê ek mag nie met jou praat nie" (Sorry, Mr Roger, but Tasmin says I am not allowed to speak to you).

What a cheek. Had her new lawyer forgotten my honourable deed? What disloyalty from my favourite client? Unbeknown to me, and contrary to our verbal agreement, Tasmin had taken it on herself to massively re-evaluate Mrs Baartjies' damages. Her new client's depression had worsened, she had ballooned in weight, and her husband had finally divorced her. In summary her loss of amenities of life, meaning quantification of her misery, was now greatly re-calculated at R950 000. This would of course destroy my plan, as the insurance was for R350 000.

With no explanation or apology, ten days later, I received a summons for R950 000, citing my negligence towards Mrs Baartjies. The enormity of my crisis struck home. My house was my only asset, valued at about R300 000. Newspapers would delight in exposing the shame of the 'negligent' human rights lawyer. I informed my wife who reminded me tersely of her firm advice not to assist Mrs Baartjies. I had no excuse, and my family faced financial ruin. We decided to go for a quick divorce to try and place the house in her name and thereby save our main asset. Negotiations around this 'fake' divorce soon became tense as questions such as "how much money will you need?" and "what about access to the children?" started to feel all too real, turning the fake divorce into a dress rehearsal. And nothing could stop the freight train steaming towards us.

In the small hours of a Sunday morning, a vivid dream woke me in a sweat. I was sweeping leaves off the street that goes past my office, and looked up to see a long stretch limousine, somewhat like a funeral hearse, driving slowly past. In the back, like a celebrity queen, sat a well-dressed Mrs Baartjies, who waved sadly, ever so sadly at me out of the tinted window. Tears rolling down her cheeks. Shaken by the image, I informed my about-to-be-ex-wife that I was off to the office. I needed to think straight. But no matter which way I turned, the die was surely cast.

Mrs Baartjies would in due course give evidence in court on the negligence part of her claim, and my naïve admission of guilt would place the nail in my coffin.

In a daze, I slumped onto my office floor. How unfair. Weighing up whether disappearing to the Okavango swamps might be better than suicide, I was lying flat on the wooden floor, with eyes shut, when the phone began to ring insistently.

After many rings, it stopped. Then seconds later it rang again. Not expecting a call on a Sunday morning, I picked up the receiver. "Mnr Chennells, het *jy* dit gedoen?" came a familiar voice (Mr Chennells, did *you* do it?). Mr Baartjies. Why on earth was he phoning me? I asked him to repeat himself, which he did, more loudly and angrily. I sat down on a chair, and asked him to explain himself. Something odd was a foot.

"Sy is dood, Mnr Chennells. Het *jy* dit gedoen?" (She is dead, Mr Chennells. Did *you* do it?)

In a tumble of words, he blurted out that he had found his ex-wife dead in her apartment early that morning. "Sal haar saak aangaan?" (Will her case proceed?) Her damages case against me. His only concern, the money. As if through a thick fog, I first asked him if he was sure, which he affirmed angrily. Yes, of course, she was dead. "Did *you* do it?" he asked again, more urgently.

Without replying, I slammed the phone down and leaped around wildly. Mrs Baartjies, dead? No applicant, no witness. The case against me as dead as she was. My initial cries of joy soon morphed into tears of release. Poor Mrs Baartjies. And lucky me. My poverty nightmare would no longer come to pass. Serve that bloody Tasmin right.

As my sobbing subsided, I imagined my former favourite client. United with her right leg, slim and smiling, coaching the angels in a heavenly game of netball. Happy at last.

18

Revenge of the Chickengod

"Komred Rodzer, we gonna tell you something very important," Patrick whispered, leaning towards me so that we could not be overheard, "but we must tell you outside the fektry." I agreed with alacrity, sensing an answer to my prayers, and hurried gratefully with him to the exit, past a workbench lined with pink parcels of product bearing the company's cheery brand – a perky white rooster with bright red comb. Overcome by a flood of relief, I burst into the light of day.

A chicken abattoir is no place for the soft of heart . . .

In the late 1980s I was mediating in a deadlocked wages and working conditions dispute between the Food and Allied Workers Union (FAWU) and a chicken-farming conglomerate near Stellenbosch. My first task was to meet the two sides, seated awkwardly opposite each other in the company's boardroom. Polished wooden table. Carved chairs with plump cushions. Bowls of sweets before each seat.

The union comrades were a robust group of Xhosa and Coloured shop stewards sporting rugged overalls and red Cosatu T-shirts, while the management team were decked out in open-necked shirts and jackets. Tea was served in delicate China cups, the union comrades ladling between five and seven spoons of sugar each. Management took sweeteners or abstained.

The mood remained tense as I went through the pre-mediation formalities, my eyes involuntarily drawn towards the company's unprepossessing factory foreman, Mr Snyman.[4] A sparse crop of upright ginger hair adorned his blotchy face, dominated by a nose, or rather beak, which loomed between darting eyes. A scrawny rooster in human form, flashed through my subversive mind.

I was struck by the high levels of vitriol between the parties. Attempts to remind one group of the possibly innocent motives of the other side were received with undisguised disdain. Shuttling back and forth between the two antagonistic sides, the company team finally requested a half-hour caucus to consider the union's latest demands and craft a clear response.

I welcomed this opportunity to cool tempers, suggesting a tour of the factory premises to kill time. The chairman of the shop stewards, a handsome Coloured man, Patrick Swartz, Petrik in his Cape accent, seemed grateful for this break.

"Okay, djulle, we are tekking komred Rodzer for a fektry toer," he announced to the shop stewards. Calling me *komred* in front of his team implied a friendship which could indicate bias. His voice was hoarse and compelling, his green-brown eyes narrowed as he spoke, conveying the mode of a man leading a dangerous mission.

First selected was Thabo, a dapper young Xhosa shop steward and union secretary, attired in Justin Bieber-style stove-pipes and an expensive looking wristwatch. Also selected to join our mission was an attractive young woman, Joleen, who glowed at the honour and skipped to her feet. Patrick's use of the word *fektry* referred to nothing short of a full-scale abattoir. The company's plant, according to official documents, boasted the slaughter and packaging of an astounding 20 000 units (a euphemism for the feathered victims) per day, yet seeing these figures on paper was no preparation for the real thing. Steeling myself to suppress all sentiment, such as the final agonies of the birds that ended their grim battery-house lives, I donned the compulsory white gumboots, and squelched with my three uninonists across the tarred yard towards the squat building. As I grimaced involuntarily at the clashing odours of disinfectant and death, Thabo pointed out a monstrous lorry parked with its rear end against the building.

"Those are today's chickens being offloaded, mister Roger, and that is where the whole story begins." Bespectacled and well spoken, he took it upon himself to mentor me during this tour. Was he perhaps also suspecting the anxiety I was suppressing?

On entering the abattoir, the unmistakeable stench of blood and entrails intensified, and I glumly lamented my impulsive request for a tour. Too late. Besides, my hosts seemed keen, even proud to show off their dismal workplace. I followed Patrick and his two allies through an aluminium door into a neon-illuminated surreal world. An appalling noise assaulted my wincing ears, like the sound track from a bizarre horror movie. Despairing squawks of a myriad doomed chickens mingled with an inhuman cacophony of rumbles, groans and squeaks emitted by the clanking machinery, namely the chicken production line where the carnage was centred.

Dotted throughout the crowded and bloody factory floor were dozens of orange-overalled and white-gumbooted workers moving as if choreographed by an invisible puppeteer. "Those are our members," mentioned Thabo proudly, with an expansive wave, explaining that nobody was entitled to work at the company without being part of the union. I nodded absentmindedly, mentally disabled by rivers of blood flowing in a drain underfoot.

My gaze lifted to the raised production line, a moving chain that carried its bird cargo two metres above the floor, snaking through distinct sections from the live chicken 'feeder' towards its destination, namely the 'products' department (packaged thighs, breasts and braaipacks) on the other side.

Open-mouthed, I gawked as Patrick hoarsely pointed out the feeder workstation. Two orange-suited men swooped on haplessly scurrying chickens in the rear of the lorry, grabbed them deftly by the legs and with fluid movements plonked them upside-down with their feet wedged between two metal vee-hooks in the clanking chain.

"You see, mister Roger," Thabo murmured in my left ear, "chickens are not clever; if they just pulled their legs together, they could fall straight out of the production chain and escape." Sure enough, the chickens that had been freshly placed into their vee-hooks hung passively from the chain, only their reproachful glares and croaks indicating discomfort.

The chicken-catchers swooped, grabbed and vee-ed chickens with the bizarre grace of ballet dancers in some hellish performance, accompanied by the orchestral gachunk-squee-doeff tempo of the chain. A line of hanging, squawking chickens, each one metre apart, swayed groovily in time to the spasmodic jerks of the feeder chain, as they clank-advanced towards their terminal moments as mortal creatures.

"Next, komred, is the elektrik shock and throat-slitting section," hissed Patrick into my ear. I mumbled that perhaps it was not necessary for me to witness this all in such um, detail. My timorous words fell on deaf ears. Patrick strode briskly to where the chicken-laden production chain dipped and headed downwards towards an opaque silver steaming container. Feathers floated innocently on the surface, like fairy ships on a seething ocean.

"This is where the hoenners get given a groot elektriek shok to stun them, komred," explained Patrick hoarsely, with a hint of pride at the efficiency of the whole setup. My stomach and bum tightened involuntarily as the wretched creatures, plunged one by one into the steaming liquid, jerked spasmodically, then became limp. Some life-loving fowls vainly arched their hanging bodies above the water in a final attempt to avoid the impending danger, before succumbing to gravity and the lethally electrified liquid. Still the chain chugged forwards, rising steadily out of the water with its soggy and comatose victims, towards a single orange-overalled man who awaited them with white-gloved left hand and a flashing blade. The throat-slitting department. The horror, the horror. The next routine of sublime abattoir choreography. Michael Jackson might have drawn inspiration for a darkly Gothic rock number. Man shoots pristinely white-gloved left hand forward, grabs lifeless chicken by scrawny head, right hand with flashing knife-blade swoops elegantly across neck to slit the jugular; head plops into yellow plastic bucket with beak opening and closing in indignant surprise; crimson jets spurt and splish into an open drain.

Each grab-slice-whoosh-release takes a mere two seconds, allowing the slitter-maestro two seconds to scratch, fiddle or pause before the next bundle awaiting his slice-dice routine. The throat-slitter's body swayed with the clanking rhythm, a thin-lipped smile hinting at the inscrutable mental defences needed to perform such artistry without descending into madness.

"This man can only work for thirty minutes before he is replaced," Thabo offered as if reading my mind. "This is one of the toughest jobs on the factory, needs full-time concentration."

I nodded, mesmerised by the whoosh-spurt of arterial blood, and wondering obliquely if he would describe his job as throat-slitter on a curriculum vitae. The next destination for the decapitated units chugging onwards with a thin stream of blood dripping from each severed neck was the plucking section. *Thank the gods the units are out of their misery,* I thought ruefully.

One worker clipped both wings and yanked off the bulk of the tail and back feathers, then the second stripped the remaining feathers with movements too rapid for the eye. The pink and pimpled object, a parody of the sentient creature that had winced prior to the shock bath, was on its way to be a company product.

Thabo, noticing my tense and pallid silence, touched my elbow gently. "You okay, mister Roger?" I gave a tight-lipped and untruthful nod, indicating all was just dandy. The next knife-wielding worker sliced the now naked chicken down the middle with one gloved hand, guiding the gush of entrails into a steaming bucket with the other. *Was this the slice and dice-unit, or the eviscerator-unit?* I pondered darkly. The stench was growing unbearable. Patrick was now conferring earnestly with his other two shop stewards. He turned and advanced towards me with a confidential air, looking left and right.

"Komred Rodz, last wiek a very bed thing heppened," began Patrick, as the other two passed each other cigarettes and gathered around. We had moved to the shade of a lone tree in the concrete parking area. "Ja komred, us workers we are still very unheppie at something what heppened," he proceeded solemnly. Thabo and Juleen drew on their cigarettes and watched their leader. They knew the story, but seemed keen to hear it again.

"Komred, you remember how the hoenners get geskok in the electric bath?" I nodded with conviction. How could I ever forget? "Ja-nee komred," he continued, as if in a trance, "no hoenner can escape from that skok, thet we all know. Well, jus' last wiek there was a problem with daai ou Snyman. He was treating us like chicken shit, and so we sommer (kind of) went on a work stoppage jus' to protest.

"So, ja, we knew it was not legal, komred, but this ou he triet us like blerrie kaffirs and the workers was gatvol, sick en tired. An so we jus' sommer downed tools, and turned off the production line switch jus like thet, gadoeff. Hoenners was jus henging. And same time we turned off the switch for the electric-stunning bath. So komred, I'm telling you, the whole blerry fektry jus' stopped! So Snyman and the bosses stripped their moer (became enraged) eksê, phoning lawyers an' making threats and warra warra warra, but we jus' refused to start the fabriek before they hear our problems. That ou Snyman, he wanted to sommer sek us all the same day. After an hour of stoppage and a lot more of hanna-hanna (talking) the bosses they get desprit, an' they agree, so okay, they will miet the union but only if we return to work. Okay, so we all agreed. But that Snyman, he is still die moer-in about the los' production. Em I raat, komreds?"

Drawing on his cigarette, Patrick checked in for affirmation with his avid audience. Approval was duly given with a mumbled chorus of "Eish, fok" and a fervent, "Ja-nee, Petrik, dit was net so gewies, hy was die *moer* (furious) in!" from an admiring Joleen. Her body language indicated she was probably more than a mere komred to Patrick, her approval of his every word bordering on adoration. We hung on the passionate retelling.

"Nou, Komred Rodzer, you saw it, hey, when a hoenner goes onto that line, it is morsdood (stone-dead) men, end of story. But when we started the engines and put on the switch for the electric-stunning bath, there was a few seconds delay before the current came on. And this one big hoenner thet's hanging on the line he goes into the water, then comes out the other side *jus' before* the electric skok current comes on. The one in front of him is morsdood, and the one behind him too. But not this big blerrie hoenner.

"So nex thing, the throat-slitting komred sees this live hoenner coming along, checking him out skeef (sideways) with those living ogies (eyes) men." Patrick was on his feet, hamming up the chicken's mad stare.

"Now this oke he slits *dead* birds man, never ever did he slit a live hoenner, so he jus' sommer jumps away like it is dangerous, and leaves it moving down the line to the next section. So the okes at the plucking section they also only seeing dead hoenners arriving with no head, so they skrik bedonnerd (get a big fright) and by now the whole fokkin' fabriek is leaving their work stations to look."

Patrick is animated, eyes flashing, arms waving.

"So, nobody is gonna touch this miracle hoenner," he continues, "we all jus' watching what heppens. So, the hoenner, he keeps going down the line, head turning left and right like he is a hoenner-chief checking out the whole situasie. By the time he gets to entrails section, the whole workforce is now gethered, an' the production line is moving, moving, moving with dead birds jus' henging, not being slit, an' this one blerrie hoenner alive as hell and no work heppening.

"Some okes are saying, 'Yo! here is a blerrie sign from God, or mebbe from the encestors.' Others is tuning thet true's god this bird mus' be medjik. The whole plek is like a blerrie sirkus. Then jus' like to prove thet he is not jus' some domgelukkig (dumb-lucky) bird, this hoenner now sommer pulls his legs together out the vee and flops onto the fektry floor making a groot kraai geraas (a big crowing noise). No hoenner has ever done thet komred, never!

"Nex thing he is standing on a drum, cheeky like a gengster, squawking at the big crowd that is starting to jol (celebrate) and sing around him." Thabo and Joleen are as engrossed as I am, nodding and interjecting with sounds and words of affirmation, their abandoned cigarettes smoking on the table.

"So, then the bosses turn off the production line," Patrick continued. "The whole fektry is now stopped. The big hoenner he starts to look for something to eat. One oke throws him a sandwich, and he starts to peck, checking us all out sideways in a cheeky way. When his eyes looks at you it feels laik he is not jus' a hoenner. I mean, komred, never has such a thing heppened to us. So, the bosses are totally bedonnerd, and Snyman, he is jumping aroun' like a headless hoenner screaming at workers to go back to work, but eish, nobody wants to lissen to him men, they jus' want to check out this hoenner and see what is going to happen next. I mean some of us workers was saying that we mus' make this special hoenner a member of the union, bring him some stukkies (girls). Nex thing he shakes his feathers to get the water off an' it sprays over some women workers who scream and laugh like it was a lekker jol. Man, it was such a partie kicking up in there, komred."

But now Patrick's hoarse tone dropped.

"Ja, komreds. So that blerrie k**t Snyman (Patrick's language starting to unravel) "was stripping his moer (losing his temper) more en more. So he gryps (grabs) a knife and sommer runs there where the workers is stending around the hoenner. His eyes looking like he is malbefok (f**king mad), he runs straight to the hoenner. Like a samurai he swaais die groet mes en kap sy kop heel af, kerTJAFF! Shwa! Jus' like thet"(He swings the big knife and chops his head clean off, kertjaff).

Patrick's eyes pop and glaze as he acts out the *coup de grâce*.

"So die spesiale hoenner is now kop-af (beheaded) flopping around on the floor blood spurting. Snyman now he screams at us, 'Sien julle, dit is maar net 'n fokking hoender; nou gaan terug na julle se werk!'" (See, it is just a fucking chicken; now get back to work).

With what sounds like a sob Patrick addressed me directly.

"My gott, komred, you see this hoenner was now not like any hoenner, an' our people was saying to kill it like thet was evil. Xhosa guys who believe in revenge by ancestors were shouting to Snyman, 'Usofa ngoku, mlungu' (you will die now, white man). It was bed man. The hoenner was still flopping, blood flowing. When he stops moving, we go back to work. No talking, we was all so shocked."

Patrick paused, staring at the ground, Joleen's hand resting on his forearm. He was still overcome by the miracle of the chicken's escape from death followed by the violent beheading. The cigarettes burned out on the table, untouched. Thabo stared at the ground, lost in thought. Joleen chimed in softly, "Ja, djys reg, Petrick, daai het ons groot geskok" (Ja, you are right, Patrick, that gave us a huge shock).

We walked back to the meeting room in silence, weighed down. What to make of it? Patrick seemed spent, and for the rest of the afternoon went through the meetings in a daze whilst the negotiations around wages and conditions of work ground on. When I was with the management team, I found myself glancing sideways at Snyman, murderer of the great survivor-chicken.

A settlement between the parties was finally reached. Time to leave. I shook Snyman's clammy hand, reluctantly, overcoming my revulsion. When I bade farewell to the union, Patrick gave me a hug and thanked me again, not for my mediation skills, I suspected, but more for having listened empathetically to their story.

Three weeks later at around 11 p.m. one night, I awoke to a phone call. Patrick. His hoarse whisper recognisable, and strangely upbeat. "Komred Roger, you won't believe what happened, men. A gang of robbers had broken into the company premises. Snyman went to challenge them, and komred, hulle het hom met messe keelaf geslag" (they cut his throat with their knives). I replaced the receiver in a daze. With a knife, with no mercy?

Was this the revenge of the chickengod?

19

Beyond Dispute

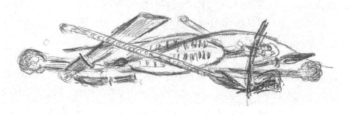

A therapist, handling a conflict between a husband and wife, first interviews the wife. She hears her story and says, "You know, you're right." Then she listens to the husband's side and responds, "You know, you're right." An apprentice overhearing this asks the therapist, "How can you say to both husband and wife 'you are right?' The therapist says, "You know, you're right."

The practice of law is all about working out who is right and then trying to persuade a magistrate or a judge on the justice of your client's case. Often, however, things are far more complex, and the law can show itself to be a blunt instrument. Seeking alternative ways of resolving conflicts has therefore become a growing field.

After decades of donning a lawyer's garb, a new role appeared on my radar – mediator. Empathy, which can be a hindrance as a litigation lawyer, becomes an asset when both parties in a dispute need to trust you. I resonated with the ethos of alternate dispute resolution (ADR) which aims at resolving conflict out of court and with retention of dignity. To trust, not a controlled outcome, but a fluid process of negotiation. Soon I was called to assist to resolve disputes all around South Africa.

Parties in conflict or dispute no longer agreeing with one another need to at least agree on a mediator. I pondered why I was often chosen above other excellent candidates. Only later did I discover that whilst struggle organisations favoured me for my history as a longstanding 'comrade' and union lawyer, companies believed that my European background would ensure I was sympathetic to their needs.

Conflict in South Africa is usually antagonistic, sometimes deadly. During a three-day mediation between the Golden Arrow Bus company and SATAWU (South African Transport and Allied Workers Union) over bus routes and workers' rights, striking workers killed five bus drivers. In struggle conflicts, threats of death for betraying the union cause were not uncommon.

To be a good ADR practitioner requires one to steady one's ego. On one occasion, the union and management delegation were in the reception area at a hotel, awaiting my arrival. As I strode confidently to meet the company directors, extending my hand in greeting, one of the union leaders greeted me loudly with a jovial, "Môre, komred Roger" (Morning, comrade Roger). The company boss looked startled, evaded my proffered handshake and said grimly, "Comrade Roger. Please be advised that this mediation is over." Identifying me as a comrade was a red flag to the company requiring an unbiased mediator. Perhaps the shortest mediation in history? Such failures struck like lightning, and were humbling.

After Mandela's release in 1990, negotiations began at the World Trade Centre in 1991 to end apartheid and usher in a democratic South Africa.[5] Sporadic violence bubbled over in Johannesburg townships between hostel dwellers, loyal to the Inkatha Freedom Party, and civic groupings, loyal to the ANC. Persistent rumours averred that the police were assisting Inkatha to scupper the peace talks. The climax to this black-on-black violence came on 17 June 1992 when the Joe Slovo informal settlement in Boipatong was attacked by about three hundred armed men from Kwa Madala hostel, killing forty-five people and maiming many more. The ANC withdrew from negotiations, blaming the government for the Boipatong killings, and the peace process derailed.

A few weeks after the Boipatong massacre, I was scheduled to join an African colleague, E, in a church hall to mediate between hostel dwellers and comrades in Sebokeng where a spate of killings had brought tensions to fever pitch. We reserved a squad of armed police to stand by in case of violence and arranged for the leaders of the warring parties to use separate entrances. At the front entrance I persuaded eight Zulu hostel leaders wearing rakish headgear of skins and bandanas to leave their weapons outside the door. Machetes, sticks, axes and home-made rifles. At the rear door, E received equally hostile civic leaders, who also left a pile of weapons outside. They filed in, suspicious, and took seats on plastic chairs about five metres apart from their counterparts. The leaders avoided eye contact, the hostility tangible. Only a week earlier, a young hostel girl had been killed in crossfire.

Our game plan was that as soon as the leaders were disarmed and seated we would start the meeting with prayer, to focus minds and to invite spiritual guidance. Opening prayers were *de rigueur* for difficult meetings, enabling a priest or a trusted elder to provide a calming message and to set an appropriate tone with words of guidance. Then we would control the exchanges, get them to vent their grievances, and to hear one another. Seeking first to understand, before being understood. After such a foundation, building trust and working towards mutual understanding should follow naturally.

E welcomed the sullen warriors in English, Zulu and Tswana, and asked if anybody would volunteer to open the meeting with a suitable prayer. After a few seconds, a tall and grizzled Zulu elder rose slowly to his feet. Excellent, I thought, exactly as planned. This man had authority in spades, and his prayerful words would surely bring calm and balance. Some took off hats, others closed their eyes in anticipation.

In a deep voice, laced with aggression and dramatic pauses, he spoke, "Wenkulunkulu wonkulunkulu," (Oh god of gods) "usilethele namuhla ekamelweni" (You have brought us together today into a room) "nezinja ezibulale abantu bakithi" (with the very dogs that have killed our people). A moment of shocked silence as the words sunk home, followed by pandemonium. Leaders rushed to grab their weapons, fierce imprecations flying, but the police swarmed expertly and forced them to leave. The mediation process died instantly.

Such events showcase the unpredictability of humans in dispute, requiring vigilance and humility on the part of mediators. We welcomed annual wage negotiations as being more predictable processes, a choreographed tussle over money between slogan-chanting union members and grim-faced management. The most potent trump cards that unions used in negotiations were the threat of a strike (which would close the business) or violent intimidation of the workforce into compliance. The union battle cry, "An injury to one is an injury to all" emphasised that collective loyalty to the union cause was compulsory.

During a bleak period in 1995 strikes spread like bad news. I was selected to mediate a wage dispute between union X and a company that manufactured brake drums in Bellville. My information was that negotiations between the workforce of a hundred and seventy and the company were deadlocked, so I anticipated the usual poker game. The union's demands being way over inflation, the company claiming unaffordability, followed by a negotiation process of bluffing and arm-wrestling towards resolution.

I was ushered into a boardroom with a pine table and plastic chairs. The union representative, Thabo X, a seasoned hothead, together with six shop stewards from the factory sat around the table, folded arms reflecting the state of impasse. Among them was Siya, the head shop steward, a broad-shouldered human buffalo. The company owner, Mr Helmut X, sat at the head of the table, looking inappropriately nonchalant considering the mood in the room. I had noticed earlier that he had pulled up to the factory in a Mercedes Benz 350 SL; an insensitive display of wealth, I thought.

I enquired whether the Human Resources department would be attending. "I am ze human resources department, Mr Mediator," said Helmut in a strong German accent, "ve don't waste money on such luxuries." Unusual. In South Africa any company with a workforce needed an HR department to manage staff and workplace issues. Perhaps this was a reason for the deadlock?

"Let's get down to business," I began, after explaining the ground rules. "In this plenary session, we will first confirm where the parties stand, and then explore how we might move towards an agreement."

"Mr Mediator," interjected Thabo, his voice raised and brittle. "Excuse me but I must interject. Mr Helmut must please stop offending our members. He has offered *zero percent* during negotiations, which is unheard of in our country. In fact, disgusting. Inflation is now eight percent, and the workers' demand of ten percent is reasonable to make up for historical backlog."

Neither Helmut nor the union shop steward flinched at this intemperate outburst. As an afterthought, Thabo blurted out petulantly, "And just look at that expensive car he drives. The man is rich. Money is no problem."

I turned to the owner. "Mr X, the workers would like you to make it clear at this point. Are you prepared to improve on your offer?"

All eyes turned to Helmut. Fleshy face, clipped beard, overweight, work-stained jeans and heavy boots. A heavy sigh escaped his large frame, an audible eye-roll, before he continued in a surprisingly soft voice. "Vel, Mr Mediator, zis whole process is such a vaste of production time." Raising his hands and shrugging shoulders, he continued, "I haf told my men, Mr Mediator, ve cannot afford ze increase zis year. Sales are right down. Ve fight to survive. I am able to pay *zero* increase, schluss." Short pause. "And I believe, my vorkers vil understand."

By the intensity of Thabo's response, the boss might well have offered his workers death by poison. A zero offer was beyond his comprehension. "You will regret this, *sir*," he said sarcastically, emphasising the word sir. "My union's members will *never* accept. You want war, we will give you war."

My control of the meeting was unravelling. I requested Helmut to leave the room so that I could confer with the union and ascertain their response. A strike was surely inevitable.

Helmut ambled out the room, Thabo still hyperventilating with indignation. "Comrade Roger," he hissed, as soon as the door closed. "Our members will never accept a zero increase; we will have to teach that Helmut boss a lesson." Siya tugged at Thabo's sleeve. "Ndicela, siyixoxe lento, mfondini" (Can we discuss this thing, please, comrade). Visibly annoyed by this, Thabo agreed. Shop stewards were normally cannon fodder in the class struggle, accepting without question the advice of union representatives.

I left the room. They would, of course, agree quickly on a unified position, namely to reject the non-increase. After a few minutes, Siya popped his head around the door and motioned for me to return. Thabo sat glowering with arms folded, Siya clearly now in control.

"Mr Roger. We respect what comrade Thabo has said. But the workers want to accept what Mr Helmut is saying. We say, no strike. We accept zero increase." I tried not to show surprise, for no union in South Africa had *ever* accepted a zero percent offer. Thabo left the room, muttering.

I was burning to know what was behind this norm-busting settlement. Unions often took their members' loyalty for granted in their struggle against the bosses. After the agreement was signed, I was finally alone with Helmut.

"Please tell me," I asked, "how did you get the workers to accept a zero increase? What is your secret?"

He was surprised at the question. "Zere is no secret, Mr Mediator," he said. "Ze vorkers trust me. Zat is all."

I needed more. How was I to understand or to even explain this victory to my colleagues? Was bribery involved? Helmut was impatient, wanting to get back to his work, but I pushed him further. "Please indulge me, Mr X. Just describe your normal day in this factory."

"Vel, so I arrive each day in my Mercedes at 7.30 a.m., zen I spend ze next two hours on ze shop floor."

"Oh, I see," I replied. "You mean you walk around and greet the workers? Nice."

"No no no, I go to each vork station, ve talk about how ze vork is going. Ve make jokes. I speak to each vorker. I know zem all by name, zeir problems, zeir children, zeir machines. Zen after about two hours, I go to my office for a nice coffee, and start my office vork."

So that was his priceless 'secret'. His genuine connection with each worker trumped their loyalty to the union cause. And I was widely, but wrongly, praised for this historic mediation settlement.

20

Rastafari Tabernacle Tales

An old Rastafari, a grey beard twirled under his chin like a sausage roll, takes the mic. He asks, soft but clear, for all present to hear, "Mista. We hear yo story. But da one ting we ALL wanta know is DO EE TINK HAILE SELASSIE BE DA ONE TRUE GOD?"

July 2007. The World Intellectual Property Organisation (WIPO), for whom I had worked previously, recommended me to assist the ten Rastafarian Mansions of Jamaica, namely the international Rastafari leadership, with their internal conflicts and intellectual property problems. During our working days I came to understand more of their world, including expressions such as *I and I* meaning we; *Irie, Irie,* expressing that things are cool; *Praise Jah,* a common interjection, greeting or thank you; *Empress* (girlfriend); *Babylon,* an oppressor of any form. And a man like me with little hair is called a *ball-head*. Letters were signed off with *One Love,* and above us all wafted the omnipresent aroma of the sacred herb – marijuana.

On the third day they invited me to their famous Nyabinghi ceremony, warning that it lasted the entire night. I had heard about this most holy of all Rastafari ceremonies, the annual gathering of the faithful held at the Holy Tabernacle, deep in the hills above Kingston town. Honoured, I gladly accepted. With companions Ras Daniel and Ras Lance, I travelled early the next evening in a battered Toyota to the Nyabinghi venue along potholed roads winding through a steamy paradise. Bananas, mangoes, breadfruits and more for sale round every corner. Hundreds of dreadlocked Rastas wearing ceremonial robes gyrated and swayed on a grassy field to hypnotic music. A massive bonfire blazed. Thumping drumbeats filled the air.

Ras Daniel hissed in my ear, "Lissen my brudda. Dat be de hartbit of Africa, e no' stop all nigh' long, e callin da brethren to come home to Africa." The word Africa was spat out with the vehemence and passion of a true believer. Wide-eyed at the sights and sitting upright in the back seat, I felt a furry weight moving on my sandalled right foot. I looked down to see a tarantula as large as my hand. "Don' worry," said Ras Daniel, noting my fear, "e don' do nobody no arm." Calmly, he picked the huge creature up in his hand and plopped it out of the window to crawl off into the darkness. "You stay 'ere brudda." Ras Daniel, placed a rough hand on my leg. "I gon' tell da warriors dis whitefella 'e one o' us." Gratefully sinking back in the seat, feet still raised in a nerdy anti-spider posture, I peered out of the window trying to make sense of the eerie scene drenched in the pervasive scent of marijuana. The sacred herb is illegal in Jamaica, but the brethren smoke it as part of their practice as a blessing from God, essential to prayer. Around the periphery of the gathering stood dozens of old vehicles interspersed with ragged tents and canvasses.

The slave trade dumped children of Africa in this tropical paradise in the 18th century to serve the British sugar barons. Rastafarianism developed in Jamaica in the 1930s, a religious movement based upon a specific interpretation of the Old Testament, and a single god named Jah. Haile Selassie (Emperor of Ethiopia 1930–1974) is regarded as Jah incarnate, a human prophet, and Africa is the motherland. "Are you Jamaican?" I once asked a Rasta elder. "No mon, I'm an African, living in Jamaica," was his indignant response.

Hypnotic drumbeats accompanied by an evocative wailing chant emanated from the circular building nearby, the Holy Tabernacle. A half-completed building, with black plastic sheeting for a roof, and a large central altar adorned with a massive painting of HIM (His Imperial Majesty), resplendent in grand and medal-festooned imperial uniform. Purposeful of gaze, the visage of Emperor Haile Selassie, otherwise known as the Lion of the North and Divine Conquering Emperor of the House of Judah, dominated the room. At his side stood his equally adorned but far plumper wife, the Royal Empress Menen Asfaw. She glared past her divine husband with a wrinkle-nosed expression of disgust as if he had just broken wind, which in no way detracted from the iconic image.

Hundreds of dancing worshippers, illuminated by the flickering fire, chanted and gyrated to the mesmerising beat. I felt alien, a proper ball-head, and more than a bit afraid. Ras Lance, sitting in the front seat, rolled a massive joint, prepared lovingly with trance-like dedication. In his mid-thirties he was one of the youngest attending, his mere six-inch dreadlocks marking him as a recent convert to the faith. Blessed with the looks of a martial arts film star, Ras Lance moved like a panther and spoke with passionate intensity about his faith. I was not surprised when he confessed that his most challenging spiritual problem was an inability to resist women. "They love me too much, mon," he complained. "And I no can say no." Gloomily he added that despite his best efforts to reform, he had already fathered seven children from no less than five women, none of them his wife. I was tempted to quip, "Hey Lance, yo' mama sho' named you well, mon," but chose not to risk this new friendship.

Drawing deeply on a fat spliff, Lance then launched into his own version of the millennium theory that prophesied death on earth for all who failed to accept the True Faith (Rastafari). Non-believers would, he added sagely, die painful deaths, and fry in their well-deserved Armageddon. Nodding and murmuring vague assent, I accepted the frequently proffered spliff, drawing the sweet smoke into my near-virginal lungs. Today was a good time to give this stuff a full go, I figured. "Yeah, brother, truly these things will come to pass," I heard myself murmuring placatingly at Lance, in between hearty puffs. Soon the joint was history, and I well stoned.

Making my escape from the divinations of prophet Lance, I lurched towards the bonfire, former anxiety replaced by a weed-induced bonhomie. The drumbeat was pervasive, its heavy vibration thumping through flesh and blood. Such hypnotic chanting had no precedent in my memories. Soon I was swaying from side to side in a sea of dreadlocked brethren who were floating on waves of fuzzy contentedness. A spider on the tabernacle wall might have enjoyed the sight of a middle-aged bald white man grooving affably in a mass of robes and tangled hair. When a dreadlocked apparition loomed out of the darkness muttering unintelligibly at me, I responded with something like, "Hi um hello, I mean, um, blessings and irie, brother." The toothless, dreadlocked old rasta was smoking a 'chalice', a sort of hookah pipe that bubbled ganja smoke via a coconut shell bowl. Exhaling wispy fume from his nostrils, he mumbled what sounded like, "Bubba wanna tel ee manshon im be alla puko mamma orwatt." "Um, excuse me, brother?" I leaned forward to catch the drift. He repeated the words louder, which didn't help. "Blessed peace, one love mon," was my corny retort, at which he held out his fist out for a street-cred Rasta-greeting and swayed off puffing contentedly. One love! I could feel it in my bones.

Another visage now appeared before me, this one aggressive and menacing. "Hey whitey, wa' you doin' 'ere a'da Nyabinghi, mon?" His face contorted with rage. "Yo' whiteys killd our pipple" was one phrase that I deciphered in a torrent which blamed all whites for racism. The raised voice caused immediate upset among the revellers who gathered round, and I tensed for a possible fight. Clearly, he had not heard Ras Daniel's spiel that I was an invited visitor. The drums thumped, adrenaline spurted as I tried to calm my antagonist. His vernacular outburst was a cloud of rage, with only a few phrases such as 'fukken whites' intelligible. He was inches from my face and gaining momentum when salvation arrived out of the smoky haze. Quivering with octogenarian rage, Ras Daniel clapped a sinewy hand on my adversary's shoulders shouting, "Rasta, shut yo mouf mon, dis whitey be bra' Roger, he be wid us."

My saviour's tirade was equally hard to follow, but included stern words sprinkled with Biblical references. Deflated, my aggressor slunk into the gloom followed by berating comments from onlookers. Knees knocking, I thanked Ras Daniel for his timely intervention, and he too disappeared into the crowd, still shaking his grey dreadlocks in anger.

Woozy and overwhelmed, I made my way back to our old Toyota, first checking for giant spiders. Lance, the pontificator, was snoring in the front seat, so I climbed into the rear, resolved to lay low until dawn. The wailing songs and the doef-doef ga-doef of the drums induced a comforting, trancelike state. Rasta Roger drifted off.

A knock at the window made me start with fright. Daybreak, and the grey-bearded lugubriosity of Ras Howie pushed up against the fogged glass. I was needed to attend the formal closure of the Nyabinghi and explain my work with them. Together we joined others moving towards the Tabernacle, whilst the drumming continued as it had all night long.

Ras Kremlin, ancient high priest of the Nyabinghi, despite having prayed, chanted and danced like a youngster all night long, still exuded a vibrant Mick Jagger-like energy. He was in charge. This amazing man was in his mid-nineties, product of a life devoted to his religion and the holy weed. Flicking his yellow-matted dreadlocks like an angry lion and waving a Rastafari flag over his head with Dumbledorian gravitas, he summoned the brethren to conclude the marathon twelve-hour worship.

Behind the imposing high priest stood the two holy drummers of the Nyabinghi, the respected theocratic order who protect the massive drums together with the hallowed rhythms of the Rastafarian legacy. Alongside them sat five junior drummers each beating progressively smaller drums with immaculate coordination. These men, not surprisingly, looked more ecstatic than exhausted, having filled the air with their ancient African heartbeat dusk to dawn. Ga-doef, ga-doef, boom boom ga-doef. We gathered around the old man. Haile Selassie and his wife gazed down benignly from the central altar as the Tabernacle filled. The drumming rose to a crescendo and then, suddenly, with a dramatic flourish of Ras Kremlin's flag, it stopped dead. A silence more intense than the pounding drums. Ras Kremlin gazed through slitted eyes at the exhausted night survivors, daring anyone to move.

"Blessings, Haile I, Lion of the House of Judah Haile I, Haile I," Ras Kremlin chanted into a microphone. "Jah!" was the response from some three hundred dreadlocked, dazed brethren, the chant repeated three times. Ras Junior Manning, leader of the Council, took the mic from Ras Kremlin, who sank exhausted into the seat behind him. Ras Junior addressed the expectant gathering, describing how in the beginning the ever-divine Emperor Selassie had ordered the Rasta brethren worldwide to speak with one voice. Yet after years of increasing discord amongst the Rasta mansions and with ongoing enemy theft of Rasta sacred property, the ideals of one voice and one love became forgotten.

"Conflict and disputes increased amongst I and I, my brethren." Muttering affirmations indicated that this discord in the brotherhood resonated strongly in the audience. "So, I and I decided it time to call fo' expert help. We asked da United Nations, an dey called on dis man bra' Roger standing here, who hav done simler work fo' da Indigenous pipples o' our home, in Africa." With this he looked directly at me and offered me the mic. How to explain my work with the Rastafari Council? After an encouraging push-nudge from Ras Daniel, I stepped forward.

Showtime, and this Rogstafarian was still high. Looking around at the forbidding gathering, I realised that nothing had prepared me for this. How much detail should I give about the conflict, what about the intellectual property issues? How to connect with the audience?

I opened my mouth. Despite my skin colour, like them, I was an African. "Irie, and greetings to all, I give thanks to be here with you Rastafari brethren." Some positive murmurs followed my hesitant introduction. Speaking slowly, I described my work with the Council on protecting Rastafari heritage, adding that we had made progress but still had work to do. Dry stuff. I added how the San peoples in Africa had similarly been conflicted, yet had formed one united council to gain strength. Polite interest, with a few murmurs of 'blessings, give thanks', etc. But a thick blanket of reserve still hung over the gathering. The Nyabinghi faithful had clearly expected, was hoping for, something more.

Before I could hand the mic back to Ras Junior, the old Rasta grabbed the mic and threw that curved ball at me. "Do ee tink Haile Selassie be da one true God?" His challenge hung in the air, then rippled through the tabernacle like shrapnel. Every Rasta jerked erect; eyes fixed on the worm squirming on the hook. A glance at my protectors Ras Daniel and Ras Lance showed them looking downwards. No help there. For *the* killer question, I was on my own. Recognising Haile Selassie as the one and only god as the overarching belief unites all Rastas in faith. Yet if I told my own truth, I would surely be lynched. Or thrown into a nest of tarantulas. Clearing my throat a few times, I formulated a way forward. Rasta necks craned. Time to plunge. "When I was a young man in Africa," I started, with a long pause for effect and for thinking, "I believed that Emperor Haile Selassie was one of the most remarkable leaders that ever lived." A murmur of dissent rippled like an irritated current through the crowd. *"Only one of the most?"* This might imply that others were his equal. Rebellious murmurings bubbled. Ras Junior, chair of the meeting, now held his head in his hands. How was he going to manage the ugly consequences of a wrong answer? I had to get out of this hole, alone. My mind spun as a cauldron of dark faces waited. "But I am glad to tell you, my brethren," still thinking furiously between words, "what I *do* know is this." The air frizzled with tension, as three hundred Rastas hung onto every word. "That if any leader on this earth *could* have been god, it *would* have been His Royal Highness Emperor Haile Selassie." For an endless second nothing happened. If they did not buy this, I was the Titanic. The beating of my heart stopped.

Suddenly, on a signal from Ras Kremlin, the chief drummer crashed a massive doem-doem ga-doeff on his big drum, the others following with a tumultuous cascade. The crowd exploded with whooping spontaneous exclamations of joy. Ras Junior first slumped with relief, then jumped up to pump my limp hand. Cheers, shouts of 'Haile Selassie' and 'Irie, irie' and 'give thanks' filled the temple, and hands groped to touch and approve the new Rasta ally. My answer had hit the jackpot in Ras Kremlin's view, and I was now fully one of them. The Rastas loved Rasta Rog. One Love it would be.

From his altar on high Emperor Haile Selassie looked down sternly, whilst the Empress sneered at my cheap escape.

21

When Harry Met Roger

In the movie *The Terminal,* based on a true story, Tom Hanks plays the role of a traveller from a fictional country who is stuck at John F. Kennedy airport terminal. This story is also set in a terminal. "Any member of the public found in the airport after hours will be guilty of an offence and arrested on sight," boomed the voice over the Heathrow public address system.

It was 9 p.m. June 1994, and I had just climbed under a table at O' Malley's airport restaurant. I pulled my legs inwards and out of sight. I would need the luck of the Irish to survive the night. Anti-IRA security was at a peak in London after a spate of bombs, and arrests took place daily. The plan to spend the night at the airport to meet my daughter Rebecca's 6.30 a.m. flight had turned into a folly. I was in the UK in the final week of a two-month research grant to study conflict resolution at the Universities of Belfast and Norfolk. Rebecca's thirteenth birthday present was to spend a week with her dad in the UK. There was no way I could get an early train to Heathrow, and I could not afford a London hotel, so the plan was to find an overnight hideout – after the airport closed. Voila! A father ready to meet the early flight.

I had arrived at eight, and surveyed all the nooks, from the shops being locked up behind steel bars, to the range of eateries, with inhospitable resting places. O' Malley's restaurant offered carpeted floors, wooden tables and benches, space to sleep beneath. The bar area was locked with a metal screen. When the last waiters locked up and left, I struck, creeping under the second table from the entrance.

The PA announcement threw me into a potential drama. I would be a mere pawn if discovered, and deemed a criminal suspect. Arrest would be a disaster. I had not brought my passport, would be thrown into custody, and would miss Becky's flight. Plus acquire a criminal record and have to refund the grant. I imagined the courtroom scene. Your profession, Mr Chennells?" "I'm a lawyer, Your Honour." A titter would run through the audience, rapidly silenced by the grim judge's gavel banging together with, "Silence in court."

From the time the airport closed, successive pairs of uniformed policemen each with an Alsatian dog in tow patrolled the area every thirty minutes. Click-click-tick, two pairs of shoes and one large dog's toenails. Under the second table, I needed to pull my legs in from the passage to avoid detection.

The next police couple and dog headed straight for O' Malley's and sat on the bench, inches above my crouching frame. Two pairs of shiny black shoes, one female, almost touching my nose. As I lay frozen in fear, a scuffling and squelchy sound from above turned out to be the two officers of the peace smooching. The Alsatian poked his head under the table and to my relief wagged its tail approvingly. Clearly, I did not fit the description of the IRA enemy. But my terror intensified. If they caught me now, witness to their no doubt illegal tryst, they would have no mercy. With a tom-tom pounding in my chest, I patted the Alsatian's head, willing it to lose interest. After an age, the love birds headed off with their still tail-wagging dog, me left in a pool of relief.

I emerged and stretched my legs, confident that I would hear the next police patrol long before they came into sight. Surely there might be a better hiding place? I searched the bar area in the hopes of finding a Guinness or some such delight left behind from the day. No such luck. Soon I heard footsteps and again dived for my lair.

The same couple returned, this time sitting at a nearby table, sharing a cigarette. I could see them clearly, and if they had glanced my way, I was a goner. They had eyes only for each other. "So when did you first take a fancy to me?" he asked. Giggles from the woman cop, and a coy reply that I could not figure out. Followed by another bout of smooching. She was younger, seemingly of Indian descent, he middle-aged and pudgy. The dog wagged its tail at me. They left.

Only 10.30 p.m. My armpits were soaked, reserves close to depletion. I *had* to get through the night without detection. But sleep kept tugging. At the click-click-tick of each police patrol, I pulled my legs in, then gratefully stretched them out into the passage. Fear and adrenaline, fuelled by desperation, kept sleep at bay. A clock chimed midnight. Patrols came and went. Each time my legs retracted like plane wheels on take-off, then stretched out on landing.

Finally, oblivion struck and I fell into a deep sleep, to be rudely awoken as my worst nightmare became reality. My leg shaken roughly, an angry voice shouting, "Get up! Get up! What are you doing here?" The horror was happening. I was truly fucked. A barrage of questions from the uniformed man. "Who are you? What are you doing here?" He looked like he was in his forties, short army haircut, uniform black and military-like, but not the London police. A few years my junior.

"Where are you from?" he persisted sternly. I mumbled a response. "I am not a danger to anybody. My name is Roger Chennells. I am from South Africa and am waiting to meet my daughter on the early flight." I gave up control, accepting my fate.

A long pause. I imagined myself in jail, Becky panicking on arrival, vainly looking for her dad. "Christ man!" the man exploded at me, his accent now oddly familiar, "You are in such deep shit. I am going to help you, just follow me quickly."

He grabbed my wrist roughly and walked fast, looking left and right for the police, then pulling out a bunch of keys and unlocking a side door. Small room with basin and bed, "Here you will be safe, Roger," he said. "You can sleep. I will unlock the door when the airport opens at 5 a.m."

"Thanks so much, man," I breathed, "but who are you? Why are you helping me?" I could not process the rapid reversal of disaster.

"I am Harry Cheadle," he replied, smiling for the first time. "I am head of night security at Heathrow, working closely with the London police."

"And?" I quizzed.

"Over twenty years ago, I was at Michaelhouse with your brother Mark. He was very good to me. Protected me from some guys who were bullying me. Anything to pay back the favour."

Phew, the old school tie. And my middle brother Mark, also known as Sparks. I could not wait to tell him how his kindness to Harry Cheadle had saved my bacon. I glanced at my watch. 3.30 a.m. I set the wrist alarm for 5.30 and fell into the sleep of the saved. The click of a lock unlocking woke me. I heard Harry walk away.

I left my haven and strode past the scene of last night's torture. O' Malley's looked friendly now, a hive of activity, the early morning cleaners busy with mops and vacuum cleaners. I sauntered past shops and stalls preparing for the day, a song in my heart. I felt like some unseen power had considered me worthy of a miracle. Heathrow belonged to me.

Becky ran into my arms a few hours later. "But how did you get here so early, Dad?" she asked. "You look a bit dishevelled."

I paused.

"Ag, it was a piece of cake, my darling. Easy-peasy." Sometimes, it's easier to bend the truth.

And, thank you, Harry. I'm forever glad it was you who discovered me, and not the kissing couple.

22

Ancestors and an Amulet

April 2010. Five a.m. on a Saturday morning. Woken by a telephone call. "Mista Rogers. Bulldozers have started grading in the sacred forest. You must please help." Phakhati, the Ramunangi leader, his voice taut.

An urgent interdict, a lawyer's nightmare. Weekend plans scuppered by the slog of drafting documents, statements, affidavits, collating photos, reports and briefing counsel. At midday an ultimatum was faxed to the Venda King ordering immediate cessation of bulldozing. By Sunday night documents signed. Monday first thing we filed the interdict at court, and served it on the king.

Phakhati phoned at midday, still short of breath and taut. "Mista Rogers, you are in danger, you mus' get protection."

"Protection from what, Phakhati?"

The king had visited the royal sangoma (witch doctor) in response to our interdict, and as the Ramunangi lawyer, I was a prime target. If I did not get proper protection, Phakhati added, something bad would happen. When my Venda friend Maria phoned minutes later expressing the same fears, I wavered still.

A lawyer seeking witchdoctor protection? What about the law? Hedging my bets, I made an appointment to see Vusi.

I had been asked to assist the Ramunangi clan a year earlier, after their king had proposed the commercial development of their sacred Phiphidi waterfall. It was my first encounter with Venda culture, where *makadzis* (old women) sit on the floor in deference to men, prostrating themselves in embarrassing (to me) self-deprecation. Traditional greetings of *Aaaa* and *Ndaaa* are uttered before speaking, accompanied by exaggerated bows, hands pressed together facing downwards. At my first meeting I stood up, bowed, and offered a confident "Aaaa" to the gathering. This brought the house down, and as the laughter and ululations subsided, Maria whispered with a shy smile, "Roger, you said, 'I greet you as a woman.' Men are meant to say 'Ndaaa.'"

The Ramunangi clan are the traditional custodians of the Phiphidi waterfall, which includes conducting special rituals and appeasing the ancestors. During the apartheid years puppet chiefs had been installed and the Ramunangi were unable to protect their sacred site. In 1980, the entire forest area, including Phiphidi waterfall, had been fenced off as a picnic site by the local chief. Too intimidated to object and unsupported by the chiefs, the clan lay low, practising their rituals in secret at the waterfall whilst the public visited their sacred site by day. With the advent of democracy in 1996, the ANC government confirmed King Tshivhase as owner of all forest reserves, including Phiphidi. Known for his love of the high life above his Venda heritage, he viewed ancient sacred sites merely as business opportunities.

During my first meeting with the clan, male elders rose to their feet, gravely saying, "Ndaaa" and then fumed at the dishonouring of their sacred site. Loud music and picnics, rubbish and condoms flung into the stream. Such insults were abhorrent to the ancestors. When it was my turn to speak, I stated, "I have heard your pain, and believe the time has come for decisive action." I resolved then and there to assist them oppose the predations of their king. Far from enthusiasm, an apprehensive cloud filled the room. The clan was terrified at the prospect of opposing the king. They had been battered into submission and, despite the atrocities, they could not access clenched-fist outrage. I sat with stomach churning in response to the injustice. How could the Ramunangi have allowed themselves to become so dominated?

The next day a makhadzi, known as Professor on account of her cultural knowledge, took Maria (coordinator of the Ramunangi) and me to the Phiphidi waterfall. Respectfully, we walked into the gloom where gnarled jackal berries lined the gurgling river. Dark swirling waters evoked an aura of magic and pixies, the *zwidutwane* (water spirits) that lived at the bottom of waterfalls, being half visible, with one eye, one leg and one arm. Roiling past sharp rocks the water crashed down a series of rapids and into Ghuvhukhuvhu, the sacred pool. The onomatopoeic name describes its foaming chaos.

"Tell mister Roger that is where the sacred python lives," Professor whispered to Maria, pointing at the turbulent pool. She was in her late eighties, but walked lightly and with energy to burn. Later I discovered that she tends vegetables daily and climbs her mango trees to harvest the fruit. For my benefit she pointed out a rock near the swirling pool, where the sacred python is said to lie. "That was where the offerings are made," she said, ensuring good rain, crops and health. "Anyone who sees the python dies immediately," she whispered via Maria, glancing quickly away in case she caught a glimpse of the dreaded serpent. Did this explain the lack of witnesses? Tugging Maria's sleeve, she continued in Venda, eyes twinkling. "She wants you to understand," Maria explained with a smile. "All of this," a flamboyant sweep of her arms taking in the forest canopy with echoing bird calls, "is holy, it is our church."

Time for action. A committee was elected, statements taken from key informants. After much research, I drafted a document confirming the role and importance of the Ramunangi clan as traditional custodians of the Phiphidi sacred site which, together with Lake Fundudzi, forms the heartbeat of Venda culture. An NGO called Dzomo la Mupo (Spokesperson for Nature) was formed to coordinate the custodian clans of this and other sacred sites. When we informed authorities that the Ramunangi intended to assert their rights, government officials became shifty. They acknowledged the Ramunangi as custodians of Phiphidi, but it was unheard of to question the king. We were on a collision course with an untouchable Venda power.

As per appointment, I drew up at Vusi's small house in the Cape Town suburbs. No indication from outside that a sangoma resided within. "So how can I assist, Roger?" asked Vusi, sitting me down in his lounge.

A genial man-mountain, dressed in flowing print robes and with a sonorous voice, he looked the part. Unknown herb aromas jostled for dominance, animal skins adorned the walls, and an array of accessories around his neck completed the picture. A modern African medicine man.

"The Ramunangi say that King Tshivhase has put a spell on me because I am helping them block his development of Phiphidi waterfall," I explained. He nodded his head gravely. "I know the Venda and their spells. You need strong protection. Their curses are not to be underestimated." My breathing had become shallow, images of Leon Schuster's movie *Mr Bones* mingling with fear of the unknown. "May we begin, Roger?" I nodded, far too quickly. If protection was available, I wanted it.

I sat on the floor facing a sort of shrine adorned by bone and skin objects, pills and powders in old bottles. On Vusi's far side an assortment of spears and knobkieries. First, he solemnly lit the *mphephu*, the acrid herb whose smoke summonses the ancestors. "Roger, are you ready?" He looked at me, as if waiting for my go-ahead to launch a nuclear missile.

I nodded, suppressing a small cough at the pungent smoke. Next, he took a swig from a half-jack of Klipdrift brandy and sprayed a misty booze-cloud around and over me, cheap grog aroma mingling with the mphephu. I glanced around furtively, conscious of being respectful to ancestors who were by now surely hovering. "Wozani okhokho!" I jumped as Vusi suddenly burst into a booming Zulu incantation. "Wozani okhokho, wozani" (Come to us, you ancestors, come). He then rattled off a string of incantations calling on the ancestors, including phrases I understood such as "Okhokho bezwa ukukhala kwethu" (Ancestors, hear our prayers), "Vimbani ingozi" (Block the danger) and "Sizani inganeyako" (Help your child), which were repeated over and over. The prayers rose and fell, intense and berating, at times pleading, and altogether quite beautiful.

Next was a ritual bath in a tub of lukewarm water filled with herbs. I felt cleansed and as spicy as a meerkat. Dressed, I returned to where Vusi now sat cross-legged and hunched over on the floor like a large housewife, deftly sewing a red leather amulet. I settled beside him. Handing me a rusty spear and knobkierie to hold, he carefully placed the red amulet around my neck. More incantations, then he began to

150

leap around me like a dervish, stomping and beseeching, shaking my shoulders every now and then like a rag doll. I clenched my eyes tight, gripping the spear and knobkierie as if my life was at stake, which perhaps it was.

At last, he came to a puffing stop, prizing the weapons from my tight grip with a satisfied smile. "Okay Roger, you can go now. Your protection is strong." As I arose his parting words were, "Wear this amulet all the time, Roger. It holds the power of the ancestors. They will protect you and the Ramunangi from the king's spells." I left fingering the soft amulet, feeling somewhat invincible.

The clan needed to gather urgently to discuss the court process. I flew to Joburg the next afternoon, overnighting in Pretoria with my girlfriend Judy, then drove early next day to Thohoyandou. As I sped up the N1 through the Soutpansberg mountains, an icy thought speared the soft tissue of my gut, garrotting my balmy mood. My amulet! I had removed the amulet for bed, and in my early departure had left it behind. Waves of nausea flooded my system. Too late to turn back. Vusi's sober warning to wear it all the time, all too fresh in mind.

On arrival at Thohoyandou, thoughts of the missing amulet faded under the demands of the day. Maria welcomed me with a hug and bundled me into a rusty taxi. The sun-glassed driver greeted me with a flash of white teeth, turned the Kwaito music to full volume as we careered down the potholed road in a cloud of fumes. Dodging potholes and people, up Thohoyandou main street, left at the BP garage and along a potted dirt road to Phiphidi where the Ramunangi committee was already assembling.

'Aaaas' from the women, 'ndaas' from the men, triple-handshaking all round interspersed with *matsherone* (hello) and *ndolivuba* (thank you). We were excited to be together. Five plastic chairs were placed under a towering marula tree, and a lithe young girl with a mosaic of neatly braided hair picked up the flotsam of plastic bags and sundry objects that littered the backyard. Scrawny chickens scratched optimistically in the red dust.

The scheduled time of the meeting, 10 a.m., was long past, and only three members of the clan had arrived. We waited and waited. I fiddled with my Blackberry and watched thin-legged children rolling an old tyre. The braided girl tended the fire (that was to cook food for the expected masses) in the nonchalant manner of one who had done this task many times. Soon I was joined by committee secretary, Walter Ramunangi, a teacher with the aura of a human Eeyore. "Why the delay, Walter?" I asked. "We arranged transport for everybody, Mista Roger," he said, gloomily looking at his watch. "I cannot understand why they are not here already."

I had learned not to expect Western time standards in Africa, but for such an important meeting this was unusual. Phakhati paced backwards and forwards receiving and answering calls, none of which seemed good news. He joined us under the tree, shaking his head. "Bad news, mista Roger," he said. "One of the taxis had an accident and some people were injured. Three of the other taxis have broken down, and they say they can't come." He looked miserable. It was now midday, and only twelve people had arrived at a meeting that should have been hundreds. We agreed to start.

After an opening prayer, I was asked to report on the state of the interdict, and on the legal fight ahead. I expressed concern at the failure of the clan to assemble and the litany of bad luck of the four taxis that had broken down. As I was speaking, an awful wailing arose from the direction of the forest. Something terrible was happening in or near Phiphidi. Some went off to see to check while I sat down. There was little more to say.

We picked at the mountain of traditional vegetarian fare with mopani worms and chicken, debating the mysterious lack of attendance. Surely four taxis with about twelve passengers each could not have crashed or broken down on the same morning? Nobody was telling the full truth it seemed; strange forces seemed to be at play. As we crammed into our taxi for the return journey, Mashudu, the youngest committee member, came running wide-eyed to the vehicle. In staccato spurts she gasped that a young girl had drowned in Ghuvhughuvu sacred pool, explaining the cries and commotion. Turning to me, Maria whispered tersely, "When ancestors are angry, they take human sacrifice!"

That evening we held a debriefing meeting in the dining room of the Fig Tree Lodge where I was booked in for the night. I did not tell the committee about forgetting my amulet, for reasons of embarrassment and pride. It was stupid to have left the amulet behind, but I also did not want to admit to the power of magic spells. We sat around a small round table as Phakhati opened our meeting. Normally positive and energetic, he was deflated. Johannes, Phakhati's cousin and the oldest man in the group, was equally sombre, his dark face blacker than usual in the dimly lit room. Walter was his usual doleful self, and Mashudu fiddled with her pencil as she sat next to Professor and prepared to take minutes.

Reviewing the day, we discussed the inexplicable no-show, the accident of one and breaking down of four taxis, and of course the drowning of a girl in the sacred pool during our meeting. I tried to move the conversation to our interdict against the king, but they were fixated on the disastrous day. The ancestors seemed to be angry, and had taken a human life. Why? At times the discussions in Venda grew heated without pause for translation, and I had to remind Maria to fill me in. We were at loggerheads, going round in circles. Reluctantly, I came clean about my missing amulet.

"Okay friends, so last week I went to see Sangoma Vusi, on Phakhati's advice," I began. They listened intently, understanding much of my deliberately slow English before Maria's translation. "The sangoma gave me strong medicine to protect us from the king's spells, and to help us fight this case." Five pairs of meerkat eyes stared alertly. "Now this is getting interesting, Roger. Go on, go on." I hesitated, but there was no going back.

"Vusi gave me this amulet to wear around my neck for protection, but to tell the truth (a long pause for a deep breath) I forgot it and left it behind in Pretoria." As Maria translated these words, Phakhati and Johannes gasped, and the others leaned forward. Meerkats spotting the same worm. Embarrassed at this rapt response, I tried to minimise my error. "Look, friends, it was just a small mistake; of course, I will wear it all the time in the future." Then with a mirthless laugh, "Hey, let's be realistic. Surely what happened today could *not* have been the ancestors punishing us because I left my amulet?"

As Maria translated this attempt to make light of my failure, an almighty explosion rocked the room. We reeled in shock, two chairs crashed to the floor, and a pungent alcoholic mist rained down upon us. Johannes leaped to his feet with a shout, and I leaned forward covering my computer from the liquid raining from above. Walter wiped the raining mist from his bald head and licked it with apparent relish. It was *magewu* (traditional fermented beer). Professor began to laugh and dance in the spray, drying her head with her waist blanket. With sweet magewu mist still in the air, we worked out what had happened. Professor had bought her weekly two-litre plastic bottle of magewu at the market that afternoon, and had placed it upright in her open bag on the floor beside her chair. At the exact moment I had said, "Surely the ancestors can't be angry?" the bottle had exploded, splashing the beer against the ceiling, and raining it down on us all. The entire committee was drenched.

Professor addressed me excitedly and I asked Maria to translate.

"What Professor is saying, Roger," said Maria, amused, "maybe after the magewu shampooing, you will understand our ancestors are present. If we do not obey, they show us their power."

"Ask Professor, please, Maria," I said, still struggling, "Has she ever seen a bottle of magewu explode?"

"No, never ever before."

That magewu shampooing did it. I wore the amulet night and day till we won the case and saved Phiphidi waterfall.

23

Messengers from the Air

Wings spread wide, the bearded vulture straddles updrafts from the vertical cliffs, slicing through the mists that swirl around escarpments. A cow, a baboon or an antelope grazing too near the edge of the cliff are all perfect prey. Commonly an unwary dassie is the creature most likely to end its life this way, but one sharp strike from this large bird, surprise the chief weapon, tumbles any unwary creature over the cliff. Gravity and the rocks below do the rest.

Exhilarated, I was standing at the southern tip of the Kingdom of Lesotho, toes six inches away from the cliff face, directing a stream of urine into South Africa below. This was the first rest on day three of a trans-Drakensberg hike, and my two older companions, Clive Craig and Mr Upfold, were resting on the pathway fifty metres back. "Just going to check out the cliff edge," I had said, feeling less exhausted than them from the morning's exertions. The rising updraft was damp on my cheeks, and the sheer drop into Natal below both scary and exciting. Tossing a large stone over the edge earlier, it took six seconds before a muffled sound from far below signalled the landing.

Well into my urination, I exhaled with relief and relaxed into a sort of trance. Vapour from my hot outbreath joined the swirling mists. Although my toes were on the brink, I felt steady, with no fear of toppling forwards; the steaming amber arc disappearing into the fog. Then, in a flash, an impulse of danger, flung from guardian angels or some higher self, exploded in my mind. I hurled myself backwards from the cliff face. A feathered missile at shoulder height, accompanied by a whooshing sound, sliced the air where I had stood. Wingspan double my height, the bearded vulture briefly cocked its feathered head as it passed, as if in surprise, and was swallowed by the mist. Hugging the rocky ground, the sting of the warm urine on my leg, I imagined the tumble through the air that would have been my final seconds. In later years, I heard about the Darwin Awards which record humans who remove themselves from the gene pool in the most foolish ways. I would surely have been a prime contender.

Decades later, I lean forwards over my lime green Kawasaki 650, late for a board meeting at !Khwa ttu, the San Culture Centre on the West Coast. I am wearing a bulky BMW jacket designed to protect one from high-speed falls, although any motorbike rider knows that nothing can deliver you from a high-speed accident. The road between Malmesbury and Darling lies ahead empty and straight. No cows, cars nor people, perfect for pushing the limits.

I was a latecomer to the world of large bikes. At age forty I was diagnosed with a mysterious autoimmune disease named CFS (chronic fatigue syndrome) or ME[6], which turned me from a healthy workaholic into a sick and depressed man. Countless visits to doctors over five years had left me depleted; struggling to continue work, to pursue the San land claim, to be a 'struggle' lawyer, and be an adequate dad to small kids. Leslee said to me one day as I was about to leave for the Kalahari, "Bassy has a new game called 'Daddy Daddy'. Perhaps you'd like to see?" Flattered, I said, "Of course."

Our five-year-old youngest trotted up holding a small toy suitcase. "Bassy, show Dad your game." "Okay, Mum," he piped. Trotting to the kitchen door, he turned and waved before leaving, shouting, "Bye everyone, be good, see you soon," and then disappeared round the corner. "He stays in the garden for a long while," Leslee said, "and then returns through the kitchen door. Leaving, being away, and then returning after a long time. That is what he sees you doing."

The sickness dragged me down. Any exertion was punished immediately by relapse with fever and headaches. Believing my active days to be over, I purchased a mean machine to compensate for my loss of life force. Like Robert M. Pirsig in *Zen and the Art of Motorcycle Maintenance* who warns against the gumption trap that blocks people from awareness, I used my illness as an invitation to engage with the mystery of my ailing body. My own healing path began. I read books on the inner journey, swam daily in the icy waters of the Eersterivier, and sought insights in new places. A persistent voice whispered, "You will heal."

Enter Credo Mutwa.

This old sangoma, famous for writing a tome on Zulu mythology, *Indaba My Children,* in English at age seventeen, had become known latterly as a mystic healer. A friend suggested I contact him, and, with nothing to lose, I rang the number.

"Dr Mutwa, I presume," I began, not trying to be cute.

"Indeed, it is he," came a thin and refined voice. "How may I assist today?"

"My name is Roger Chennells, Dr Mutwa," I said, "I am unwell."

"Of course, you are," was his reply. "May I call you Mr Rogers?"

"Certainly, sir," I said, as polite as can be, "would you like me to describe my symptoms?"

"No, Mr Rogers," he said, "that will not be necessary. Why don't I tell *you* what your symptoms are, and you can please correct me if I am wrong?"

Intrigued, I agreed, and he proceeded.

"You begin each day, Mr Rogers, with a small tickle in the back of your throat. This soon turns into an annoying cough. So despite being a man of considerable energy, you are exhausted all the time. The slightest exertion causes your body to rebel with flu symptoms and a fever. This has been going on for at least five years, and you are desperate. You are starting to believe that you will never heal."

157

Long pause. "How am I doing, Mr Rogers?"

Bull's eye. "Please go on, Dr Mutwa," I gulped.

"You have the oldest sickness in Africa," he proceeded. "No need for shame. Even Shaka Zulu suffered from this malady for two years, and recovered using the technique that I am about to tell you. So Mr Rogers, let's get down to the cure. Do you perhaps have access to a young goat for slaughter, some milkweed thistle and African Wild Potato of the *Hypoxis* family in your garden?

"I am afraid not, sir."

"I thought not," he responded, with a chortle. "In that case, please go at once to your nearest Link Pharmacy and order the following." He listed four medicines, which I wrote down. "This is only half the cure, Mr Rogers." He went on. The second, and more important half, is the spiritual component. You need to value and love your life more and more, in every possible way; get rid of *all* sources of negative energy. You have important work to do with indigenous peoples as well as your family. Follow my advice, and your health will return."

"Thanks so much, Dr Mutwa." (How *did* he know about my work with indigenous peoples, I wondered? I had said nothing.) "How can I repay you? I mean, what do I owe you?"

"Mr Rogers," he responded, again with that chuckle, "you owe me everything, and at the same time, nothing. If you feel I have been of value, here are my bank details." I paid him generously, vowing to follow his advice.

Despite my steady healing, I drove that dangerous motorbike for the next twenty years. And on that empty West Coast road, hurtling towards !Khwa ttu, the throttle was wide open. At 180 km/h, any collision would have spelled oblivion. Unbeknownst, however, the universe was not done with large birds and me. Two guinea fowl flying side by side from my right to my left, at head height, aimed to land on the field to the left. In a sensual blur, I felt a whoosh as the first shaved my visor inches from my nose, and the second clipped the satchel on my back. At such speed and momentum, either of them would have broken my neck on direct impact. As they landed squawking on the field, my bike stuttered to a halt on the verge, stalled and fell onto me. In shock I hugged the earth, left leg trapped under the steaming engine, wet from spilled petrol.

Death had been foiled with another dramatic wake-up call. I limped into the room, late for the meeting, and sat blankly throughout, stinking of petrol and processing cell shock. Such a message from the universe could not be ignored. If I did not get it now, I never would.

'Rapping, rapping at my chamber's door', like the raven in Edgar Allan Poe's poem, were the words of Credo Mutwa, for which I had shown such a careless disregard. "Love and value your life," he had said, again and again. It was time to avoid the gumption trap, to take in the messages that were sent from the sky.

Imagining the old sangoma's chuckle, I sold the Kawasaki the next day.

24

Luaviavi the Chameleon

I was an attorney in my mid-fifties, with decades of practice under my chin. Generally, I tried to adopt a conciliatory approach to legal disputes but when no settlement seemed possible, I would reluctantly resort to traditional law. When that took place, the litigation that followed inevitably damaged relationships, and no matter the outcome, innocent parties suffered.

July 2010. I was urgently approached to assist with a legal drama of the worst kind – involving the ambitious and charismatic CEO of an environmental NGO operating in the Venda region. Jezi Madonsela firmly believed that she was far more important than the NGO board and refused to be bound by what she regarded scornfully as their 'Western management requirements'. This attitude had become increasingly detrimental to the organisation and a long period of conflict ensued. She seemed impervious to criticism or correction.

The board finally resorted to the most drastic of all actions. Summary dismissal. Sure enough, as the original founder and star of the organisation, Jezi was understandably beyond livid at the indignity. Within days of her being fired it became clear that she was not only determined to challenge her dismissal in court, demanding a massive payment in compensation, but was also intent on mobilising the local communities to take her side. This was serious stuff. I had often witnessed the sheer power of Jezi's personality in mobilising popular support, and my heart sank at the task of facing such a powerful antagonist. The dispute had already hampered the work of the organisation for years and the beneficiary communities suffered whilst she and the board remained in a deadlock.

My initial investigations showed that the board had failed to follow the formal legal procedures, making real the possibility of our failure in court. Naturally, I felt out the possibility of negotiating an amicable solution. This idea was squashed like a gnat, my approach being met with Jezi's white-hot fury. No middle ground. A fight to the finish, with only one winner, and collateral damage all round. Feeling gloomy I phoned Joan, the NGO director responsible for the case. Her response was most unusual.

"The funders are concerned about the damage this case with Jezi can do to the organisation. Whilst respecting your legal abilities, they suggest that you visit Sangoma Vusi." This could be translated to mean, "We would feel safer with paranormal support." I have already told the story in this book of how Vusi provided me with protection from the Venda King, so I knew him to be a powerful traditional healer. But what self-respecting lawyer would accept a sangoma's assistance for a difficult case? If this became known, imagine my shame? And could a spell or curse *really* affect the outcome of the law? I vacillated. Yet I was acutely aware of our frail case, and the implacable power of an angry Jezi.

I phoned Vusi.

Sitting on the floor of his unremarkable suburban home, I tried not to be distracted by the assorted skins, bones and potions that surrounded us, emitting a musty, acrid-sweet aroma. Vusi was a commanding presence; his portly frame swathed in blankets and beads, his bass voice reassuring. After a brief discussion, he proceeded to throw the bones onto his grass mat, intensely examining the tumbled objects. After mumbling and fiddling with the bones, he informed me gravely, "Your opponent has assembled a strong legal team as well as community supporters. This will present you with a formidable, if not unbeatable case."

I was intrigued at how Vusi had deduced these facts from the tumbled fall of the bones. Neither Joan nor I had not shared details of the Jezi story with him. I was all ears. "There is only one way to go from here," he rumbled, after a further period of thought, "your opponent is simply too powerful to fight head on, so our only option is to invoke Luaviavi the chameleon spell."

"The what?" I exclaimed.

"When your adversary is too strong, rather than fight directly, invoking the chameleon spell changes the opponent's very nature or 'colour,' thereby diffusing the case. Shandu-shanduka, fana na luaviavi," (to change colour, just like the chameleon) Vusi explained. "It is somewhat like the principles of Judo," he offered, as if an afterthought.

"That sounds excellent to me, Vusi. Let's do it," I responded, suppressing a niggling voice of disbelief.

It was settled then, the chameleon spell it would be. Vusi lit the *mphephu* herbs, enabling their sweet and acrid smoke to invoke the spirits of the ancestors. He then stomped around, chanting imprecations in a rumbling torrent of fluent Nguni. Finally, he concluded the ritual by taking a deep swig of cheap brandy from a half-jack, spraying an alcoholic cloud all over me.

An impressive performance to be sure.

I left him, stifling my doubts and carrying a small leather amulet filled with unknown substances, which he said carried the essence of the spell. All I had to do was to trust the ancestors and keep the amulet on my person leading up to the court case.

Jezi duly filed her case for wrongful dismissal with the Commission for Conciliation, Mediation and Arbitration (CCMA) in Polokwane. In her documents she demanded full re-instatement, alternatively six months' salary. This would cripple the NGO. I drafted a comprehensive array of documents in support of the NGO's defence, including Heads of Argument bolstering our case. My faith in the chameleon spell had receded. If we were to win, I needed to apply all my accumulated legal knowledge in the usual way and other skills in an unusual way.

By the time the court date drew near, I had filed twenty-five pages of evidence, including affidavits describing the board's attempts to correct Jezi's disruptive behaviour, with dozens of case references supporting an employer's right to dismiss an errant director. It would take at least a day in court to lead all of this evidence. Then we would have to deal with her response which challenged our Achilles heel, namely the faulty process that had preceded the dismissal.

On the date of the hearing, with anxious heart and laden briefcase, I accompanied Joan, director and chief witness for the NGO, to the forbidding building that was the Polokwane CCMA court. The senior clerk consulted her files and confirmed that applicant Jezi was registered to prosecute her application at 9 a.m. and was supported by a local lawyer and several witnesses. Anticipating her arrival with an entourage of witnesses and supporters, we sat down nervously in the reception area going over our documents a last time. Joan, a doughty activist with decades of experience, looked exhausted and grey.

Hearing a sound at the door, I looked up. There was Jezi alone, looking dishevelled, and somehow different. No lawyer, no entourage? Gone was that haughty demeanour, that arrogance and seething anger. Instead, she looked a picture of humility and appeared to be crying. Walking quickly across the room she approached Joan and flung her arms around her neck, weeping loudly. "I'm so sorry, I'm so sorry, Joan!" she repeated over and over. "I have changed my mind about the case. I was so wrong. I want nothing at all from the organisation and want to withdraw the case."

I couldn't believe my ears. When she had calmed down, I led her quickly over to the clerk, in case she came to her senses. Jezi duly signed a formal notice of withdrawal. The crisis was over. This fierce and powerful woman, who had never been known to apologise or to admit she was wrong, had inexplicably transformed and changed her nature.

Just like Luaviavi.

Some might doubt the authenticity of this story, so I place my hand on the metaphorical Bible. "Nothing but the truth."

I felt like a failing water diviner who abandons his state-of-the-art sound equipment in favour of the old divining rods and finds an aquifer.

And I was praised for this victory that truly belonged to the chameleon.

25

Kudus, Ancestors and Black Label

Winter 1992. And that beautiful hazard of African roads. Driving out of Windhoek at dusk with my friend Axel at the wheel of his Musso 4X4, we were heading for Harmony, a seminar centre, about ten kilometres out of town. The massive beast appeared suddenly in our headlights, crashed into the bonnet with a bone-crunching thud, then hit the windshield, flattening the roof on its flight over the top. A clattering of horns, hooves, bones on metal.

I was squashed to the left of the front passenger seat as the roof collapsed and both front doors sprung open. Axel was crumpled to the right behind the steering wheel. Painfully we crawled out, dazed in shock. "You okay, Axel?" I called, fearing the worst and nursing a bashed knee and bruised temple. "Fine, I think," answered Axel, voice guttural and laboured, "but I think the car is buggered, and the kudu too!" Limping to the rear of the smashed Musso, there was the injured kudu, illuminated by a nearby street light, wheezing and struggling to get onto its feet. After such an impact, how could any creature survive?

The noble beast was facing me, blood oozing from impact wounds. Massive spiral horns glinting in the faint light. In my peripheral vision I noted a car had stopped and people were coming. With extreme effort the kudu heaved itself up to balance on three legs, one front leg uselessly hanging, lifting its proud head until its eyes gazed directly at mine. For long seconds we stared at each other, while a thin stream of blood dribbled from its nose, our laboured breaths shutting out all other sounds. Finally, it swayed to the left, then to the right, still holding my awe-struck gaze, until with a trembling cough it collapsed onto the road. One shuddering sigh, and it was dead. More cars had now stopped and a small crowd gathered around the kudu, prodding, firing questions. One opportunist asked if he could take it away for its meat. Another answered, "Why not?" Reliving the awful last moments of the kudu, I retreated into the darkness and cried soundlessly.

Axel made calls and a tow truck took us to a panel beater where a swarthy man with grimy overalls clambered about the Musso assessing damage. "Look here, misters," he said to us, pointing past the crumpled passenger door at what was my seat. "See this, here right in the middle of the seat?" He stuck his thumb into a large hole. "This is where the kudu's horn pierced as it rolled over the bonnet and the roof. Passenger should have been killed."

Hours later, we arrived at the conference centre where about thirty San representatives were preparing for the meeting scheduled for the next three days. Harmony, a favourite venue for San meetings, covered about twenty hectares of indigenous Namibian bush, surrounded by a high game fence. Scenically placed buildings amongst hardy acacia, erythrina and mopane trees. Shaken and exhausted, we were shown to our accommodation. Still dressed, I fell immediately into a troubled sleep.

Images of the kudu relentlessly tormented my dreams. Accusing brown eyes drilled into my brain where there was no escape, blood drizzling and then pouring from the dying animal's shiny muzzle. Resentful, fatally wounded. Majestic horns spiralled into splintering metal, fur making way for bruised and bloody flesh, gasping for life as it swayed left and right, before crashing down. Heart pounding, I woke shakily to find that my bedside light was still on. One thirty a.m. Relieved to escape the psychic assault I stepped out into the night.

Half asleep, eyes lidded, I stepped onto the patch of grass that lay outside my room and zipped open my fly. As I was fumbling, a strange feeling of being watched came over me. I opened my eyes. Three stately kudu does, ears pitched forward, stood in a semi-circle less than two metres away, gazing intently at me. For stretched-out seconds none of us moved. Trying to take in the surreal scene, I shyly hid my private part. It sunk in that these three kudus were watching me, in flesh and blood, and it felt personal. Abruptly, and after at least a minute or two, the middle doe turned away firmly, as if she had seen enough. She was followed closely by the other two and they disappeared into the darkness. Stunned, I remained in pee position for a long time.

The next morning there was work to do and I was still overwhelmed, not only by the drama of the accident but also, even more, by the midnight visitation. Before breakfast I knocked on the office door of Ewald Hurter, the owner of Harmony and our host for the days to come. A powerful German in his fifties, his impressive belly and matching personality exuded genial confidence. Two Rottweiler dogs lay at his feet, office festooned with animal skins, trophies and memorabilia. After greeting him I got straight to the point.

"Ewald, how many tame kudus do you have here? I have never seen them on my previous visits, but last night three of them came right close to me ouside my room." He looked at me quizzically, as if I had said something stupid.

"Are you sure you saw ze kudus, Roger? I don't zink so." His German accent seemed stronger than ever.

When I asked why he thought I was mistaken, he explained. "Tventy years I have owned zis farm. Ze fence is six foot six. Not vunce have I seen ze kudu on zis place. Zo I don't zink you saw ze zudu." His dogs kept any antelope from entering his farm. Whilst a kudu could possibly clear the fence, he had never ever seen them on the property.

I changed the subject, my head spinning, then took leave. Were those kudu does the 'wives' of the dead kudu? And if so, what was the message for me? What should I do? As I walked back to my cottage, my mind raced back to a previous visitation from the animal world. At a tormented time in my life, I had moved away from wife and children to a cob house in Jonkershoek Valley, near Stellenbosch. Agonising about the life-changing wrench that loomed, a friend arranged a visit to the highly recommended Sangoma John. "What can you lose anyway?" was his persuasive argument.

167

Within days I was sitting meekly on a grass mat in front of the stern healer who, without ado, lit the mphephu to alert the spirit world, and prepared to throw the bones. After checking that I had come for a reading, and with no preliminary discussions during which he might have gleaned information about my issues, he launched into the ritual. Chanting Nguni imprecations, he first rattled and shook a grubby bag, then with an oath hurled a clattering of bones and other objects onto the mat. Studying the seeming chaos intently, touching one, shifting another, muttering all the while. I felt strangely unmoved, as if challenging the ancestors to make sense of my quandary.

Time ticked on. "A truly remarkable throw," John stated, gently. I have never seen this permutation before." I perked up. "See this bone in front here?" he went on. "It is a lion vertebra, representing the cat spirit. The way it has separated from and dominates the others is significant. This entire reading is dominated by the cat spirit, which represents spiritual power and change."

He went on to describe other bones and their meanings. And then he uttered words that would remain with me forever. "You are about to take the step that you have been preparing for for much of your adult life. You have no choice but to leave your family. Your wife will be angry (pointing at one sharp bone), your children will suffer too (pointing at three similar knuckle bones together). Your heart will know deep pain (pointing at a cowrie shell lying face up, representing vulnerability). What you must take is a spiritual, as much as a physical step. This reading is so important, the cat spirit will send you a message within the next day to ensure that you have got the message." He emphasised that the cat energy represents the force of the spirit to seek the right path. As I left, his words followed me, "Keep an eye out for that cat message, Roger, and let me know please."

I returned to the clay house in the forest, bemused by the fact that I had never ever seen a cat in the ten years I had known the farm. What cat message? What nonsense! As I was drifting off to sleep at around 10 p.m. I heard a scratching sound on the roof. Grabbing torch and golf stick, I opened the door and looked into the darkness. Nothing. Then a sound above and behind me. On the roof, one metre from my torch, crouched, a gorgeously spotted genet cat. Not darting away, but looking at me intently. My heart pounded. Its behaviour was not that of a wild creature. "Are you an ancestor? Are you from the ancestors?" I asked. Silence, and keen stare. After at least a minute, it climbed unhurriedly into the oak above the roof and disappeared from the light.

I returned to bed, heart racing. A visit from the ancestors? It was so tame, its behaviour so unlike a wild creature. But then the doubts creeping in. Pure coincidence? What if the genet just *happened* to be on my roof, tame and unafraid, on the night I awaited a cat message? Soon my doubting mind won the debate and I figured it was *just* a cat. Not a message from the wild.

Slipping back into sleep a noise again jerked me awake. This time louder, and outside the door. Golf stick and torch in hand, I eased open the door. The genet cat on the pathway, less than two metres outside the door, now stood on its hind legs. Facing me, as if for a chat. Not moving, fearless. I breathed deeply, awed, and in the presence of mystery. "Okay, Mr Cat, "now I truly get it. I understand. You *are* from the ancestors and bring a message as the sangoma warned." It did not nod its head but in every other way seemed to hear my words. I carried on chatting, warming to this new reality. After a while, it sank to its four legs, and in an almost bored manner, walked down the path and out of sight.

The next morning I phoned John. "You won't guess what happened last night, John." Without waiting for his response, I continued excitedly, "As you warned me. A genet cat visited me, twice! What must I do?" He sounded pleased, but not surprised. "I am glad. That was confirmation that the spirits are with you on your journey. Now if you do not want a cat visit every night for the next week, you should buy a quart of Black Label beer, take a swig, and then pour a libation over where the cat visited you, tonight. Then the ancestors will know that you know." I did so that night, and never ever saw the genet cat again.

Back at Harmony estate, I knew what to do. I bought a quart of Windhoek Lager as they had no Black Label. At about midnight, I stepped out of my cottage. Taking a massive swig from the bottle, I poured the rest liberally over the hoof prints of the previous night's visitors. "Be assured, lovely ladies," I spoke aloud, "your man's death and your visit will never be forgotten." After all, as Goethe once said, 'superstition is the poetry of life'.

KALAHARI SAN

26

Rotman, a Minister and an Arrow

One morning, my friend Antony Osler – human rights lawyer, Buddhist, philosopher and author – phoned. "Rog, you will get a call from a friend of mine. Cait Andrew. She's unusual, but nice. It's about Bushmen." Within days Cait had phoned and we were driving to visit a small clan of Bushmen living at Kagga Kamma in the Cederberg.

Cait was intense, with the rugged features of an Apache warrior; high cheekbones, between beautiful and scary. During the three-hour journey via Ceres, she smoked continuously while describing the musicology research that she was doing with the clan leader, Regopstaan Kruiper, the last known player of the San mouth bow. In passing, she added, "There's a big eclipse of the moon happening later today. It's gonna be special."

We were met by fifteen small people dressed in skins, who swarmed around us excitedly. Before long all (including children) were puffing on the dagga zols from Cait. She led me briskly to meet the San patriarch Regopstaan, now in his eighties. He wore a tiny loincloth and lay crumpled in a heap on a grimy blanket. He had been tall for a Bushman, his rugged face ravaged by furrows and gaunt with pain. He became animated, aided by long draws on Cait's offered spliff, and whispered in between a hacking cough that he had long awaited this day.

"Gaan jy vir ons sing en speel, Regopstaan?" (Will you sing and play for us?) asked Cait.

"Ja, mies. Dis 'n ou liedjie wat ek gaan sing. Hoe eendag, wanneer die son verduister, 'n bleek man gaan kom om ons te help" (Yes, miss. It is an old song that I will sing. How one day, when the sun goes dim, a pale man will come to help us).

As the marijuana kicked in he pointed at the sun that was darkening and announced that he was going to perform the old eclipse song. Taking out what looked like a hunting bow with a hollow gourd at one end and mouthpiece at the other, he leaned on one elbow and rested the bow in a space conveniently left by a missing lower tooth. Twanging the string a few times with a thin reed arrow, he chanted a haunting refrain in the San/Nama dialect, while family members gathered around and clapped an edgy beat. Arms draped unreservedly around one another. Repeated, again and again, the melody gathered strength with the family joining in the refrain, timeless cadences echoing off the sandstone rocks. I accepted puffs of the spliff, freely shared, as the eclipse darkened the earth and floated dreamily above the stone-age scene.

On Cait's insistence and with the sun now seriously darkening, we went from Regopstaan's bed to a nearby sandstone cave where I was to address the Kruiper clan. Cait's introduction was swift. "Hierdie man is 'n lawyer. Hy is 'n vriend. Hy sal julle help om julle grond in die Kalahari terug te kry" (This man is a lawyer. He is a friend. He will help you get your land back in the Kalahari).

Swaying in front of them and far from sober, their new lawyer beamed drunkenly at the gathered clan as they in turn smiled back happily, young and old. Dawid Kruiper and his wife Sanna sat cross-legged in front on the sandy floor. Many of the young kids carried sticks or small bows in their hands. Drawing a deep breath prior to launching into the legal implications of a land claim, I noticed a kitten-sized rat sitting upright about two metres away, gazing inquisitively at me, his nose whiffling. Surreal images jostled in my struggling mind: large cave, eclipse of the sun behind moon, semi-naked San audience and attentive rat. And me, higher than a vulture, about to speak.

After a long pause my training kicked in. I suggested we start with an attendance register, Cait agreeing to write down names that were sung out to her. When the list got to twenty-four names and my befuddled brain could clearly count only fifteen adults in the space, seeing a name I did not recognise, I asked Cait, "Who is Abram?"

Laughing, Oom Dawid explained that Abram, Regopstaan's long-deceased father, was in attendance, together with his wife and other long-passed family members. At least nine recorded on the list as present were ancestors, ghosts, present in spirit only. The San's insistence on the participation of departed spirits at important gatherings would still take time to understand.

While digesting that many of my audience belonged to another realm, I began to describe what we needed to do to lodge a claim for their ancestral land. I would assist them to elect a committee to represent their extended family, and their legal case would be based upon the Restitution of Land Rights Act, still in the process of being promulgated.

They listened intently and click-chattered among themselves, quick to burst into laughter at any hint of levity. Every so often I glanced at the rat, reassured that at least *it* was engrossed in what I was saying, seemingly following my every word. I even felt sure it was nodding at the appropriate places. Suddenly, as if it had just recalled an urgent engagement, he dropped to all fours and dashed at full speed for the cave exit.

A bad mistake for Mr Rat, and what happened next took place in a blur. A youngster of about twelve, whom I later got to know as Am-Am, had his bow and arrow at the ready. As the rat scampered past, he took a rapid shot, piercing the poor creature through the stomach. With a squeak the rodent collapsed in a heap, legs making futile death kicks.

For me the meeting was over. I rushed to the rat's side and helplessly witnessed the sleek creature's agonised dying spasms. Shocked by the needless cruelty, I was also grudgingly impressed by Am-Am's effortless hunting skills. My audience was overjoyed at the unexpected turn of developments, and intrigued by their new lawyer's apparent close bond with the deceased rat. When Cait and I left the cave, the sound of happy laughter still in our ears, I had been given the nickname which has stuck to this day. Rotman.

Two months after the cave and rat experience, I stood with Oom Dawid on a red sand dune near the Molopo River, approximately fifty kilometres outside the Kgalagadi Transfrontier Park. Ancient camel thorn trees dotted the river bed, some containing the hulking shapes of the white backed vultures that had chosen this stretch of river as a nesting colony. Kalahari dune grasses, waving in all directions, provided proof of recent good rains.

"Oom Dawid, waar presies was julle eie grond?"(Oom Dawid, where exactly was your own land?)

I needed to describe their land with clarity to lodge a legal claim, and also attach a map to the court documents. The old Bushman made an expansive gesture with a wrinkled arm.

"Alles, Rotman. Alles wat jy kan sien, en baie verder" (All, Rotman, that you can see, and much further).

Trying to understand, I asked whether what he described was in fact, *their own land*. Laughing heartily at this, he took a deep draw on his dagga and Boxer blend home-rolled spliff. "Rotman, kyk nou!" (Rotman, look!) Picking up a handful of fine red sand, he dribbled it through his fingers. "Hierdie grond is my ma en my pa, my oupa en ouma, al my voorouers. As ek doodgaan word ek ook deel daarvan (This sand is my mother and father, my grandfather and grandmother, and all their predecessors. When I die, I too become part of it).

His splayed toes wriggled into the red sand. "Ons Boesmans weet nie van *eienaars* nie, Rotman. Ons *behoort aan* die grond" (We Bushmen do not know about ownership, Rotman. We *belong to* the land). Taking notes furiously, I realised that I was traversing the cusp of modern and indigenous cosmology. "Elke boom, klip, bok of dier is soos familie vir ons" (Every tree, stone, antelope and animal, is like family to us).

After a year of working with the Kruiper clan both at Kagga Kamma and in the Kalahari, it was time to formulate their legal claim. Monthly meetings with the elected committee, research into the San origins in the

Kalahari Gemsbok Park and countless discussions took place on red sandy floors. The work provided new challenges to one trained in a Western paradigm. My job was to teach a hunter-gatherer clan with ancient survival skills and belonging in Kalahari wilderness how to negotiate a world of committees, law and rights to land. Negotiations needed to be held with the distant government in terms of the Restitution Act of 1996. *Ownership* of land, the concept central to Western economies, needed to be proved for the case to succeed.

How to convert the beliefs shared on the banks of the Molopo River into a claim for land ownership in our law? Notions entirely foreign to Western legal systems, where owners fence in, own and dominate their land. Adam's curse in Genesis was to go forth into the world to conquer the birds of the air, the beasts of the field: not to regard them as family.

As Dawid and his family explained, every place, feature and being in their territory is named, is known like a mother does her children, and woven into a fine blanket of knowing which floats over generations and is passed on by word of mouth. This invisible blanket settles over the land they inhabit as evident and as tangible as a title deed. When the San return to their land after being away, they pick up the red sand, placing some on tongue, rubbing the rest into hair. Children roll in it gleefully. This was the virtual map that proved their land, one that lives on skin, in hearts and in minds. But how was I to draw such a map?

Researching the claim of the group then referred to as the Southern Kalahari San, retired Professor HP Steyn provided crucial assistance. He had previously gathered reams of unpublished material on the Kruiper family, as well as the /Auni, !Khomani and N/amani language groups. The Kruipers were the last San living in a semi-traditional manner in South Africa, and who still retained much of the lifestyle and knowledge that had died out elsewhere. A diaspora had caused their clan members to spread far and wide, including into Namibia and Botswana. Our task was to unravel decades of this diaspora, and to bring some form of restitution for South Africa's first peoples.

One day, Oom Dawid called a special meeting of the clan at Kagga Kamma, announcing that they had something special for me. With swaggering showmanship, he flung off an old blanket that covered an object in his hands, revealing a decorated hunting bow with leather quiver and arrows. "Rotman," he said smiling broadly, "jy is aan ons gestuur met die maan se duister, om die pad vorentoe oop te skiet" (Rotman, you were sent to us during the moon's eclipse to shoot our way into the future).

Pointing at a chicken about ten metres away, clucking and scratching in the sandy soil, he thrust the bow towards me and suggested that I now take the first symbolic shot. Despite my Robin Hood-adoring childhood when I had made bows and fired countless arrows, I feared the high expectations. What if I aimed at the chicken and missed by a mile? And what had the chicken done to deserve this fate? As I wavered, Dawid picked up a tiny child's shoe lying in the sand, strutted off on thin bandy legs and placed it about fifteen to twenty metres away, the toe facing us. This was my target. There was absolutely no way I would hit such a small object, and what an omen a miss would be.

Inspiration arrived. I responded earnestly that whilst I gladly accepted the gift of the bow and arrows, my job was to stand behind them as they shoot the way forward. I was there to support *them* on their way. Nodding and murmuring indicated ready assent, so I asked for the best archer amongst them to step forward. I would then support him whilst he took the shot.

After some excited chattering they pushed forward a wizened man of about forty. Abidjol, a famous hunter, chosen by the clan to shoot that symbolic arrow from my new bow. He bent and strung the bow between his bandy legs in a fluid movement, took out one of the small arrows and leaned forward plucking the bowstring to test its tension. A hush settled over the gathering, with me standing behind him, my right hand on his shoulder.

Thwuk! The bow twanged and the arrow flew with a perfect arc right into the shoe. Whoops and laughter erupted as Dawid picked up the target, arrow sticking out of the toe, and gave it to me as a memento. All agreed it was a great omen for the land claim, and within minutes a host of aromatic springbok-shin spliffs of marijuana were doing the rounds.

Back in the 'real' world, the formal legal document was duly lodged with the Department of Land Affairs, and the San land claim launched. This was a significant event, the first indigenous land claim ever to be lodged in South Africa, so I thought that we should meet the Minister of Land Affairs to ensure that he was aware of the significance. Soon I had an appointment to meet with Minister Derek Hanekom, and a date set for our delegation to meet with him in Parliament. This was to be a make or break meeting for us, the task being to persuade him of the significance of the only first people's claim in the country. An impressive presentation was required.

Workshops and long discussions prepared the committee: Dawid Kruiper, his brother Buks, Dawid's son Toppies, his daughter Oulet, cousins Ricky and Isak. Not one of them could read or write, nor had ever been to Cape Town, let alone to the Houses of Parliament. The game plan was that the charismatic leader Dawid would describe their diaspora since eviction from the park in 1931, while others would contribute additional information on selected topics.

With a week to go, anticipation for the great ministerial meeting was rising, so I requested the manager of Kagga Kamma, Michael Daiber, to assist with final preparations. The committee needed decent clothes, as I doubted Parliament would grant admission to semi-naked loincloth-dressed San. Dagga and weapons such as bows, arrows and knives were to be left behind. Michael entered the spirit and undertook to drive them to Parliament for the historic meeting. The team was understandably skittish, he added, but up for it, and committed to put on an excellent performance. The day before the meeting, also feeling skittish, I phoned Michael at midday to check on things. "Don't worry, Rot," he said cheerily, "we will be there on time tomorrow, no problem."

The next morning as I was dressing in my best suit, I received an anxious phone call. The usually calm Michael was close to incoherent. "Rot, sorry man eish, so sorry man, we have a huge problem. I went to fetch the committee just now, and they are all totally unconscious!" I asked him to slow down, calm down, explain. "They started drinking last night, Rot, and this morning they are all totally pissed. I just cannot wake them up."

This was miles beyond my worst nightmare.

"Throw water on them Mike, give them coffee, slap them, whatever is needed. They *have* to be with the Minister this morning."

An hour later he phoned again, his voice now flat. "So sorry, Rot. I have tried everything, but they are totally out of it. I cannot even wake one. You will have to go alone."

Just before 11 a.m. I arrived at Minister Hanekom's rooms in Parliament. He arose from behind his large desk as I was ushered in, a frown on his face. "Where are your clients, Mr Chennells? I am expecting the San delegation."

He had clearly done his homework, and was expecting me plus a committee of five. Six chairs were arranged around the coffee table.

"I am sorry, Minister," I said, wondering how much truth would be wise. "I am afraid that my delegation is . . . um . . . er. . . . well . . . indisposed."

"What?" he exclaimed, eyes widening. "What do you mean, indisposed?"

Nothing to lose, I thought, so I went for honesty and explained that as far as I could tell, the very idea of meeting with him, a minister of the government, had been simply too stressful for my clients. Their response to this pressure was to drink enough alcohol to knock them out for an entire day so that the problem would disappear. "I apologise, Minister, but the truth is my clients are all dead drunk!"

This catastrophe turned out to be a godsend. Hanekom had been no stranger to mind-altering substances in his younger days, and was tickled by the very idea of this indisposed delegation. Leaning forwards, he pressed me. "Please tell me all you can, Chennells: their history, background and the significance of this land claim." It was clear from his attentiveness that he found their story captivating as well as historically significant, and felt destined to assist with their plight.

By the time I left his office, hours later, we had established a solid understanding, and he had undertaken to give our land claim his personal attention. As far as he was concerned any group too vulnerable, too overwhelmed to even show up at such an important meeting *really* needed additional assistance, and he was going to give it.

The Minister was as good as his word, ensuring that the case received priority right until the official promulgation of the historic land claim on 21 February 1999. The San delegation and the !Khomani community owe him a lifelong debt of gratitude.

The arrow had struck its parliamentary target.

27

A Dance for Abidjol

Just before Upington, Oom Dawid tapped me on the shoulder. "Dis Abidjol, Rotman. Ons moet hom gaan haal" (It's Abidjol, Rotman. We must go and fetch him). We were heading for the Kalahari in the Rooi Donkie (red donkey), my Toyota Condor. Abidjol, the San huntsman who had fired my symbolic arrow at Kagga Kamma years earlier, was said to be close to death. He had moved into Botshabelo – a sprawling Upington township famous for all the most unsavoury reasons – with his new girlfriend a year or two back, and was in trouble. Abidjol was a favourite. Sanna, Dawid's wife, nephew Isak and three other San, cramped together in the vehicle, all gave directions at once, chattering excitedly over each other.

After countless wrong turns, directions and counter-directions, we pulled up in a potholed alley and approached an unnumbered tin shanty. On the covered stoep, on a rotten mattress, we found an emaciated Abidjol curled in foetal position alongside two mangy dogs. A crumpled relic of his former self, he was unable to walk or talk, depressed and listless. His girlfriend had left him for the black man who owned the shack, forcing him to sleep and be fed outside with the two dogs. Without ceremony, we carried the pitiful heap to the Rooi Donkie and drove two hours on the North Road to the clan base at Welkom, outside the park.

Word quickly spread about Abidjol's arrival in the Kalahari. The next day a delegation from the family informed me that they needed extra wood so that they could dance for him. The wood was bought and the dance scheduled for the next night. When I arrived at Oom Dawid's grass hut before sunset, Abidjol was curled up on a crumpled blanket much as I had left him a day before, still refusing to eat or talk. His look was entirely blank, that of a man on death row, who had lost the will to live. *Why go to all this effort*, I wondered. He seemed clearly beyond rescue, too far gone.

The fire was lit and the clan had gathered, dressed in skins with rattles on their wiry legs. Ricky was in charge, despite Oom Dawid's senior status, and soon the women began an off-beat clapping, evocative of millennia of such human gatherings. Toppies, Pien and Ou Jon, all Dawid's children, followed Ricky as he shuffle-hopped around the growing fire, then one by one others joined in, the giraffe-thorn pods around their thin legs adding a rattle to the hypnotic beat. Small children knew their place around the fire as spectators and clappers, whilst early teenagers such as Ping, Am-Am and Leeukos were allowed to join the dance. After a while Isak and his wife Lys fetched the prostrate bundle of misery that was Abidjol and seated him inside the growing circle of shuffle-stamping dancers.

With Abidjol's arrival the intensity of the clapping and dancing grew, until finally he started to take notice of what was happening. With a massive effort he fought gravity, and in a series of minuscule hesitant moves, reminiscent of a chameleon, rose shakily to his feet. He was going to join the dance. With shuffling steps, he started, still held by willing arms on both sides as the beat entered his body, injecting an inexplicable life force into his gaunt frame. One by one the dancers shuffled behind him placing hands firmly on his shoulders, each one seemingly imparting healing energy before making way for another. By the time he had shuffled around the fire five or six times, his emaciated body gained life force from these interactions like a tick on a vein of blood. His shuffling feet kicked up their own puffs of dust. And still the beat rose in intensity.

Eyes glazed, rhythmically shuffling and swaying, the participants had now entered into a deep trance and were headed towards some kind of climax. Ricky then laid both hands on Abidjol's shoulders, first from behind, then from the front, whilst the chanting and clapping continued to rise. For long seconds, a crescendo was sustained, pregnant with tension. Suddenly, accompanied by an otherworldly shriek, both leader and patient collapsed to the ground in a tangle of brown limbs. I was unable to see exactly what was happening as the other dancers crowded around the two on the ground, who seemed to have passed out. The singing stuttered to a stop.

Ricky disentangled from Abidjol and rose slowly, exhausted, his trance broken, his role as dance leader accomplished. Abidjol remained spreadeagled and unconscious. One by one the dancers and clappers drifted away from the circle of red earth that had been pounded for the past hours. Someone placed a blanket over Abidjol and checked on him. Presumably the patient was still alive.

I went early the next morning to visit Abidjol. *Had he survived the night?* I wondered. I expected to find him still sick, but hopefully not too damaged by the exertions of the dance. To my wonderment, the tiny Bushman was standing near a fire with a tin mug of coffee in his hand, bright-eyed and smiling. Upright, alert, the old Abidjol. Not a trace of the depression and misery that had gripped him for so long.

"Rotman!" he called out with a cheeky smile, "Onthou jy daardie ou pyltjie wat ek vir jou geskiet het?" (Do you remember that old arrow I shot for you?) Of course I did, I assured him. "Daardie pyltjie maak die toekoms oop, ne?" (That arrow shoots the way into the future, correct?) We chatted excitedly about that, and then more. Abidjol was back, and his future lay ahead. Sharp as the tip of that first arrow.

Meanwhile, back at Kagga Kamma the legal team was hard at work on the land claim, well aware that the old clan leader's time on earth was slipping away. Regularly I checked on the old man Regopstaan, desperate that he would survive long enough to witness success. Speaking in a hoarse whisper, now an apparition of parchment skin and bone, Regopstaan gripped my hand like a drowning man.

"Rotman, ek sê vir jou, wanneer ons ons grond terrugkry, sal dit in die Kalahari reën, soos nooit vantevore nie" (Rotman, I tell you, when we get our land back, it will rain in the Kalahari, like never before). After repeating this prophecy twice, he sank back onto his blanket, exhausted.

Six years had passed since we had met during the full moon eclipse, when the !Khomani land claim was gathering steam. The government was committed to negotiations, Minister Hanekom was taking a personal interest in the progress, and our focus was on ensuring that this unique land claim arrow struck its mark. Regopstaan was a shadow of the San patriarch who had once killed a gemsbok singlehandedly with a spear, and who had thought nothing of running forty-kilometre errands for the park manager, Le Riche, before breakfast. His gravitas, even in this reduced state, was still compelling.

Gripping my hand and gazing intently at me through cloudy eyes, he thanked me again for my role in taking on his people's claim, and asked if I understood his prediction. "Dankie, Regopstaan," I squeezed through a constricted throat, "ek waardeer jou woorde. En ek sal onthou wat jy sê oor die reën" (Thank you, Regopstaan. I appreciate your words. And I will remember what you said about the rain). He died soon after this, and was given a hero's burial by the now greatly expanded San clan, deep in the red dunes of the Kalahari. Wrapped in his old blanket, accompanied by his mouth bow, snuff and sticks for the journey, he was returned to the red earth of the mother.

After the land claim had been finalised, two years later on 21 March 1999 Thabo Mbeki presided over a grand ceremony at the Molopo Lodge, near the town of Askham, to return over 40 000 hectares of Kalahari land plus heritage rights in the Kgalagadi National Park to the San. Dawid Kruiper, the new clan leader, and Petrus Vaalbooi the elected San chairperson, shared the raised podium with Mbeki. Stirring speeches about return of land and first peoples of the continent mingled with the fine red dust hanging in the hot afternoon.

The much-loved Ouma /Una Rooi, one of three old sisters who still spoke the original N/uu language, then spoke passionately in both N/uu and Afrikaans. "Ons taal en ons kultuur is soos bloed gespil, en toegemaak onder die rooi sand" (Our language and our culture were spilled like blood, and covered by the red sand). Gripping the mic far too tightly and hissing through lips inappropriately dabbed with red lipstick, her words plopped like heavy raindrops on the enthralled audience. "En nou, vandag, maak ons dit weer oop!" (And now, today, we are opening it up, at last) she crowed triumphantly, this weathered warrior, to an eruption of joyful cheers. The entire San community that I had got to know over the past decade sat patiently in rows of plastic chairs, soaking in every word and gesture of the historic celebration.

I felt choked up throughout the ceremony and when the crowd started to disperse towards the end of the proceedings a few tantalising drops of rain fell on the dusty earth. Regopstaan and his prediction suddenly flooded my mind. I took off my hat so as to feel the unmistakeable wet plops on my head. Suppressing tears, I realised that these few raindrops were no more than a harbinger. An omen and a messenger. Oom Dawid had interpreted his father's prophecy as meaning that the rain would only truly fall when *legal ownership* of the land was transferred to the San, which made more sense. To be honest, my own belief or faith in Regopstaan's prediction had become tentative. I mean, let's be real! How on earth could rainfall be regulated or predicted years in the future by a dying Bushman?

After the Molopo ceremony we worked hard on the legal documentation required to transfer the eight farms to the San. By early December 1999 the State Attorney was poised to legally pass ownership to the !Khomani San Communal Property Association, scheduled to take place on the 16th December 1999. Appropriately, this was a public holiday, the Day of Reconciliation. The land claim journey would be over, and the San finally legal owners of the land.

Early that morning, well over a hundred excited and weapon-brandishing San, many flaunting bows and arrows and spears, gathered at the gates of Scotty's Fort,[7] the most central and best-known of the San farms. A fired-up and charismatic Petrus Vaalbooi, leader of the claim, led the group, emphasising the peaceful nature of their celebration. His mother, Ouma Elsie, had been discovered early during the land claim research to be one of the last speakers of the 'extinct'[8] N/uu language (together with Ouma /Una and her sisters). Ouma Elsie had become one of the inspirational icons of the reconstituting San diaspora, and had recently, like Regopstaan, passed away before the return of their land. Petrus, gave an emotional address to his gathered 'militia'.

Scotty's Fort farm boasted a luxurious thatched house built by the then owner Mr van Zyl,[9] who was a non-repentant alcoholic of volatile demeanour. Having either forgotten or refusing to believe that his farm was to be transferred to the San on that very day, his customary morning hangover was rudely pierced by a cacophony of dancing and singing swelling from his front lawn. Apoplectic with rage he brandished his loaded shotgun through the upstairs window and threatened to open fire on the exuberant dancing crowd below. Thankfully, he was persuaded to calm down and through an alcohol-induced fog, finally twigged that he was no longer the owner of his property. Those that he was threatening to shoot were the lawful owners of Scotty's Fort. Typically, the San took no umbrage at his aggression, and a good-natured ceasefire was soon negotiated.

As the San revellers started to leave Scotty's Fort farm, the rains began.

Precisely as Regopstaan had predicted, it poured solidly across the Kalahari for over two weeks, until both the Auob and the Nossob dry rivers flooded their banks, and tourist travel in the park became impossible. Nature responded with outrageous abundance. Insects, whose eggs had lain dormant for decades waiting for moisture, hatched in huge numbers; fish emerged from nowhere to swim in the once-dry riverbed; birds that preyed upon the teeming insects walked full-bellied on the ground, no longer able to fly. Outbreaks of flying ants and songololo millipedes provided a nutritious feast for all.

Petrus phoned, describing the torrential rains over the farm. He knew about the Regopstaan prophecy. I rushed to the Kalahari to witness the phenomenon, unprepared for the sights that awaited. The red semi-desert had been transformed into a garden of Eden, with vegetation and all forms of life burgeoning in mad profusion. Massive Wahlberg's eagles plodded and hopped on the ground, their crops full of termites, too stuffed to fly. Moths, butterflies and beetles crawled and flew in their armies, cramming their lives into their allotted few hot weeks, whilst the entire food chain from frogs and lizards to mice and jackals partook of the bounty.

Overwhelmed by the cornucopia and by the visible manifestation of Regopstaan's prediction, I wrestled with my own disbelief. Could the timing of this rare deluge simply be a delicious coincidence? Or was it another version of the San mysteries? Still open-minded, I booked into the Alpha guest cottage nearby the San farms. During a visit to the outside toilet that evening, I counted fifteen species of moths swarming around the light.

Later, whilst I enjoyed supper on the stoep together with some tourists, our attention was drawn to a massive male gecko using the wall light to lure his prey. He had quirkily been named Gordon, after the character Gordon Gecko played by Michael Douglas in the movie *Wall Street*, whose most famous line delivered to a shareholders' meeting was, 'Greed is good. Greed will save America!' As the moths fluttered helplessly towards the light, Gordon gulped them down, one by one. Living by his motto on greed, his stomach was already distended by the abundant food. Would he ever know how to stop?

Conversation revolved around the once-in-a-lifetime rains and whether they had been caused by normal weather cycles, or other natural causes. One guest insisted that climate change was to blame and that such weather extreme events were proof of that. Another believed that the rains might represent the phenomenon known as the 'fifty-year flood'. "What would you guys think," I added to the conversation, "if I told you that these floods were predicted with precise timing by a San leader six years ago?" Polite interest turned into good-natured teasing. Imagine such a silly notion.

The next morning, I woke early to coffee and a glorious Kalahari sunrise. I needed to first meet Oom Dawid, then return to Upington and then home. On the stoep floor, lying spreadeagled on his back with large belly facing upwards, was Gordon, his face in death set in a contented smile. He had eaten that final moth, a gulp too far, and had fallen off the wall onto his back. A lesson on the nature of greed?

I found Oom Dawid sitting in front of a small fire, smoking as usual, and shifting 'askoekies' on the coals. This was our first opportunity, after all the celebrations, speeches and public events, to quietly review the long journey that had brought us from my first meeting with the clan to its joyous conclusion. Time to reminisce, and be thankful. He stood up, creakily, holding his painful back and greeted me with a warm hug. "Rotman, Rotman."

After preliminary chats, I raised the business of the day. The eight farms identified for the San land claim had now been purchased, I informed him, and a sum of R2.4 million remained from the original R15 million allocated by the government. I needed his and the committee's views on investing this money so that the community would continue to benefit and prosper.

He shifted a few logs and took a deep draw on his spliff, a sign that something important was about to be shared. After a long silence, he told me seriously, "Rotman, ek het nou baie diep gedink oor daardie geld," (I have pondered very deeply about that money). Another draw and slow exhale, whilst I awaited his considered wisdom. He had reached his decision.

"Rotman. Jy moet nou vir ons 'n helikogter gaan koop" (You need to go buy us a helicopter). Clearly, he wasn't joking.

Suppressing a smile, I asked, "Why a helicopter, Dawid?"

"Rotman," he responded seriously, with only the tiniest hint of mirth, "Die wêreld het nou so baie probleme. Met 'n helikogter kan ek vir President Ronald Reagan gaan ontmoet. Ons leiers moet 'n slag bymekaarkom" (The world is now in such a bad way. With a helicopter I can go and meet President Ronald Reagan. Us leaders need to get together).

And why not? If their ears were open, world leaders of Reagan's ilk might have learned much wisdom from Oom Dawid Kruiper, First Nations prophet.

28

A Mouse, a Leopard and the Eland

"So how good *are* the San as trackers, really?" My answer to this frequent question was, "They are simply amazing. They are Master Trackers." Then the questioner would press on with, "But HOW good are they really? And *why* are they so good"?

I had my personal theories, which included their understanding of all creatures, making their behaviour easy to predict. Louis Liebenberg in *The Art of Tracking* claims that the San were the first scientists, their discoveries about nature providing a crucial step in human evolution. Closely observing all aspects of nature, the San use hypothesis and knowledge to predict the behaviour of their prey.

One day in the Kalahari an uptight white woman, the senior ranger's wife, challenged Oom Dawid about certain tracks she had asked him to identify. With no hesitation, Oom Dawid identified the scratchy marks as being the footprints of a small bird. No, she insisted, claiming that she had done an advanced course on tracking. These were definitely the tracks of a field mouse. "See, Oom Dawid," she said, patronisingly, "look here at how the mouse hops. I am sure that you are wrong today. This is a mouse."

Oom Dawid smiled benignly, and again insisted gently on his interpretation of the marks. But she was not buying it, nor prepared to leave it there, but suggested now more firmly that he was wrong. Oom Dawid pondered this impasse awhile. It was not his way to argue with her or to make her lose face. Finally, with a sly grin, he announced a plan. "Alright, miesies," he said to the lady, "let's just follow your little mouse's tracks for a while and see what happens." We followed him as he pointed at the spoor.

After a few metres he stood up, in mock surprise. "Now, look here miesies, a very strange thing has happened." Pointing at the red sand he continued. "See, the tracks have stopped right here, and your little mouse seems to have suddenly grown wings and flown away." She looked at the unmistakeable end of the bird's trail, the kick as it flew off, and flushed. Dawid was seldom wrong.

Perched on the front bumper of a Land Rover and at speeds up to about 25 km/h, Dawid's brother Buks could read tracks on a sandy road as if from a large page. Which animals had passed by, how recently, hasty or relaxed, nervous or peaceful. "Female lion with two cubs, in a hurry, moving towards those trees." And sure enough, there they would be. But Buks was never able to explain or put his art to words. "Agge nee, Rotman, d-d-d di's moelik" (Ag no, Rotman, it is difficult) he responded, with his trademark stammer.

Once he tried to clarify how San seem to know when lions are nearby. "Sien Rotman, ons Boesmans *ken* mos 'n leeu of 'n luiperd so goed. Hulle is familie. Ons kan *voel* wanneer hulle naby is" (You see, we Bushmen just *know* a lion or a leopard so well, just like family. We can *feel* when they are nearby). He tapped his forehead to signify a feeling in the head. What did he actually mean by that feeling in the head, I pondered. There was something to that feeling, but what could it be?

One hot day, four of us friends including a San tracker, Ou Jan, stood in the open back of a Land Cruiser, driving along a dirt track a few metres south of the game fence in the park. To spice up a long Kalahari day, my friend Stef suggested that we place a bet. The deal was that he would owe me a hundred beers if we spotted a leopard, and I would owe him ten beers for a lion. The odds seemed fair and Ou Jan was asked to help us find one of the big cats.

At a speed of about 40 km/h a plume of red dust kicked up behind the Cruiser on the sandy road and beyond the high park fence sloped red dunes, dotted with small shepherd's bush trees. Kilometres went by with no sign of life on the baking dunes other than the usual steenbok and ground squirrels. Suddenly Ou Jan stiffened, raised his right hand high and hissed, "Stop, meneer, stop."

I banged on the roof and the driver hit the brakes. All our intent gazing at the veld beyond the park fence revealed nothing but red sandy grassland and half a dozen shepherd's bush trees. "Wat sien jy, Ou Jan"? (What do you see, Ou Jan?) Scanning the hillside through slit eyes, he admitted that he could not yet see anything, but he could *feel* that a big cat was nearby. This did not sound convincing, as the veld looked entirely devoid of life. He had this feeling in his head, he explained, tapping forehead with finger. It was possibly hiding behind one of those small bushes. Diffidently, as if embarrassed to ask us to do such a silly thing, he requested us to look together at one bush at a time. If the cat is in that particular bush, "Sal hy ongemaklik voel," Ou Jan explained. It will feel uncomfortable and will probably show itself.

So we all gazed at the first small bush on our left. Nothing. Then on to the next bush. Again, no response. But bush number three delivered an explosive revelation. Seconds after we had stared at the bush, a male leopard burst out and charged up the slope, over the dune and out of sight. Whoops of delight, while Ou Jan smiled complacently. We drove away slowly, excited by yet another display of San magic. Stef still owes me those beers.

Vet Piet, a renowned San tracker, was a cousin to Oom Dawid and Buks, and worked for SAN Parks. He shared his tracking gift with many admiring tourists, yet was still unable to explain how the tracking ability worked. At about midday on a normal Kgalagadi day, dry and 38 degrees in the shade, while driving my Land Rover with Vet Piet and friends, we came across a large herd of eland, charging in the same direction about fifty metres to the right of our dirt track. The earth shook from the pounding hooves of Africa's largest antelope and a plume of red dust rose into the sky.

Someone pleaded that I turn the vehicle sharp right and head towards the moving herd so he could get a few close-up photos. I looked at Vet

Piet who shook his head. Instead, Vet Piet indicated, we should rather drive straight towards a tree about three hundred metres ahead, and wait there. "Rotman, daar sal die eland ophou hardloop. Hulle sal links draai, en by ons verbygestap kom" (Rotman, there the eland will stop running, they will then turn to the left, and will walk right past us).

I knew to not ask questions, so drove towards the small tree as instructed. Intuitively it seemed the wrong thing to do. Surely the eland would carry on running away from us? As if being guided by some magic control panel, the galloping herd slowed to a canter, then to a trot and finally to a brisk walk. Next the leaders swung to the left and within minutes close to three hundred eland walked past our vehicle, no more than thirty metres away, precisely as Vet Piet had predicted. Cameras clicked amidst joyful exclamations as the unforgettable scene unfolded.

I needed to understand what we had witnessed. When our tents were pitched, I strolled to where the stocky Bushman sat under a camel thorn tree puffing on a Lexington. "Vet Piet. How on earth were you able to predict the behaviour of those eland?" Amused by my question, his response was, "Ai Rotman. Ek het sommer net geweet" (Ai Rotman, I simply knew). I was not satisfied. There had to be a train of logic, even if subconscious, behind such an accurate prediction. I asked him to please go and think carefully about what knowledge he had utilised. "Hoe het jy geweet *presies* wat daardie eland sou doen?" (How did you know *precisely* what those eland would do?)

He agreed good-naturedly and sat pondering my request. After a while he returned to where I was sitting, smiling shyly as if having discovered something surprising. "Rotman. Ek het baie diep gedink. Maar dit was moeilik" (Rotman, I have thought deeply. But it was difficult).

He went on to say that he had now worked out every step in the process. It was all about observation, he explained, followed by deduction. His observations were firstly that the herd of eland, heaviest of all African antelope, were running for fun on that day, and not out of fear, for example, from lions. Secondly, they had already been running at full speed for about seven hundred metres, which one could deduce from the height and length of the plume of dust behind them. Thirdly, the wind was blowing from their left to their right, in other words across them, which one could also tell from the plume. Finally, it was a particularly hot day.

Then his deductions: One, an eland's body gets hot quickly, when running so hard. They soon overheat, and in about 300 metres' time (approximately near that single tree) they would need to cool down urgently; two, eland cool down through their nostrils, so they would need to turn into the wind blowing from left to right; and three, the herd would thus need to walk that way, towards that tree. And so the huge herd walked slowly in front of our vehicle, as predicted.

"Good explanation, Vet Piet," I said.

But something important was missing. He had explained the basics of the recipe. A vital ingredient, that intuitive, almost magical knowledge that comes from aeons of observation, was missing. !Ngate Xgamxebe[10] said that 'tracking is like dancing, because your body is happy…You feel it in the dance. It tells you when you love tracking and dancing, you are talking with God.' Vet Piet would have chuckled and shaken his head. "Jammer, Rotman. Daai ding kan ek nie verduidelik nie."

"Sorry, Rotman. That thing I can't explain."

29

Rich Man for a Day

Ricky Kruiper was born to be noticed. At first glance, a lean and intense Bushman, but closer acquaintance revealed a burning intensity that could animate his features with an unpredictable array of human passions. Unusually young to be the lead trance dancer for the Kruiper San clan, he was acknowledged for his precocious spirituality and life force. When the joy of living was flowing, which was often, Ricky would draw others towards him like a magnet, and the laughter would spurt and bubble for hours with him at the epicentre. But when drunk or upset, a vicious side emerged. Bad things happened, and nobody was safe, least of all himself. That was Ricky.

One night, under the influence of the spirits and probably also marijuana, he raped four women of his clan at Kagga Kamma, including his wife Oulet. The next morning he was arrested and taken to the Ceres Police Station in the boot of the farmer's car, judged far too dangerous to be allowed inside. Nobody dared testify against him. On his return as a free man, he was shrunken in misery at the shame of his deeds. As is customary, he was soon forgiven by the close-knit San community.

One day in February 1997, an American filmmaker sought out Ricky, then living with his wife and children at Welkom, a San hamlet near the Kgalagadi Park, to act in a beer commercial. With the quirky humour that would emerge at unlikely moments, Ricky responded with a rare English sentence. "Jus' don' talk to me man, talk to my lawyer," adding that his lawyer's name was Rotman.

The next day I answered the phone to a hesitant American voice, "Er, is that Mr Rotman?" I replied cautiously in the affirmative, realising this was Bushman business, and negotiated the best film contract that I could for Ricky. He would be paid R25 000 for one morning's filming. On completion paid in one roll of one-hundred-rand bank notes. This was Ricky's request. I was excited at his good fortune, imagining all the uses this massive amount could be put to. Perhaps an education fund for their many children, an investment for a 'rainy day?'

Weeks later I received an anxious call from the film director. "Mr Rotman, we have finished filming. Ricky was excellent. And I handed him a huge wad of one-hundred-rand notes as per the contract." There was a long silence. "But I think you had better get here as soon as you possibly can." He would not elaborate, and it sounded ominous.

Urgently I tried to phone Ricky but the lines just rang and rang. Something peculiar was going on. With rising unease, I booked the first plane to the Kalahari, arriving in Upington at 4 p.m. the next afternoon, and gunning the hired car over the remaining two hundred kilometres towards the red dunes of Welkom. Alerted by the American's agitated tone, my intuition stirred and I imagined the worst. As the last light illuminated another glorious Kalahari sunset, I pulled into Welkom having resolved to deal calmly with whatever lay ahead.

Scenes of unimaginable horror unfolded as I walked between the shacks in the smoke-laden twilight. Semi-naked human bodies groaned and writhed on the ground in between the humble shacks, as if the victims had suffered from a gruesome massacre. Lumps of meat and gristle, bones of all sizes, remains of intestines and charred animal skin were strewn in all directions, some still being gnawed by scrawny San dogs. An aroma of smoke and charred meat hung in the air.

If this had been a Steven Spielberg movie set depicting a post battle scene one would feel that the special effects crew had overdone the hype. Children played happily amidst the repulsive carnage, tossing bones and bottles to one another, oblivious of the lurid obscenity around them.

Empty bottles of wine and beer provided the only indication that this was a modern, rather than an ancient, disaster. Some of the dogs, stomachs distended from this rare opportunity to feast, could no longer stand with comfort, and lay amongst the groaning human bodies.

With heart now thumping I picked my way through the debris towards the remains of a mighty fire that was still smouldering, gagging at a heightened stench of charred fat and intestines. Some San adults uttered slurred cries of recognition, but were too drunk to provide any answers. The remains of the fire indicated it had burned for the entire previous night, and from the bones and skulls in evidence at least two donkeys and two sheep had given their lives for this Armageddon.

Repeatedly I asked, "Waar is Ricky?" (Where is Ricky?) Nobody knew. Some mumbled words about money being burned, which sounded ill-omened. Eventually a half-sober woman said to me, "Haai Rotman, Ricky is gesteek, hy is by die hospitaal" (Rotman, Ricky was stabbed. He is in hospital).

I sped from the horror scene towards the humble clinic that served as the 'hospital' in the nearby village of Askham. There I found Ricky in the emergency ward, blissfully unconscious, a large bloodstained bandage around his neck, and intravenous tubes indicating the seriousness of his condition. The strong disinfectant was not enough to erase the alcoholic odours pervading the air around his bed. Ricky snoozed on peacefully, a faint smile softening his scarred and battered face. I staggered off to a local B & B where I spent a disturbed and restless night.

The next morning, Ricky was sitting up in bed, looking very much alive and beaming around him like a battered but cherubic choir boy. He seemed not to have a care in the world and greeted me with a smile. "Haai, Rotman, hoe gaan dit?" (Hi, Rotman, how are you?) I resisted the burning desire to pontificate, so simply asked him to tell me the story. What follows is based on Ricky's own version, bolstered by inputs from some of the party survivors that I spoke to later in the day.

Ricky had invited the entire population of the surrounding Kalahari to celebrate his windfall. The bush telegraph spread the news like wildfire, and soon San and Coloured people from miles around were streaming towards Welkom. Ricky strode into the local bottle store, a grubby building with one fridge and shelves laden with cheap liquor, and waving his roll of notes at the baffled assistant, ordered the entire contents of the shop. All the beer, wine and hard liquor. From a local farmer he ordered a lorry-load of firewood, two sheep and two donkeys, all to be delivered immediately. He paid by peeling notes off the cash roll. By midday the fires were burning high, the animals were slaughtered, and the contents of the Molopo bottle store delivered in four large crates piled outside Ricky's shack.

Guests streaming in were encouraged to eat and drink and be merry, with no thought of the morrow. I imagine little persuasion was necessary. The party went on all through the night and deep into the hot Kalahari morning. At 10 a.m., with the fire almost burned out and most people semi-conscious, Ricky rounded everyone up. Yanking people from drunken comas, he demanded that all guests should urgently join him at the fire. Only the truly unconscious were left to sleep in peace. Logs were thrown onto the fire until it was again burning fiercely, whilst the groaning and still-drunken survivors gathered around. Ricky, benefactor of this memorable feast, had demanded their presence, and with throbbing heads, they awaited his words.

Plunging into his shack, Ricky emerged carrying between his two hands what remained of the original wad of one-hundred-rand notes. According to eyewitnesses, he held it theatrically above his head, and shouted out loudly. "Het julle almal genoeg gedrink? Het julle almal genoeg geëet?" (Have you all drunk enough? Have you all eaten enough?) I imagine the murmured and slurred groans of assent from the puzzled and drunken mob. All had indeed drunk and eaten enough.

"Kyk nou mooi! Kyk nou almal wat maak ek met hierdie fokken geld" (Look carefully now, all of you, look what I am going to do with this fucking money). Ricky dramatically hurled his remaining bundle of money into the middle of the fire. His guests were stunned, the poorest of the poor witnessing untold wealth burning. One soul tried to jump into the fire to rescue some notes, but Ricky beat him over the back with a stick which stopped him and all other attempts. Ricky beamed around drunkenly, and the befuddled crowd gazed transfixed as the beautiful blue buffalo one-hundred-rand notes crinkled up and turned into ash.

Ten minutes later, an exhausted newcomer came jostling through the crowd and up to the fire, calling loudly for Ricky. This was a San man who had lent twenty rand to Ricky some years previously. Hearing on the bush telegraph that Ricky had come into money, he had run through the night from Philandersbron, a settlement about fifty kilometres away, to recover his old debt. Ricky was still swaying by the fire watching his new riches going up in smoke when the newcomer ran up. Overjoyed at the prospect of finally recovering his money he announced himself to Ricky, who responded contritely, one would imagine, that he was unfortunately just a few minutes too late. Without a cent in the world, he could not repay his twenty-rand debt. The newcomer pulled his knife and plunged it into Ricky's neck.

"So why did you do it, Ricky?" was my question. "The money could have educated your children, fed many people, built a better house, assisted with your old age."

"Rotman," said Ricky with a warm but patronising smile, whilst gingerly fingering the bandage on his neck. "How can I explain this to you? Before I got the money, I knew exactly who I was. I was Ricky, the poor Boesman. But getting that money changed everything. That money was dangerous, like poison. Everyone wanted it, I could never rest. Everyone wanted to be my friend. Now that the money is gone, I have a sore throat, but I have peace, and I know again who I am.

"I am still Ricky, the Boesman."

30

Five Fags for a Story

The San are famous as storytellers, weaving fireside tales that seek primarily to entertain. 'A story is like the wind, it comes from a far-off place, and we feel it . . .'[11] Oom Dawid Kruiper was one such storyteller with an innate feeling for a good story. Sometimes he would while away the long hours on our monthly trips, entertaining his fellow passengers with stories. Once a month we drove from Kagga Kamma to the Kalahari while working on the land claim, a journey of straight roads and endless vistas. Calvinia to Kenhart, 140 kilometres of arid semi-desert scrub. Kenhart to Brandvlei, 160 kilometres of the same. An occasional squished road kill, and here and there a kink in the dead-straight road to interrupt the tedium.

One day, Oom Dawid picked up a rubber dinosaur (Brontosaurus) that my son Oliver had left in the car, and asked, "Rottie, watter dier is hierdie?" (Rottie, what animal is this?) When I explained that it was an ancient creature that had lived in the swamps long before humans came to earth, his imagination fired up. Before long he created a sequence where the dinosaur squelched through a muddy swamp, each footstep marked by a gurgling sound. Warming to his theme, the dinosaur bent down to eat, fall over, defecate, burp, and let out massive farts. For each of the bodily functions he provided fitting sound effects and milked his audience shamelessly for a laugh.

Since the creature was lonely and had last seen his mate many moons ago, he had it craning its neck to look around for her, emitting a pleading, pining, love-sick roar. Of course, the performance bulged with sexual innuendo, and by now the audience was in stitches. On he would go, inventing new encounters and ideas, each one retained in the next telling if they went down well. The show concluded with the dinosaur spotting his mate across the swamp and gleefully galloping off, together with squelching, grunting and puffing side effects, pertinent to the eventual meeting and joyful coupling. Not much of a storyline, yet the dinosaur provided endless entertainment.

April 1997. A group of San were travelling in a Kombi from Kagga Kamma to the Kalahari for our monthly meeting. I was already in the Kalahari, so my partner Glyn Williams and a friend Wayne Hamman had offered to drive. On the gravel road about halfway between Ceres and Calvinia the right front tire burst. The Kombi rolled twice, spewing out its occupants in all directions. The accident claimed two San lives, and would leave scars upon the close-knit family for years to come. Toppies' wife !Xude as well as Buks' son Baliep were killed on impact, whilst many others including Oom Dawid, his wife Sanna and a number of children were badly injured. The injured members of the Kruiper family were rushed to Carl Bremer Hospital in Cape Town and placed in different wards according to their injuries. Two days after the accident I went to the hospital, finding them all in various stages of repair.

Oom Dawid, the worst injured, having broken his hip as well as his leg and some ribs, was lying in bed strapped up with one leg raised in traction. He was glad to see me, and teared up when we discussed the accident and those who had died. It was still a mystery as to how the accident had occurred. Glyn had provided a cryptic version which went something like, "Man, it all happened so fast. A tyre burst, we rolled twice, and it was over!" At his bedside I asked Dawid if he remembered anything about the accident, and a detail-drenched story emerged.

Firstly, he described who was sitting where in the back of the Kombi, all nine occupants. Then he added what each of them had purchased in Ceres before departing, and where each one and their various packets of groceries were in the vehicle. He then pointed out who was smoking a cigarette, and with whom it was being shared, this clearly being a point worthy of observing. "Ons het mooi gery, Rotman, en ek het lekker op my eie sigaret getrek" (We were driving nicely, Rotman, and I was drawing deliciously on my own cigarette). Nobody on earth so revelled in the delicious inhaling of tobacco substances as he did. He would pause with eyes closed to emphasise the contentment of that inhalation.

He then recounted, with bewildering clarity, as if he was reading from a script. "Rotman, first I heard a small sound, like doef. Then I saw the steering wheel shake, then Wayne, the driver, tightened his grip on the wheel. Then the Kombi swerved sharply to the left and the wheels made a squealing sound, 'squeeee'. Then Sanna let out a small cry, 'Haai' and she grabbed my hand.

"Then the Kombi started to turn over, that way, and a packet of white flower that Ou Jon had bought in Ceres flew past my head and hit the roof up there, making a cloud of white dust. Then the Kombi was upside down and my head hit the roof, and the white flower was everywhere. Then it rolled back the right way up, but everyone was flying around and now Sanna's hand broke away from mine and YY went through the window on the other side. Two of the children screamed, windows were now breaking from the impact," he said.

"And then we rolled over a second time. This time I crashed into the front seat with my stomach and I felt some bones breaking," he said pointing at ribs and hips. "Now Sanna landed on her head and as we went over the second time, YY went through another window and her shoulder was full of blood. Then we were upside down again and I was flying through a window when my leg got hurt here," he said pointing to his plastered thigh.

"Then the Kombi came to a stop on its side. I was sitting on the road, facing the direction we had come from with dust in the air, and I could see three people lying next to the road. My chest and hip were sore, I could not move, I had pissed in my pants, and I was making a wheezing sound as wind escaped from my lungs. YY was crying so I knew she was okay.

"There was dust everywhere, and the Kombi engine was still going. Then the engine went quiet, and more people started groaning and crying. And then I went to sleep. And when I woke up, I was here in hospital."

201

He fell back, exhausted by the telling. A small group of about ten people had gathered around the bed during the story, including a nurse, two nurse assistants, visitors and patients. Despite his exhaustion that famous San opportunism flickered to life, and he murmured drowsily to the group through lidded eyes, "Gee maar 'n entjie of twee as julle die story geniet het. Ek vertel hom weer môre selfde tyd" (Give a cigarette or two if you enjoyed the story, and I will tell it again tomorrow same time).

When I visited Dawid and the others a week later, his storytelling had created a hospital dilemma. Pulling me aside, the kindly ward sister explained, with a hand on my arm, "Your Oom Dawid is becoming such a problem. Word spread so fast about the storytelling in Ward D every afternoon at 3 p.m. Soon people started flocking to attend from all over the hospital, causing crowding in the ward. Doctors were rescheduling operations, nurses were forsaking sick patients, even patients left their beds to get to hear the story. The ward got overcrowded, and the applause at the end could be heard all over the hospital," she added gloomily. It was like a play performance.

"So what did you do, sister?" I asked, suppressing a smile. She was not seeing the funny side. "I have now issued a hospital order," the sister concluded gravely, "that no more than twenty-five people may attend per afternoon, and they have to book through my staff. We are fully booked for the next three days." She added in something of a stage whisper that taking bookings for bedside storytelling was probably not what the Hippocratic oath had in mind, but nobody had complained yet. "This afternoon's story is due in ten minutes," she added. "And by the way, Oom Dawid has now raised his price from two to five cigarettes per person."

I went to greet Dawid who was flat on his back with his leg in traction, clearly still in pain.

"Hoe gaan dit, Dawid?" I asked.

"Rotman, dit gaan baie goed, en jy's net betyds vir my storie" (Rotman, it's going well, and you are just in time for my story).

As we chatted the ward started filling up. Nurses pulled back the curtains around Dawid's bed and ushered the selected twenty-five people, including doctors and senior nurses, into a half-circle. The atmosphere that of an audience awaiting the maestro's performance.

Effortlessly he greeted everyone, and then launched into his tale. The new version was much expanded from my first hearing, crammed with more details, sound effects and jokes, tossing the audience from bursts of laughter to pathos. Finally, he arrived at his sitting on the dusty road after the accident in his own urine, before passing out.

A collective sigh came from the onlookers, followed by exclamations and loud applause. With a sly wink aimed at me, Oom Dawid held out a plastic bag, for the five-cigarette fee. This was the cue for the ward Sister to chivvy people out of the 'theatre', and with farewells and messages of encouragement they left the ward.

Holding up the plastic bag, now bulging with cigarettes, he quipped, "Rotman. Daai ongeluk het my nie gedood nie, maar al hierdie sigarette? Eish!"

That accident couldn't kill me, but all these cigarettes? Eish!

31

The San and the City

July 2002. We board Swissair Flight S272, Cape Town to Zurich. Oom Dawid was determined to travel to the United Nations in his full cultural dress, namely a skimpy leather loincloth and springbok-skin shoulder bag. He is allocated a middle seat next to a well-groomed society lady. She panics as the semi-naked Kalahari warrior settles in the seat next to her. Frantically, she jabs the emergency button. "Stewardess," she shrills, "this man next to me is naked. I won't stand for it." Dawid was amused rather than injured at the woman's hysteria, saying, "Ai, Rotman, die arme antie het seker baie min mans se lywe gesien" (Oh, Rotman, the poor auntie has probably not seen many men's bodies). Huffing indignantly the offended lady was moved to a business class seat, and we settled down to enjoy the flight.

During the 90s, whilst the land claim was progressing, I'd worked with the San on other legal issues, including contributing to the international indigenous peoples' movement. The UN Declaration on the Rights of Indigenous Peoples[12] was in its final stages of negotiation, with up to a thousand indigenous representatives from around the world converging on Geneva each July to attend the annual week-long deliberations. The

San attended for the first time in July 1999 and had been warmly welcomed by the gathering of Aboriginals, Maoris, Native Americans, Arctic Inuit, Papua New Guinea Indians and others as one of the iconic indigenous nations of the world.

The San delegation I accompanied to the UN, courtesy of Swissair's generous donation, included both Oom Dawid Kruiper and his cousin, master-tracker Vet Piet Kleinman. Oom Dawid was a born showman and his fame had rocketed since the conclusion of the land claim. A natural orator with trickster slyness, he never lost an opportunity to size up an occasion, and to either impress, surprise, stun or confuse his audience, depending upon his whim at the time. Vet Piet bore the natural reticence of the San, with a desire to be as far from the limelight as possible.

Our arrival in Geneva was tortuous. Curt, efficient customs officials pulled Dawid aside as his flints, arrowheads and knife in the springbok bag set off multiple alarms. They soon changed their attitude when Dawid crinkled his famous grin and explained their cultural purposes. They waved us through with reserved smiles. The next day we entered the foreboding buildings of the United Nations, where Oom Dawid, semi-naked in his loincloth, headband and springbok-skin bag again set off the alarm, with red lights flashing. The contents of his springbok-skin bag when inspected also revealed a hunting bow, flint, knife, arrows, plus a bulging packet of marijuana.

These illegal items breached an entire range of UN security laws, and attracted a phalanx of stiffly humourless officials. Patiently I explained that Dawid was akin to royalty in his native country, and an exception should surely be made to allow him to attend the Indigenous Peoples working group, together with his cultural dress and items. He had been specially invited, I added, and the marijuana was a significant traditional medicine to be used at important gatherings.

Whilst the stiffs debated his future in the neon-lit offices, Dawid struck a whimsical figure, smoking a cigarette and oblivious of the stress around him. Exasperated and probably nervous about triggering a diplomatic incident by incarcerating the near-naked Bushman, the officials finally allowed us to proceed. Dawid smiled cheekily and clicked an effusive clicky thanks in Khoekhoab.

An intense day of United Nations resolutions and debates lay ahead. Both Dawid and Vet Piet impressed with their authentic responses during caucus discussions, ensuring that their presence was widely appreciated. It was clear from their contributions that they were rooted in their ancient culture, in contrast to career indigenous politicians who made eloquent speeches but had scant relationship with the hardships of their people.

At day's end we walked around the old city of Geneva. Both San walked barefoot after a day squeezed into formal shoes, although they wore normal clothes so as not to attract attention. Truth is their rugged looks caused genteel local peoples' heads to swing continuously as we meandered down the streets. In front of one of the stone statues outside the WIPO[13] head office, Vet Piet stopped, transfixed. A naked maiden standing whimsically on a rock. He was mesmerised by her beauty, and ogled at her from all angles.

When I teased him about the danger of falling in love with this unavailable young girl, he nodded ruefully. "Ja, Rotman," he went on. "Dit is waar wat jy sê, maar sy kyk vir my op daardie verlang manier" (Yes, Rotman, it is true what you say, but she looks at me in that longing way). I realised that this was beyond a silly joke; he really meant it, and felt truly moved by the image. I took a photo of Vet Piet gazing longingly at this statuette, and finally managed to coax him away, casting wistful backward glances.

Up and down the cobbled streets we walked, passing a zoo, Lake Geneva, countless restaurants, musicians, food vendors and marvelling and commenting on the narrow streets and quaint buildings. We stopped at a tourist pub that served beers in a long glass boot; both Kalahari lads revelling in the joy of coaxing the foamy waves into their mouths. After two delicious boot beers I managed to cajole them away, and used my tourist map to lead us to the old city centre, past gardens, museums and parks.

Soon it was dark. We had walked many miles, and to my embarrassment, I realised I had no idea how to get back to our hotel. As I squinted at my map by the dim street lights, Dawid asked, "Rotman, jy lyk bekommered. Wat's fout?" (You look worried. What's the problem?)

"We are lost," I said.

Dawid chuckled and slapped his thigh as if this was the silliest thing he had ever heard. "How can we be lost, Rotman?" he said, incredulously.

Sceptically I replied, "Okay then, Dawid, you lead us back. If you can."

My sarcasm was lost on him as he struck out, his sinewy legs shuffling barefoot and nimble over the cobbles. At each corner, he told me what he expected to see next. Every imaginable feature, a sleeping dog, a small tree, a plant, funny signposts, unusual doorways were all captured perfectly in his mind; nothing escaped the observation and recall programme refined by years of hunting in the Kalahari. Following our bandy-legged leader, we arrived at our hotel.

A week after our return I visited the two friends in the Kalahari. Dawid reminisced fondly about the swooshing waves of the long boot beers, by far his most memorable experience of his entire UN trip. Vet Piet agreed this was a highlight of his own first and only trip to Geneva, up there with his statue girlfriend. When I surprised Vet Piet with a photograph of the naked damsel statue with the words on the back, "Aan my liewe Vet Piet, met liefde" (To my dear Vet Piet, with love), his face crumpled with longing. "Ai, Rotman, ek verlang so na daai meisietjie" (Oh, Rotman, I do so miss that little girl). A stray tear disappeared into the cracks of his walnut cheek.

I reminded them of my own most memorable experience, that being when Oom Dawid retraced our steps back to the hotel. An impossible feat for any normal person.

The two old buddies nudged each other and chuckled. "Ai Rotman, dit was *so* maklik," said Dawid. "Ons het net ons spore terug gevolg."

Ai Rotman, it was *so* easy. We just followed our tracks back.

THE OUTBACK

32

Cupladrinx at Curtin Springs

Without knocking, a giant of a man burst into my office, leaned against the doorway, and boomed, "Hey, Roggah, so you comin' to th' local, Froiday?" It was Mike (pronounced Moike), the supremely confident Chief Engineer. He literally bristled with energy.

"Um, what, er, where's the local, Mike?" I had prepared myself mentally to encounter no booze for months on end, so the prospect of alcohol after only one week suddenly seemed attractive.

"Curtin Springs, mate. Only 240 moiles away. Noice lil' pub mate, best boozer in these parts."

"That's local?" I said *sotto voce*, then more loudly, "Um, ja, thanks. Count me in, Mike."

When the Anangu Pitjantjatjara (AP) Aboriginal government appointed me as their lawyer, I was contractually required not to drink alcohol at any time during my employment. The Pitjantjatjara Land Rights Act in 1981, following the first successful land claim in Australia, had created the sprawling and remote AP lands – about 300 by 500 kilometres, five hours' drive south of Alice Springs. There were about 1 500 souls spread across the massive area, which had been pronounced *dry* by the national government in response to the high rate of alcohol abuse in the Aboriginal community.

I had duly reported for Outback duty at Umuwa, main settlement of the AP lands. In a baking January I was uneasy about working within an entirely new legal system and having to survive so many months without an end-of-day beer. Despite decades of experience as a lawyer, I felt apprehensive and ill-equipped for the challenges ahead.

The first week was bleak. Temperatures hovered around 40 degrees Celsius, the Aboriginal leaders seemed inscrutably hostile, and my Aussie colleagues were difficult to like. Hovering above us all, the problems facing the small team tasked with trying to bring 'order' to a massive chunk of Aboriginal land seemed insurmountable. I found myself gazing through the window of my matchbox office onto arid semi-desert whilst noisy parakeets screeched overhead, an alien on a strange planet. With head in hands, I darkly pondered resignation.

Friday 4 p.m. came around and the chosen AP staff eagerly boarded Mike's Land Cruiser. Within seconds, we kicked up dust on the gravel road towards the famous Uluṟu. Time to check out my work companions, whom I was about to get to know.

Mike, the self-appointed leader of this mission, was in his early forties, testosterone-laden and determined. A Bruce Willis look-alike (albeit with large paunch), he was what you might call 'a man's man', or more appropriately, an Ozzie bloke – through and through. With him in the front passenger seat sat his better half, Nellie. A large lass, she chewed gum with quiet aggression, staring impassively ahead. She was chief accountant. Then old Bill, the amiable AP mechanic, who sat next to me, gazing under bushy eyebrows into the far distance. A man of few words, Bill had spent his working life repairing heavy equipment in the Aussie sun which had burned his face and forearms to the scarred texture of the Outback. Ridges and furrows every which way. Trevor, the social anthropologist, on my other side. I would work closely with him during my time with the AP community. He was the youngest, a soft-spoken youth with floppy hair. Trevor seemed out of place in this rough company, and I sensed a solidarity. Finally, and least conspicuously, Jilpie Jim slumped alone in the rear seat. The most senior of the group at fifty-nine, Jim carried the moniker 'jilpie', a Pitjantjatjara word for an esteemed old fella. He had worked in the Outback his entire life as community liaison person, and was said to carry scars from a failed marriage. Whatever the reason, an Eeyore-like moroseness ensured the solitary existence he seemed to desire. So that was our six-pack team.

A plume of angry red dust traced our headlong charge through the arid vistas. Spiky spinifex grass waved above russet earth, deceptively inviting. Spinifex is thorny and devastating in its damage to human legs, whilst being home to an array of creatures. After three hours of hard driving, Mike finally brought the steaming vehicle to a halt in an empty parking lot next to a set of low buildings and white gum tree ghosts. A humble sign on a not-quite-upright rusted metal pole announced: Curtin Springs Public Bar.

With Mike and Nellie in the lead, our thirsty group burst through swing doors into the bar and blinked in the sudden dimness. From somewhere in the shadows, a gravelly woman's voice greeted us, more ghost than human. "So, what'll it be, gennelmen?" Sarcastic emphasis on the last word. A stick-thin bar lady, owner of the voice, emerged from the gloom. Narrow lips, set in lemon-sucking disapproval, dominated a lean and pockmarked face.

Unphased, Mike boomed in our hostess's direction, "Goodday there, foive Coopers and a double rum, willya, an' makeit one for yourself too, hey Sheila?" The double rum was clearly for Nellie, the beers for us boys. Wincing visibly at being called Sheila, the bar lady plonked five half pint Coopers bottles on the counter with a thin-lipped grimace. Nowhere near a smile. As we set about these first drinks, I marvelled at the absence of outer and inner beauty in our hostess, resolving to stay out of her way.

"Fukkinnell that's good shit, mates, am I roit or am I *roit?*" boomed Mike, letting out a loud belch. Nellie frowned disapprovingly in our direction until we responded to her beau's rallying call with corresponding levels of gusto. My breathy, "Ja, it sure is, Mike," sounded prim and out of place. Assuaged Nellie hurled the rum down her throat in two massive glugs as I mentally added her to the list of scary females to be avoided.

Just then, the batwing bar doors opened with a loud crash, like in the movies. An enormous Aboriginal man with untidy hair and a scraggly white beard stumbled into the room. Nellie's greeting of, "G'day, Cookie!" surprised me as much as her friendly smile at the newcomer.

Cookie was a jilpie, deep in his sixties, with a dishevelled demeanour. Without acknowledging Nellie's greeting, he grabbed the beer in front of him, took a huge slug, and wiped his lips on a grubby sleeve. Avoiding eye contact, his rudeness was strangely consistent with his appearance.

"Who the heck's this guy?" I asked Trevor in a whisper.

"That is old Cookie, mate. Bin here his whole fukkin loife. Never left Curtin Springs." Trevor took a long swig. "Cooks the food," he continued, "that's why he's called Cookie."

I nodded at this crystal logic and took a long pull on my beer. I was learning fast in Outback school.

"So, who's boi-ing next, mates?" thundered Mike, staring around at his merry men with an expectant grin. Round one had become history, its only purpose being a prelude to many more. An overdeveloped sense of duty, combined with the need to be liked, kicked in. My own voice now piped up with forced casualness, "Okay guys, next round's on me." I slapped a wad of notes on the counter like this was a Western movie, and I its reluctant star.

"Good on yer, Roger," rumbled two or three of my new best mates-to-be as the bonhomie grew. "Nunta palya mulpa" (you are a good guy, friend) came from old Jilpie Jim, whom I discovered, when drinking, spoke Pitjantjatjara instead of English. Beers were lined up and drunk with increasing speed as the room began to shimmer and slide. With growing lightheadedness, I wondered whether my AP contractual commitment to avoid all alcohol applied to a Friday evening? Or was there a Friday night amnesty? If it did, I was not alone, I figured, and the unpleasant thought dissolved in bubbles of beer.

Gadoef! The batwing doors bashed open again, and all heads swung. This time an unshaven and bronzed James Dean look-alike in leather gear, accompanied by two equally rough sidekicks, swaggered into the room. With them came a pungent reek of camels and sweat, which soon blended in with the barroom fug. Barlady raked the newcomers with laser eyes, and within seconds slapped three beers on the counter with trademark veiled aggression. "Cheers, Vixie," growled the first tanned camel man, taking a three-second slurp on the bottle. *So scary barlady has a name,* I mused.

"Roggie, my mate," said Mike, placing a bunch of banana fingers on my shoulder. His face too close to mine, set in a benign expression of affection. Something about being his drinking buddy and confidante set off alarm bells, both disturbing and inconvenient. "Have ya heard Nellie's joke about the abbos?"

I heard myself assuring Mike that no, I hadn't and couldn't wait to do so. Again, that lack of authenticity, subtle relic of peer pressure, reminiscent of school days. How could I ever show my real self to these people or deal with the racism, which would surely emerge with Nellie's joke? I peeked at Cookie who seemed in another realm, gazing into the middle distance. Others gathered around Nellie, who allowed herself a rare flash of vulnerability as she glanced coyly at her man. "Go on, Nellie," said Mike proudly. "Tells a winner joke, she does," he added proudly, gazing lovingly at her.

Taking a deep breath, she plunged into a bar joke involving a man who comes home unexpectedly to find his wife in bed with two Aboriginal men. The story was predictably vulgar and punctuated by crude expletives as she built towards the climax with practiced timing. Thankfully the joke was more about errant wives and illicit sex rather than Aboriginals and race. Smirking and gaining confidence in her audience, she finally spat out the crude punchline, "Well gennelmen, now she is fuckin' yours" blurted out by the cuckolded husband. The assembled faithful exploded in coarse laughter, whilst my smirk concealed a growing internal disturbance. Any criticism of the crude humour would surely have brought about Mike's disapproval. Despite the beer now flooding my system, I cringed inwardly; I had now become fully part of the general vulgarity in the room.

Round four (or was it five?) appeared as if by magic. Jilpie had thrown down notes, saying, "Tjuta pukulpa, my mates" (Let's be happy). "Don't countem mate, drinkem!" is the secret to good parties, as an Aboriginal friend called Frank once proclaimed. This advice is good only if you do not intend to stay sober, and true to Frank's advice, I gave up all attempts to count.

Nellie's demeanour and Vixie's hostility became less burdensome, and I sniggered inwardly as Mike greeted each new round like a patriarch welcoming home a prodigal son. The camel drivers were also buying rounds, and I was swigging with the best. Anything seemed possible. Cookie, after chugging three beers, had shuffled off to the kitchen carrying two more in his baggy bum pockets, while the tanned camel man was busy showing Trevor a nasty camel bite wound on his back. This required removing his shirt and exposing a lean, tanned body, the injury soon examined by the whole pub.

The wheels of life were loose, and I was slurring, long past that famous point of no return at which the option to stop briefly presents itself. Bloodstreams were awash with beer, food desperately needed. Exuding a flushed energy, Nellie told another filthy joke, with Mike's arm lovingly draped around her. Gagging inwardly from the toxic joke bonhomie, I left the bar counter and tried to start a conversation with loner Jilpie Jim, sitting on his own in a corner.

"So wadda fuck you doing in this gofforsaken place, hey Roggah?" Small talk was clearly not Jilpie's thing.

"My wife and kidsh," I started, shaking my head morosely, figuring that it was too complicated to explain.

My words grabbed Jilpie's interest, and with clenched jaw he responded that his own wife had left him many years ago, taking his only kid. He gazed angrily at the floor as if the answer lay there. Whilst we slurred our sad stories to each other, a thought began to form, then to flash. Not only Jilpie Jim, but all in the room were outsiders, probably in the Outback to escape the normal world. Including me.

How far, and estranged, my wife and children felt. It had been my choice to come to this remotest of all destinations, alone. But what about them? An image of my daughter Clara, aged eleven, loomed large. "Don't worry, Dad, we *know* you love the Bushmen more than us!" she would say with an annoying smirk. She knew how to get to me. Like a pearl in an oyster, a nugget of resolve grew in the thicket of Jilpie's dronings. My kids were my purpose. Period. "Fuckemall!" Jilpie blurted suddenly, after a long silence, gulping a huge quaff in a way that seemed to put a full stop on our dialogue. Taking no offence, I wandered back to the fray.

215

The world unravelled, steadily. Vixie kept a river of drinks flowing in stony silence whilst nursing a glass of milk behind the counter, and Trevor was locked in conversation with the festering-wounded camel driver. His hand was now resting intimately and high on the latter's thigh. "Good on you, Trevor," I thought with drunken affection, approving the blooming of this unexpected romance.

Noise and smoke levels rising, I found myself joining in a drunken rendition of "Walzing Matilda" led by a camel man who knew the words. Platters of Cookie's greasy food clattered onto the bar to loud cheers; massive hamburgers, generous chips and ketchup sloshed on the side. These were greedily devoured in short-lived silence. Soon plates made way for beer bottles, drunken laughter bubbling and erupting like rolling thunder in a storm. *How long could this all last*, I wondered, *before things started falling apart?*

Without warning, Vixie picked up a brass bell from behind the counter, rang it loudly into the din and through clenched teeth shouled, "Last round, gennelmen!"

"Keeriste, Vixie! Already?" barked Mike, quickly ordering four double rum-and-cokes "for the road." How the hell was this drunken man going to drive us home? The diehards crowded the bar for last orders, every man for himself.

A sense of relief poked a wet nose into my befuddled being. I had not only survived this epic booze-up, but this old scrum half had become a central player in the game that was nearly over. Flawed, but loyal to each other. Clinging to a fragment of sanity, I took in the state of the Curtin Springs team. Mike and Nellie giggling together, chugging their last drinks with the exaggerated movements of the inebriated. Trevor and camel man had slipped out, hand in hand, into the night, which made me strangely happy. Jilpie Jim was slouched in a corner with old Bill and the other camel men, draining their drinks to the last.

Squinting through the fog, I found to my shock that Vixie was smiling warmly, directly at me. One eye twitched in what could have, *must* have been a long wink. Ye gods, was that hostile woman hitting on me? Long seconds passed as I looked away, flustered, gazed at my feet, and then again around the room. Anywhere but at her. Long seconds more, until I finally glanced back. Too late, for she had spun on her heels whilst I dithered, leaving the pub without a backward glance. My brain churned. Old Vixie had looked so attractive for those few moments. Had I ever been so drunk?

Mike and Nellie staggered arm in arm into the night, whooping loudly as they headed for the Land Cruiser. Yip, he was going to drive. Jilpie was next, limp and supported by one of the camel men. Bill lurched out too, bashing the swing door noisily and stumbling towards the car park. Last to leave, I glanced at the stained-glass mirror behind the bar, and beheld a bald and familiar figure leering back at me through the haze. That reflected image belonged to another version, one that had survived Curtin Springs, intact. I raised my glass to the distorted alter-ego, then staggered out into the night.

Mike drove like a gladiator, rock solid and silent despite having drunk enough to sink a barge. His powerful intent was on the road, and nobody doubted that he would get us safely home. My god, one could go to war with such a guy, never mind his rough ways. Nellie was curled up like a large poodle on the front passenger seat. Jilpie's grizzled head rested snoring on my shoulder, and Bill puffed rhythmically on the back seat. Through the night we roared. Twice we stopped to relieve bladders into the bristling darkness, with spinifex, ghostlike in the moonlight, pricking our legs. Nellie woke up and leaned over, "Are you boys alright then, lovvies?" I smiled at her. "Thanks, Nellie," I murmured, touched.

At Curtin Springs pub I had mingled with what my gran would have called a bunch of "hoodlums and ne'er-do-wells". But I now felt the opposite. Rare seeds of bonding and even love had taken root, which would grow more significant over the months ahead. Above all, that flashback of Clara's taunt and my nugget of resolve towards my children was a turning point. Like the spinifex grasses that accompanied our journey home, these new shoots, spiky and even hostile to the observer, would prove resilient and strong.

33

Burning Tempers

Battered Toyota Land Cruisers, the only vehicles tough enough for this wild country, converged on the quiet community centre at Umuwa. Noisily and dustily, they had brought the important men – the leaders of the vast Anangu Pitjantjatjara (AP) Aboriginal lands. The day of the big meeting – my first encounter as the new AP lawyer with indigenous governance in Australia and with my collective Aboriginal bosses (known as the 'zekkativs').

Executive meeting. At the door to the humble Umuwa community hall, an ancient mongrel lay scrunched against the door. Battered and exhausted from his Outback life, he made a ragged canine doorstop. His scarred neck and head were poised nobly above his body, as if separate from it, his nose held at a regal tilt. Was he simply catching the first delicious rays of the sun, or receiving messages from a higher spiritual plane? I bent over to pat the meditating dog, but withdrew my hand rapidly, thinking of fleas, germs and the like; doorstop dog chose to ignore the insult, eyelids fluttering softly in sun-induced bliss.

The gloomy room was furnished with tables in a circle and plastic chairs. The meeting was running only about an hour late, which translator Trev informed me was unusually punctual for these parts. A burly man with wild hair, a thin moustache and a lugubrious demeanor, Trev had been appointed by the AP as my personal guide and translator, tasked to keep me up to speed. My indulgent smile to Trev at this snippet felt unintentionally patronising, so I issued a note-to-self: *just chill, mate, make no waves.*

Some of the massive men introduced themselves, others simply shuffled past, many barefooted, towards their seats. First to shake my hand was Rodney Kalpipi. A man mountain, six foot six of sun-blocking bulk, with bushy eyebrows looming over a surprisingly kind face. My hand disappeared inside his, a tiny white insect engulfed by a bunch of giant, warm and, mercifully gentle, black bananas. His wide-brimmed black hat was affixed to a bush of wild grey hair.

Trev pointed out Desmond Frost, the most famous of the Pitjantjatjara leaders. At first, I did not see him, for he wasn't sitting like the others but was draped horizontally over three chairs on the far side of the table. Only his size 12 leather boots and ample belly, peeping coyly above the melamine tabletop, indicated his presence. Was he perhaps praying or meditating? Then an unmistakable snore thrust aside such speculations. Desmond Frost was, unashamedly, asleep.

Presently, Chairman Oscar clumped into the room, his heavy leather boots and massive hat marking him as one for centre stage. A man of dark presence and unpredictable power, he sat heavily at the head of the long table, shuffling papers and exuding a hostile nonchalance. He was dressed like a car salesman, smooth and flashy, with oily black hair slicked back Elvis-style. Looking around languidly at the slowly filling room, he seemed unperturbed by the prevailing sense of disorder.

I took the time to observe. Oscar's older brother, Len, stood smoking despite the no-smoking signs on the wall. He was sharing his cigarette with another greybeard at the far end of the table, and the two were giggling like naughty kids at some private source of amusement. Big Rodney Kilpipi's chair now leaned dangerously backwards against the wall. With his monster boots on the tabletop and tent-sized hat tipped over his face, his body language declared, 'Until this gets interesting, I am gonna rest awhile.' Meanwhile, Desmond Frost's boots and belly had not budged and his snores had subsided into a rhythmic rumbling.

Seven or eight other jilpie zekkativs (esteemed oldfellas) occupied the remaining seats in the dingy room. The general garb was surprisingly consistent, as if the dress code for the meeting was (one) tease your hair for a week so it stands up in the wildest manner, (two) grab the oldest hat and clothes you own, (three) drag 'em around in the dust for a day, and finally (four) just stick 'em on! With my clean khaki longs and white shirt I felt overdressed and incongruous.

No pen or paper in the room besides mine, and no one looked remotely ready for such an important meeting. Where were the minutes? How would they record and remember their decisions? My open laptop seemed increasingly out of place and I fidgeted, in anticipation of what lay ahead. Trev, sensing my hesitance, whispered, "No computers here, loyya, no minutes allowed at zekkativ meetings. You godda puddit away, okay?" Strange indeed, but who was I to buck the system at this early stage of my employment? I closed my laptop and waited. *Just chill, mate.* Intercultural competence, I had once learned, was the ability to understand and interact with cultural systems other than one's own. This meeting was going to be a good test.

"Owa, owa (hello, hello), gennelmen, gmornin', forst aadem onna genna," growled Oscar, addressing a grubby whiteboard scrawled with a list of incomprehensible 'agenna aadems'. His English was mumbled and distorted, which seemed strangely appropriate, considering how the English settlers had so devastated his people.

The first aadem was the case of the AP Director, Bamaki Thompson, whose misconduct and refusal to leave his post had become a crisis. By title and status, the most senior leader in the lands. Immediately the zekkativ members started talking loudly at each other in Pitjantjatjara, which to my ear sounded like an impenetrable "warra-warra-warra".

Bamaki rose ponderously to his feet, seemingly without permission, and the hubbub dried up at once. An impressive figure, Bamaki was a jilpie in his weathered prime, his mop of slate hair and barrel-like chest exuding a wrestler aura. Aggressive brows adorned piercing eyes, perched above industrial-strength nostrils which dominated all other facial features. A prominent folk hero in the land struggle twenty years back, he had been rewarded with the plum position of AP Director, and had happily appropriated the status, salary and 'toyoda' (vehicle) that went with the job. Apparently, and this was the problem, he had failed to display responsibility and, well, directorship. Buckets of money missing, whilst his family grew visibly more prosperous. Countless attempts to discipline or dislodge him over the years had failed. Hence the current crisis. Culturally, a jilpie of such high honour and status should never be sacked, but Bamaki had pushed the boundaries of his jilpie-immunity for too long. Oozing wounded dignity at the insinuations against him, he delivered a vehement statement denying all fault.

Reluctantly, he agreed to leave the room.

The jilpies had assembled to decide his fate and all former Bamaki admirers and colleagues were now to be the unwilling hangmen. The air fizzled with tension as they all spoke at once, at, over, and across one another. I closed my eyes, and marvelled at the incomprehensible babble. Trev whispered that a consensus was being sought to a solution, namely that they should instruct Bamaki to resign today, with honour intact, failing which he would be fired. An ultimatum with a clear and harsh consequence of his non-compliance. To some, this was an unheard of insult to such a respected jilpie; to others, it was what was required. The debate raged on.

As this ethical conundrum roared around the room, I became aware of the sound of a young boy's voice coming from the yard outside. To my astonishment, he was singing an old sixties hit at the top of his voice: "Oooohhh, yeah babeh, (yeah babeh), da da da da da da, won't you be maa gal, won't you be maa gal." Nobody seemed to notice or be disturbed by this surreal aural intrusion, though the same line was repeated again and again.

Peeping out a window, I saw a curly-haired Aboriginal boy of about eleven, standing on a metal drum in the dusty yard. Some younger kids were standing at his feet, and he was singing at the top of his voice, his confidence that of an Outback Michael Jackson. What would become of such a talent? Would he end up sniffing petrol like so many others? Waving in my direction with a flashing smile, he carried on singing. He only knew the first lines of that silly song, and sang it melodiously, again and again.

The debate had now reached the fever pitch of a verbal brawl. Storms of passion raged to and fro. Was the Bamaki conundrum going to be solvable? Loyalty by some to an esteemed comrade at odds with 'whitefella' rules against corruption. An unresolved dispute with the hero Bamaki would surely split the community in two? A Catch-22 deadlock loomed, and Chairman Oscar fidgeted, unable to gauge the mood of the room.

Suddenly, a deep and authoritative voice, seemingly from nowhere, sliced through the gloom. It came from the still horizontal hulk of jilpie Desmond Frost, who had not yet deemed it necessary to rise from his three-chair snooze. His growled words landed like blows from Muhammad Ali on a hapless opponent, snuffing out all possible challenges. Game changer. Head-nodding, whispered conversations and mumblings followed Desmond's intervention, which I could tell were the initial expressions of grudging compromise.

Within minutes of Desmond's words, the jilpies had arrived at full consensus. Bamaki was to be firmly told, Trev whispered, that he could resign with honour, today, or be fired in disgrace. The erstwhile discord and tumult was replaced by a sense of harmony, a contrast which had me blinking in surprise. As I had just witnessed, consensus had been sought in preference to a voting system where status and loss of dignity were at stake.

Bamaki now returned to the room and gravely took his seat, bearing the demeanor of a martyr approaching the hangman's noose. The tension hung heavily. Before the chairman could announce the agreed-to ultimatum, Bamaki leaped to his feet, kicking his plastic chair over backwards, and stood with arms akimbo. Legs wide apart. With the theatrical flair of a Shakespearean actor, he grasped the initiative and milked the drama to the full: not for *him* to passively await a fate determined by others.

Then with a histrionic flourish, he whipped out two crumpled documents from somewhere deep in the folds of his shirt and dramatically struck a match under one. Ablaze in seconds, the document dropped from his outstretched hand and landed on the wooden floor, burning fiercely near his bare right foot. Nobody moved whilst the mystery page curled into blackened oblivion, drawing all eyes. Even the imperturbable Desmond Frost was compelled to rise languidly onto one elbow, his hat at a jaunty angle over his face, to observe the unfolding drama. Transfixed, I marvelled at Bamaki's streetfighter wiles and anarchic timing.

Ignoring the paper smouldering a hair's breadth from his dusty trouser leg, he began to read pompously from the unburned letter in gravelly but barely recognisable English, the formal language of governance on the lands. Quoting recent ill-health and motivated solely by noble sentiments towards the communadee, he graciously wished the zekkativ all prosperedy in the future. Half-closed eyes in the rugged countenance conveyed powerful and conflicting emotions as he came to the climax of his statement. Speaking gruffly, through clenched teeth, and focusing his gaze on Oscar, his words landed like grenades in the expectant quietness. It took me a moment to be sure I had heard right, but his final sentence concluded with the words, "An so now I resign as AP Director!"

A stunned silence followed this bombshell. Pointing to the charred document at his feet, a visibly calmer Bamaki explained that the burned letter had contained his declaration of war against the Pitjantjatjara zekkativ, which he would have used should they have opted to fire him in the whitefella way. Phew. A palpable sense of relief settled over the gathered jilpies, grateful to be spared what was heading for a tense standoff. Now there would be no loss of face, no further conflict or civil war in this fragile community. A complex crisis had been diffused by a seemingly incomprehensible process, but nobody seemed surprised.

Within seconds Desmond had resumed his reclining position. Oscar was rubbing the first aadem off the whiteboard agenna, and Len was offering Bamaki a cigarette, smirking with him over some private joke. Calm had returned to the zekkativ gathering, whilst tendrils of smoke still rose from the ashes of the discarded declaration of war.

Gazing around the table, I noticed that everyone other than the reclining Desmond was now smoking despite the no-smoking sign. Oscar rose to his feet, pointing at the scruffy flipchart. "Sekken aadem onna agenna, gennelmen," he growled. Next up was the long-simmering dispute between the Anangu Pitjantjatjara (AP) and its service provider, the Pitjantjatjara Council (PC). I tensed, in anticipation of another chestnut. From discussions the previous week, I had gathered that the PC was a separate non-governmental organisation that had been formed to serve the AP executive, but was now critical of them and competing for the support of government and funder agencies. For a year the dispute had all but crippled governance structures on the lands. Again, strong action was required.

The new loyya was unexpectedly asked for his opinion on a strategy against this now antagonistic organisation. Finally, time for me to provide the leaders with wise legal advice. In measured and pedantic words, I motivated a cautious, responsible approach to the threat, including a process involving further discussions supported by relationship building. Trev translated my words, which gave me a chance to observe their less than enthusiastic reactions. Increasingly glum looks around the table signalled their growing disappointment. This zekkativ was clearly tired of measured words and was expecting fighting talk from their new lawyer.

My short address was followed by an awkward lull. Too polite to criticise openly, the leaders lapsed into a state of uneasy, long seconds silence. The chairman was particularly unimpressed by my pacifist advice and launched into a torrent of angry Pitjantjatjara. Like a man possessed, he fiercely denounced a certain Garth Lennox, leader of the PC, and cursed those behind the scurrilous attack on the AP zekkativ. Others weighed in with further declarations of war, which Trev failed to and did not need to translate.

Watching the storms rage, I privately prayed that I would never get on the wrong side of these traditional jilpies. I had been reliably told that they preferred to hurl long spears to settle serious disputes in preference to the more 'civilised' methods of dispute resolution such as votes and mediations. As Oscar raged on, I looked anxiously around the room to gauge the responses. Was it time for spears?

Jilpie Len now entered the fray to hurl angry words back at his brother Oscar, who in turn retaliated with heightened passion. Whatever was now going on was not 'onna agenna', and felt even more dangerous than the still-fresh Bamaki debate. Other leaders previously silent now weighed in, at least two or three speaking loudly over each other at any one time. The decibels ramped up, and Desmond Frost finally sat upright for the first time, heaving himself vertical with a deep grunt. Trev had long forgotten to translate, so I simply observed the body language as the inter-sibling melee raged.

Oscar's anger was at fever pitch. Pushing his chair backwards he crashed out of the room like an angry buffalo, leaving the zekkativ momentarily stunned into silence. Oscar's cowboy boots stomped down the wooden passage, and a door banged. Trev finally translated. Len had accused his brother of serious corruption concerning Toyotas and community money, insisting that Oscar's behaviour caused people to believe "that we cannot manage our affairs". As I took this in, Len now exploded to his feet and stomped out in the direction of his departed brother. Glowering eyebrows, narrowed eyes. This sibling argument seemed serious, but the remaining zekkativs seemed unfazed and struck up cigarettes. Desmond and Rodney returned to their different under-hat reposes. Surely something should be done?

I got up and went after Len and Oscar, fearing that these two, my bosses, had left to fight to the death. Only last year, according to Trev, Len had thrown a spear into the neck of an opponent during an argument, and had not even been charged with an offence. Such retaliation is regarded as Anangu business, entirely acceptable, and *not* open to comparison with whitefella justice. Apparently, the speared man had walked down the Umuwa main road to the doctor with the spear sticking out either side of his neck, and had lived to tell the tale.

As I hurried down the passage towards loud voices in the tea room, my heart leaping like a roo, I wondered where they kept the spears. Timidly, I peeped around the tea room door, expecting mayhem. A new surprise met my eyes. The two belligerent brothers were chatting away, waving cups of tea in the air, and slapping each other on the shoulders. Whatever violent storm had raged had somehow abated, leaving happy brotherhood in its wake. No doubt apologies had been offered and accepted. I closed the door on this amiable scene, and staggered back to the council chamber. If I had been allowed to take minutes, what on earth would I have written? What had I just witnessed?

The other zekkativs were chatting quietly, wisps of smoke rising between them, whilst both big Rodney and Desmond snored like contented bears. I had much to learn in the Pitantjadjara world. Following the doorway dog, I closed my eyes and chose his way.

Just allow events to unfold.

34

Sentient Beings of the Outback

"Owa, owa, owa, owa!" (Yes, yes, yes, yes). Oscar, the Chairman of the Pitjantjatjara Aboriginal Council, held the mic far too close as his distorted words of greeting crackled among the humble shacks at the meeting place in Amata settlement, Central Australia. A village that appears on no map, Amata is home to about five hundred Aboriginal souls in the Pitjantjatjara heartland. This is where the famous Uluru negotiations and land claim were finalised in 1980, a glorious and recent milestone in the annals of Aboriginal struggle.

We were gathered for the annual general meeting of the organisation known as the AP (Anangu Pitjantjatjara), or simply the Pitjantjatjara people. Three giant gum trees provided the only shade in the red sandy clearing where the assembled community wrangled for position with scores of mangy shade-seeking mongrels.

"Palya, palya, palya, palya!" (Good, good, good, good) the honourable Oscar shouted encouragingly at the ragged bunch slouching under the gums, trying to elicit some reaction. He appeared unconcerned that nobody took the slightest notice of his efforts to start the meeting and smiled vaguely at the slowly gathering crowd. Clearly this was all normal to the locals. As my eyes wandered over the seated and reclining shapes, a deathly thin and bearded man rose slowly from the dust and walked unsteadily towards the chairman, one hand stretched out in front like a holy prophet blessing the ground. His other hand clasped a silver jam tin firmly below his mouth.

"No, loyya, he is not going to pray," Trev answered my whispered question with a suppressed snigger. "His brain damaged bad," he added in an unemotional aside. "Dead not long time."

Before I could respond, the man who was now halfway to the mic paused, teetered, and in agonising slow motion, fell backwards. Landing hard on his backside with a loud grunt, he narrowly missed a reclining mongrel whose tail thumped appreciatively at his good luck. The man then lurched over onto his left side, all the while holding the tin, expertly tilted to save the precious drops of whatever was inside. He lay half-turned, breathing deeply, while flies crawled all over his face and half-closed eyes. I stared, aghast, but nobody else seemed keen to assist.

After glancing at my face, Trev hurried to reassure me that this was totally normal in the AP lands. What I was witnessing was a person in the final stages of brain damage, after a lifetime of sniffing hallucinogenic petrol fumes. So that's what was in the tin. Wow, like Scott Fitzgerald said, 'First you take a drink, then the drink takes a drink, then the drink takes you.'

This man was barely functional, yet, as Trev explained, petrol sniffers were accepted, living between the cracks of their communal society as they neared death. He gestured vaguely to the crowd, implying that at least a third of those gathered were in some stage of addiction. They could be disruptive and inconvenient but were always cared for, and were already being mourned. They were no longer able to function in their families as Anangu or persons, for they had chosen to 'wake up' from this earthly dream and return to the source of all life.

"They do not die, loyya, but they return to life," Trev added, attempting a sort of gentle explanation of the whole sorry business.

As I pondered this reverse-take on life and death, watching the man twitching spasmodically in the hot sun, a bedraggled woman in a filthy dress staggered to her feet and lurched in his direction. She had a small baby clutched precariously on her hip and was holding an identical silver jam tin below her mouth. First, she placed the baby carefully on the ground, and then with her non-tin hand, heaved the fallen one into a sitting position. And there they sat together, comrades in arms.

Still Oscar fiddled busily with the mic and speakers, still the crowd steadfastly showed no interest – at least now I had a good idea why. My gaze drifted over to the canine members of the congregation. A bitch on heat scurried across the hot red sand, pursued by an assortment of scrawny dogs jostling for pole position. Feeling morose, I thought about the misery of life as a female mongrel in these parts, and wondered whether the males' unwelcome pursuit constituted 'sexual harassment', or perhaps 'unsolicited sexual advances?' We have such words and legal protections for people. Where were this dog's rights to dignity, or bodily integrity? I mused unhappily as she snarled and fended off her suitors.

The crowd had now swelled, comprised of a scattering of large dark figures squatting cross-legged in the dappled shade. Clothes were ragged beyond the telling, and if it were not for the microphone and battered toyodas (vehicles) parked in the background, the scene could have resembled a stone-age gathering ten thousand years back.

Oscar now bobbed vigorously at the front like a jack-in-the-box, rudely interrupting my sentimental daydreams. A Tom Jones lookalike, with luxuriant black hair slicked over his ears and shirt half open to reveal a bushy chest and golden chain, he exuded the confidence of an alpha male philanderer. Giving the mic cord an Elvis-like showbiz shake, he was ready to rock and roll.

Out of the corner of my eye, I noticed that the bitch on heat had scored a victory by creeping under a toyoda. Her mangy persecutors circled the car like hungry sharks around a boat, some still wagging tails optimistically. I applauded her pluck, wishing her continued success in saying no.

Chairman Oscar now began his oration in earnest, rattling away in the impenetrable (to me) Pitjantjatjara language. In between a hypermanic torrent of what sounded like 'warra-warra-warra', I kept hearing the word *loyya*, referring to me. My heart sank. I had hoped to sit this one out or perhaps, at most, wave to the group after an introduction to say, "Hi folks, nice to meetcha." No such luck. Oscar stopped abruptly in mid-warra and, turning to me with a patronisingly fond gaze, murmured, "So you gonna say sumpin, loyya?" Translator Trev, who had not bothered to translate what Oscar told the gathering, now explained simply, "Oscar tellem you noo loyya. You say sumpin, okay? I translate."

No escape. The crowd seemed peaceful enough, so what could go wrong? As I got to my feet, trying to build up confidence, a manic shriek pierced the air. I cringed, automatically assuming it was an insult directed at me. Perhaps somebody knew something bad or disliked my looks? Unable to identify the shrieker, and with confidence levels ebbing perilously low, I stumbled towards the podium.

"G'day everyone," I said into the mic, trying to sound confident (and just a tad Aussie). "I am very pleased to be here with you t'day." Blank stares from the crowd; clearly nobody understood a single word. Not a good start. Trev grabbed the mic and proceeded to talk animatedly for about a minute. At the end of his speech, an excited roar of applause erupted from the now-cheering crowd. Confused but relieved, I smiled at the dark shapes under the trees. Again, the loud shriek pierced the air, but this time I noticed with relief that the sound came from another of the damaged folks, shouting at hallucinatory demons. The community ignored him and I tried to do the same as Trev handed the mic back.

I wondered what on earth Trev could have said to elicit such an exuberant response. Feeling emboldened and with confidence rising, I proceeded with a few more safe and unexciting words. "We have a lot to do in the Pitjantjatjara lands, and I am really looking forward to working with you all." Keep it simple and safe. Warming to this new game, Trev again grabbed the mic from my hand and 'translated' my simple words into an impassioned oration. This time, when he paused for breath, the crowd cheered as if I had just offered them free beers for life. I smiled nervously. Great to feel so appreciated, but what had Trev said? "

Okay, you can sit down now, loyya, I tol' dem everyting," said Trev with a smug look on his face. Still confused, I sat down in the sand. Who cared if Trev misled them totally, the crowd loved me and surely that was a great start?

The charismatic Oscar took over again and started going through the AGM agenna, scrawled untidily on a grubby flip chart. Grazing licences, mining exploration in the lands, constitutional changes; each item was subjected to intense debate from the unstoned minority.

Men and women confidently articulated their views into the circulating mic. Lack of assertiveness was not a problem amongst the Pitjantjatjara. I liked it. How different from the general reticence and shyness of the San indigenous communities in Africa.

Proceedings briefly halted when the petrol-sniffing mother I had observed earlier began smacking her screaming child. She had clearly tried to sniff her mama's petrol and was being sternly punished. And not, I realised with growing shock, to warn her off the danger but more along the lines of, 'Bad girl, don't touch my petrol!'

The shadows lengthened as the meeting drew to a close. Heavy shapes rose from the cross-legged positions they had held for hours. I had participated little, but had observed keenly how resilient this community was, despite the poverty and slow-dying addicts in its midst. In this humble meeting place, they had participated actively and made their voices heard in an effective form of democracy. With a pang of sorrow, I had noticed that my hopeful story about bitches successfully rebuffing unwanted sex had come to a predictable end. The plucky lass had unwisely left her car shelter and had been brutally raped by the largest dog in the pack. She slunk off into the lonely evening.

A ragged man now staggered towards me, extending a filthy hand in greeting. One of the stoned people. I recognised him as the source of the mad shrieks that had almost derailed my debut. With wild eyes and saliva-dribbling mouth, he joyfully addressed me with the words "Loyya! Loyya!" Resisting a reflex to recoil I gingerly reached out to take his bony hand. As we made contact the strangest thing happened. My abhorrence drained away. I felt a connection with the soul inside the grisly façade. Behind that mad stare, glassy eyes and toothless grin, resided a fellow sentient being. Not a sad caricature of a human, stoned, lost and forlorn, but a person who felt accepted in his community, whose people would take care of him until his inevitable death. Our holding hands, smiling at each other for long moments burned into my memory.

To my surprise, he then drew out an Aussie expression, buried deep in his addled mind as our hands parted.

"No worries, mate!"

35

A Rooful Interlude

Ginger Rick gripped the Toyota Land Cruiser's wheel. He and his like were known to treat 'toyodas' as beasts that respond to dominance rather than sensitivity. A jilpie and renowned hunter, Rick exuded a sullen arrogance towards others that in polite circles might be described as 'he does not suffer fools gladly'. A pissed-off, unpleasant guy.

15 February 2001. Another harsh sizzling day under the Outback sun. At midday, an important meeting of Aboriginal leaders was scheduled in the settlement of Iwantja, three hours' hard driving south of Umuwa on a hot gravel road. As their new lawyer, I had prepared the Pitjantjatjara leaders on the key issues, their vital contribution to the meeting. Our vehicle was prepared and our team was scheduled to leave at 10 a.m.

Rick's battered hat nestled in a wild tangle of orangy hair (hence the name), and his greeting of the arriving lawyer was a triumph of understatement. If he acknowledged me at all, it was in the manner of an eagle noticing a rabbit far, far down on the earth below. This was no surprise. In my weeks at Umuwa, I had become accustomed to the, let's say, rough way in which respect and acceptance are earned and shared in this harsh world. Small talk and rules of politeness did not flourish in the AP lands.

Two other rugby front-row figures were already slouched in the rear seat. A resident cloud of giant flies buzzed happily around blobs of congealed blood and fat, spattered freely over the seats, doors and upholstery. These toyodas, used for hunting on the sly, also conveyed dead creatures.

Trying not to dwell on the precise nature of these grim stains, I climbed cautiously into the back seat, dodging the worst of the blobs, and suppressed a gag reflex as the assorted odours reached my nostrils. The furthest backseat companion ignored my arrival, whereas the other issued a mellow grunt. This was Rodney Kalpipi, a giant man whose frame would inspire fear equally in a boxing ring or a dark alley. The Stetson hat perched low over his eyes conveyed a do-not-disturb message, but I welcomed his acknowledgement as my friendliest greeting so far, by far.

Ruben Cox occupied the prized front passenger seat. Less bulky than the others and deep into his sixties, he emitted an air of refinement, unusual for a jilpie, enhanced by his tweed deerstalker that would have looked more at home in an English shooting party. A more sensitive guy than the others, I imagined, although the thicket of curly hair above bushy eyebrows and rough Aboriginal features confirmed that we were indeed far from the English countryside.

Ruben fiddled expertly with an old carburettor with grimy hands that had long last known soap and water. Without warning Rick started the motor, crunched the Land Cruiser into gear and we thundered off in a cloud of choking red dust. Already late for the important noon meeting, we needed to drive hard to deliver our well-prepared contribution. Surprised at first that my tough companions all had their seatbelts buckled and after we had careened dangerously around the first corner, I too buckled up for the ride ahead. Mercilessly the sun beat down on the un-airconditioned vehicle; the contented buzzing of flies audible above the hard-revving engine. We lurched into each other as the Toyota swayed to and fro on the crude road, with sporadic bursts of conversation between my companions in Pitjantjatjara.

Ginger Rick aggressively chewed a pungent herb that the locals use to relieve the boredom, rolling it around from left to right in an aromatic soggy ball, and occasionally spitting a brown stream out the window. I had not yet tried out this habit that they said does wonders for the chewer, but emits a foul pong which lingers for days on the breath.

After an hour or so of the hot and dusty roller-coaster, my nose had adjusted to the road-kill aromas. We were making good time. I was impressed by the team's dedication, driving at such relentless speed to make the meeting. Miraculously, Rodney's hat-over-eyes slumber continued throughout the journey, which might be, I thought, his meditative preparation for the presentation that lay ahead.

As we rounded a long bend, four large kangaroos bounced rhythmically in single file across the road ahead. Rick's eyes narrowed, his massive hands clenching on the wheel. *How nice,* I pondered, observing his response, *this guy sure appreciates the wonders of nature.* Oddly, in my opinion, the leaping roos accelerated on seeing our vehicle, more urgently than necessary it seemed, pole-vaulting over the road and into the scrubby bush beyond. *Why are they so scared,* I wondered? My question was answered seconds later as we reached the spot where the roos had disappeared. Without warning, Rick crunched the vehicle into a lower gear and wrenched the wheel to the left. Airborne for long seconds, we crashed over the sandy verge and plunged into the rank mulga scrublands in deadly pursuit. Breathless and shocked, I glanced quickly around. Ruben had dropped the carburettor on the floor and was gripping his seat with both hands, eyes transfixed on the quarry. Big Rodney's hat remained low over his eyes, in meditation pose; both hands grasping the seat. Mulga branches screeched against the metalwork and smaller trees crashed under us as Rick charted a direct course after the quarry, dodging the gum trees.

I gripped my seat, awash with adrenaline, noting that both humans and roos were now in mortal danger. Into an open clearing we crashed, the leaping animals now so close I could sense the panic fuelling their desperate escape. Hunched over the wheel, Rick was breathing hard, like a deranged Darth Vadar, steering his wildly bucking spaceship. Big Rodney finally raised his hat and sat upright, now alert and eager. As we plunged through ditches and over trees, my sympathy for the wildly leaping creatures was eclipsed by fear for my own safety. Despite their frantic efforts, we were rapidly gaining on the leaping roos.

With a sickening thud, different to all those before, the bull bar struck solid bone and flesh. The roo was flung in the air, landing on its broken back, powerful rear legs kicking frantically. Gasping and speechless, I witnessed this horror. Before the vehicle had even stopped, the 'sensitive'

Ruben had leaped out and with a brutish kick to the head, terminated the victim's agony. The engine was turned off. And in the few seconds of silence, while I gathered my wits, Rodney and Rick had already built a fire. The others gathered more wood, and Ruben idly turned over the dead roo with his foot, commenting wryly on the sizeable male genitalia to the jovial guffaws of his mates. I could only assume the gist of the joke, but clearly the boys were happy and the anticipation sky high.

Except for me. By now I was popping with anxiety, and could stifle it no more. "Excuse me, Rick," I stuttered, approaching our leader's formidable hulk. "Um, what about our meeting? We'll be late if we don't leave now," I stated, glancing pointedly at my watch.

"Don' worry, loyya, fust we eat sum roo," he growled in a manner that was not unfriendly but did not encourage further debate. I was the White Rabbit in *Alice in Wonderland*, the refrain "we'll be late, we'll be late," repeating in my programmed mind. I urgently needed to give in to Outback democracy.

Rick hoisted the roo by the tail, turning it over the flames to sear off the fur. A sickening smell of burning hair filled the air, the creature's wide-open eyes seeming to register amazement at this new indignity. Without any removal of the guts, the now-blackened roo was then thrown bodily into the fire, whilst more branches were piled on top.

No pre-fire preparation, nor removal of entrails. I imagined Bear Grylls, British adventurer, writer, television presenter, with an upper-class sneer about such lack of bushcraft. But the big guys were more energised than I had ever seen them, conversation animated, their laughter frequent and explosive. Big Rodney's massive face had transformed into an infectious grin as he made some joke about the new loyya's responses.

I found a large branch of dead wood and dragged it to the fire (if you can't beatem, joinem). This addition to the roo barbie was warmly acknowledged with nods and grunts. I was fast becoming part of this barbecue brotherhood, and we were here to eat roo! Time had become irrelevant, as had our oh so important meeting, a mere hour's drive away, that had by now already begun.

The roo smouldered and charred, barely visible within the fireball of crackling dry wood. The stench of burning fur was soon replaced by the more welcome aroma of barbecued meat. The lads smoked, chatted, and laughed, while playing with the fire, like boys playing truant and bucking authority. Ginger Rick, chief executioner and roo cooker, hooked the blackened carcass out of the fire with a stick and flung it on the ground. Not a sight for Aussie chefs or the foodie pages. The eyes were charred to dark raisins, the yellowish herbivore teeth bared in a defiant death-grin. Worse was to come, as it was time to prepare this dish for consumption.

Whipping a sharp penknife from his pocket, he sliced the stomach open from chest to groin. With a whoosh the reek of charred meat and entrails filled the air as Rick cut off a choice fatty lump and gulped it down. For the second time that day I suppressed a strong urge to gag when the opened stomach emitted the stench of par-cremated entrails. The feast that now lay before us was a charred heap of skin, meat, entrails, and shit. An old saying by Alton Brown found its way into my head. 'There are no bad foods: only bad food habits.'

Oblivious to the unappetising smell emanating from the corpse, the lads now ripped and tore into it with gusto. Each had his own sharp knife, preferring the barely cooked and ponging entrails to the well-done meat nearer the surface. Big Rodney was in his element, gesticulating with a bloody lump of par-cooked entrail in one hand while he held forth. The others laughed along, ripping into their own lumps of bloody meat, immune to lack of cutlery, condiments and the like. Fatty hands and mouths were wiped on shirt sleeves. What else?

Rick then turned to me and proffered a chunk of fatty flesh on the end of his penknife. Unwilling to refuse this rare gesture of friendship, I responded with, "Gosh, thank you Rick," grasping the morsel gingerly between thumb and forefinger. Repressing my squeamishness, I took a nibble, only to find it tasted even more awful than I had imagined. Horrible-looking, smelling and tasting, beyond description. Burned skin, fat and especially stomach contents have a ghastly odour, which brought this gastronomic nightmare to a climax.

Somehow, I had to pretend to eat, but get rid of the worst of my meat without the others finding out. Smuggle morsel into left hand whilst chewing and swallowing. Drop it onto sand and bury with shoe. Avoid signs of distaste. The feast was on, and I managed to avoid attention as my newly bonding friends ate and ate, ate and laughed, and ate again. I was included in the bonhomie, offered hunks which I pretended to eat, causing roars of laughter at my squeamishness. Their now-adopted whitefella was part of the feasting and every ghastly morsel chewed boosted acceptance. A high price to pay, I admit.

About two hours after the roo family had unwisely crossed the road, the eating and laughter slowed right down, unembarrassed burps around the smouldering ashes indicating satiation. Time to hoist the 'roo-mains' (three or four grisly pieces) onto the toyoda.

Soon we were back on the dusty road to Iwantja, evidence of the bloody feast still visible on unwashed hands, faces and clothes. Flies buzzing more merrily than before, and again we were speeding down the dusty road. According to my watch the meeting would be nearly over by now, but to my surprise I had stopped worrying.

In a cloud of red dust, we lurched to a halt outside a large community hall. Our grimy group shuffled unapologetically into the meeting room. The acrid pong of smoke and charred meat which followed our arrival drew curious, perhaps even envious looks, I imagined, as we headed towards empty chairs and sat down.

Whatever they had been debating seemed forgotten as about a hundred Aboriginal leaders gazed at us, obviously expecting an apology or explanation. Ginger Rick paused at his chair, gazing amiably around the room. Then before sitting down, he languidly slapped some dust off his grubby sleeves and announced gruffly to the room at large. "Hey you mob,[14] we gotta roo! That whadappened." Nods around the room. No further details given, no questions asked, no apology or explanation. It was enough.

It was too late for the Pitjantjatjara team to deliver our prepared contribution, and the meeting soon closed. This wasted opportunity would normally have rated as a disaster, but I felt strangely unconcerned. Boarding the old Toyota to drive home with the buzzing flies, I had become one of the mob.

From that day on, Rick, Ruben, Rodney and the others trusted me, which influenced others and changed my life on the lands. "Hey, loyya. How about we go get anudda roo?" would often be flung my way, with a sly chuckle. But that grinning roo face haunts me; my life as a carnivore forever 'roo-ined'.

36

Dreamtime

Alice Springs High Court. In the stifling courtroom, I sat near the dock watching the accused impassively listening to two days of preliminary state evidence. The deterioration of each of the deceased was described in clinical and heart-wrenching detail. Photographs beamed onto a large screen showed three beautiful young boys transforming into emaciated wraiths, the most recent pictures depicting them as pathetic creatures, fast approaching death. Sniffing petrol had had the boys in its deadly grip. Despite the availability of medical assistance, they had chosen to persist with the toxic escape. Three sets of Aboriginal parents from the A settlement had been charged with murder for allowing their teenage children Jonson Smith, Daniel Roberts and Will Owens to die from petrol-sniffing. The teenagers had grown up as 'bunjis'[15] in the humble settlement, and had died within two weeks of each other from addiction.

Aboriginal culture fascinates me, though my ability to understand is limited. Despite a six-month tenure as the lawyer of the Pitjantjatjara tribe in central Australia, living within their community as one of few whitefellas, the ancient cosmology of the Australasian Aboriginals remains an alien universe. My glimpses and understandings inescapably distorted. I remain a novice.

Most of the Aboriginal tribes that once inhabited Australia are now extinct. Ever-dwindling numbers speak their indigenous languages. Whilst particulars of their practiced cultures vary, certain foundational beliefs such as deeply held stories of origin as well as of the nature of life on earth are shared. Aboriginal cosmology is founded upon reverence for the land, upon belief in the Dreamtime and creation myths or songlines, particular to each tribe. Everything on earth is regarded as truly alive, from mountains and rivers to forests and living creatures. The same spirit energises them in perpetual cycles of life and death. Humans are part of this natural world rather than superior beings, obliged to treat all forms of life with respect. This is the polar opposite of homocentric belief systems that consider humans as the most important beings on earth, with the right to use and abuse nature at will. In this limited paradigm, enunciated in Genesis, God bestowed upon Adam ' . . . dominion over the fish of the sea, and over the fowl of the air . . . and over all the earth, and over every creeping thing that creepeth upon the earth.'[16]

I first gazed upon Uluru in 1991. Its brooding presence still ghosts in my psyche. Uluru is in the Kata Tjuta National Park in Central Australia, about 360 kilometres south-west of Alice Springs. Kata Tjuta – many heads in the Pitjantjatjara language – consists of some twenty-five red domed peaks of which Uluru is the most famous. This iconic desert mountain is generally known as Ayers Rock, the most important of all Aboriginal sacred sites. Central to vital songlines and creation myths, it inspires awe and dominates the surrounding desert. Aboriginal mistrust of the Western world runs deep, so the Pitjantjatjara elders insist that large sections of the entire mountain base be cordoned off from the curious tourists that flock annually to witness it. Key spiritual places are designated as 'off-limits' for sightseers, and not even the reasons for their importance are to be disclosed.

Western hunger to learn about Aboriginal culture thus faces an intrinsic challenge, for elders do not share their culture with outsiders. They believe – and I think it is true – that allowing stories to be published, written down or displayed for tourists runs the risk of their being captured, debased and distorted. During my time as Pitjantjatjara lawyer, I listened avidly to stories relating to their origins, myths and beliefs, appreciative of their sharing privileged information with a mere whitefella. (After the trial I heard these beliefs amplified from the mouths of the three mothers.)

The Dreamtime, central to Aboriginal beliefs, refers to the ancient time of creation when the earth was formed. This remains a potent metaphor for present-day life, referred to as the Dreaming. Dreamtime stories are myths dating from that early time when animal ancestors as well as creatures with supernatural powers populated the Earth. One of the best known of these mythical ancestors is the Rainbow Serpent who travelled through the continent, marking the earth wherever she went. One story goes that when she called on the frogs to show themselves, they came out of streams with their bellies full of water. She then tickled them so that they laughed, and the water from their stomachs ran all over the earth, forming lakes and rivers. The Rainbow Serpent then made laws for the entire earth, decreeing that those who disobeyed would become inanimate creatures such as mountains and hills. Those who obeyed became humans.

Trying to fathom the Pitjantjatjara belief system from what I had read and gleaned from my new friends, particularly from the mothers, was a slow but fascinating task. Well-meaning whitefellas were only allowed a potted version, like giving a recipe but excluding key ingredients. The stories are complicated, requiring a suspension of disbelief. Similarly, they carry an alternative logic that defies Western understanding. For example, in another Dreamtime story the koala bear mates with a butterfly. The San story of the desert lark, hopelessly in love with a springbok, has a similar thread of fabled humour. In his book *Songlines*, Bruce Chatwin describes how the ancient ballads record the origins of each tribe right from the Dreamtime, describing all important geographic features and events that have marked their ancestors' and their own paths right up to modern time. Individuals have a personal songline tagged onto their collective one in their own indigenous language, which describes his or her origins and life events.

Back to the trial. The thrust of the criminal charge was that the parents should have stopped their children's addictions; that by failing to do so they were responsible for their deaths. In my view, charging the grieving parents with the children's deaths was a crude attempt by the Australian government to enforce parental responsibility, and criminally cruel to boot. At the time of the court case, I did not realise the extent of teenage suicides amongst indigenous peoples all over the world. My research soon revealed this disturbing trend. Over recent decades an initial steady trickle of such suicides had grown into a flood, robbing vulnerable tribes of their best youth, and leaving governments confused. Whilst a number of theories jostled for support and policymakers tut-tutted helplessly, three factors remained undisputed. The suicides were an innate rebellion. Aboriginal cultures imagine and occupy a different universe. And are unable to prepare their children for schools that force adoption of the idiom of the dominant culture. There was a strong spiritual or existential component to these drastic, terminal acts of protest.

During the indigenous leaders' meeting in 1990 in Geneva San leader Dawid Kruiper and I had met with Innu leaders from Davis Inlet, a community in Labrador, Canada, which had over the years experienced a spate of teenage suicides. In the most recent event, nine teenagers were about to write their final exams. In a joint suicide note they stated that their parents no longer led the way, that they had nothing worth living for on this earth and were choosing to 'return' to the place they had come from. Officials were mystified. Some commentators blamed the helplessness, anger and depression that followed the tribe's physical and spiritual displacement from their ancient traditional lands. Photos of Davis Inlet showed a bleak and ugly resettlement village where both elders and unemployed youth lounged on street corners and sought escape via substance addiction. In Pitjantjatjara country, a similar malady was decimating the young. A social and economic impact study report compiled in 2001 stated that 'young people drift away from the Tjukurpa (Pitantjatjara term for a coherent land-based life filled with cultural meaning) towards a chaotic life of materialism on the bleak margins of the global economy'.[17] What a contrast to my own children of similar vulnerable ages, living secure suburban lives back in South Africa, whose biggest problems revolved around finding their paths in a relatively safe world whilst seeking social acceptance and belonging.

The Australian government's misguided response to its own Aboriginal deaths failed to comprehend the roots of the problem. Its decision to criminally prosecute the parents of the three teenagers was clearly designed to teach Aboriginal parents a strong lesson. In 38-degree heat the court case playing out in the Alice Springs High Court felt like an official attempt to deflect blame for rampant Aboriginal youth deaths onto the grieving parents. Despite the horrific evidence presented, recording each Aboriginal boy's inevitable trajectory towards death, the State was not able to prove criminal intention or negligence on the part of the parents. Medical services in the outstations were sparse, rehabilitation facilities non-existent and there was no proof that the parents had neglected their teenagers, rebellious by very nature against all forms of authority, and particularly against parents.

After cross-examination dismantled state evidence, the legal aid counsel applied for dismissal of the case. To our joy, the judge pronounced that the State had failed to prove that the parents were *prima facie* guilty of a criminal act. Charges were duly dismissed and the parents pronounced not guilty, free to return home. Our celebrations of this victory were muted, even though the government's strategy to blame the parents had backfired spectacularly. There was little to be happy about other than closing the sorry chapter.

During the five-hour drive back from Alice Springs to Umuwa in our hired minibus, I felt drawn to find out more from the parents. We had grown closer during the trial, and I had to an extent won their trust. The three fathers huddled at the rear of the vehicle, sharing cigarettes, averse to conversation, but Rebecca Smith, mother of Jonson, dishevelled and with unusually green eyes, was keen to talk. In her Outback version of the colonial conqueror's language, she addressed me softly. "You see, loyya, dat whitefella guvment ee be stoopid." The mothers of Daniel and Will nodded, smiling indulgently at Rebecca's gross understatement, willing her to continue. "Dat whitefella guvment, ee not unnerstand black fellas. Our mob[18] call all dis an evryting (waving her hand expansively around at the harsh environment flashing by) da Dreaming, and when ma boy Jonson ee wanting wake up from dis dream, he wanting go back dat life. Back dat place we all coming from." The words 'wake up' spoken with strong emphasis, hand gestures and raised eyebrows to denote importance.

I had not connected the Dreaming to these suicides. Rebecca continued quietly, leaning forward to emphasise her words. "So loyya, when ma boy Jonson ee having bad Dreaming, ee got no Tjukurpa (traditional lifestyle), ee not liking school and all dat, ee start taking dat petrol; cos he want *wake up* from dis dream. For me and his daddy, it not be right to

244

stop-im. We godda look otter chillens, even if dey choosing take dat petrol, our job be look otter dem up to time dey wake up."

Sarah, the mother of Will Owens, now chimed in, "Dat's right, loyya. Our chillens who took petrol not dead you see, loyya. When we say dey *wake up*, dey now be living, dey gone back to da *real life*." The words of an Aboriginal proverb returned to me. 'We are all visitors to this time, this place . . . just passing through. Our purpose here is to observe, to learn, to grow, to love . . . and then we return home.' The mothers became more animated, speaking with and over one another. My head spun. This was radical, upside down, antithetical to everything I had been taught, namely that life on earth ends finally with death.

We drove in silence homewards. As the red desert flashed past in the dark, I mused at the notion that our strivings on earth are part of a unique dream which ends when we return 'home'. How significant. That each passing moment of our earthly struggle takes its place in memory as an extension of our own personal unfolding dream.

37

Safety in the Outback

"No more risks," said James to me on my last day at AP Pitantjatjara. "Today my brand-new Nissan Patrol 4X4 arrives, with the best satellite phone, rocket flares and a de-luxe survival pack: twenty-five litres of water and food for a week." And as if to drum his point home, "Zero risk in the Outback. That is what I am aiming for."

James, my replacement as Pitantjatjara legal officer, had arrived two weeks earlier in a waft of after-shave lotion and enthusiasm. Of middle age and nattily dressed, he had debonair manners and grey sideburns, a Sean Connery's more elegant brother look-alike. As my contract neared its end, we had selected him from a bunch of applicants with high hopes for his success. The bulk of his experience with Aboriginals had been as a politician in the Northern Territory rather than as a lawyer, so he was to live and work with me for two weeks until I left.

Early on the first morning in my tiny cottage the aroma of roasting coffee woke me. There was James in the kitchen, sporting a silk dressing gown, silk cravat, leather slippers and fussing over a bubbling coffee maker. "Can't live without good coffee!" I accepted a cup of this excellent brew and idly wondered what other luxuries this elegant fellow would be expecting. Herve Wiener came to mind. 'Remember when the peacock struts his stuff, he shows his backside to half the world.'

After introducing James to the AP staff, I took him to a wall map of the 128 000 square kilometres of Pitjantjatjara lands in my office – soon to be his. Larger than the average American state, with ten remote Aboriginal settlements that he would be required to regularly visit. Blood drained from his ruddy cheeks as he took in the rugged terrain, while I pressed on. Outback Australia is known to be harsh, and it was my job to prepare him for the task. Dozens succumb to disorientation and heat in the Outback every year, so safety was crucial. Pointing out the far-flung Aboriginal settlements falling under James's jurisdiction, I emphasised the need for strict protocols to ensure survival. Aboriginal survival for millennia in such inhospitable landscapes is no comfort to Europeans, and remains a mystery.

"What happens down there, Roger?" asked James, pointing at a region in the south of the territory, with sparse tracks and no settlements.

"That is called Spinifex country, a no-go area, inhabited by a dangerous Aboriginal grouping known as the Spinifex people."

I recounted how some years back an enthusiastic anthropologist had ignored warnings to stay away, had driven there to see for himself, and was speared through the upper right leg as a mark of their displeasure. Luckily for him, they chose a leg rather than a chest spearing. He drove with the spear in his thigh all the way back to Umuwa, the shaft poking out the passenger window. "Since then," I proceeded, "the Spinifex people are left strictly alone."

James's gulp and widening eyes indicated that he was finally digesting the challenges ahead.

That afternoon I suggested that he join me for a short trip of about 150 kilometres to Kaltjiti, one of the closer aboriginal settlements. As we boarded my ancient Toyota, James kicked its worn tyres and gave the dated instrument panel a disapproving look. "Don't tell me that I will have to drive this rattletrap?" He climbed cautiously the passenger seat. "It has done over 560 000 miles!" His nose twitched as he sniffed the aroma in the car. "What is that *smell*?" He asked, opening the window to let in air. I chose silence. The previous week I had given a lift to a hunter with a six-foot dead iguana, whose now-congealed blood had leaked onto the back seat.

Through vast valleys and plains, flanked by pristine mountain ranges and orange rock faces, we drove, my companion seemingly immune to the beauty. A resentment prickled. I mean why come to this beautiful and remote place if it does not speak to you? To him the Outback seemed primarily inconvenient and fearsome (all true), and by no means a gorgeous wonderland. After bruising driving through a rocky river bed, a white-lipped James tersely asked, with an edge in his usually modulated voice, "So what happens if we break down here, Roger? Hey mate? We must be at least two hours from any settlement, and I haven't seen a single car on these roads."

I'd been expecting this. "Good question. Well, in the cubby hole over there you will find a compass and some energy bars. And perhaps some old Zoo biscuits. And then behind my seat there should be a few litres of water, if the cans were filled up last time, which could keep us alive for at least a day or two." James's tautening features were bringing out the worst in me, and I warmed to the theme. "And if we are not rescued within a day or two, well, sadly you and I will die together." Glumly he pondered this bleak scenario as we drove back to Umuwa in silence.

Whether we were bonding or not I still needed to explain the important aspects of the AP job to him. After our field trip, instead of shadowing me and learning from my work on legal matters, he became obsessed with acquiring a new vehicle. Not for him to risk his life in that smelly Toyota. With his connections in high places, he got approval to order a brand-new vehicle. What a loss it would be if a lawyer of James's importance were to die miserably due to an unreliable vehicle. When I reminded him that our time was running out, his breezy response was, "Don't worry, mate," he said, adding that all those complex mining and environmental legal issues I wanted to explain were "a piece of cake".

My last day dawned, together with delivery of James's brand-new steed. Zero risk, and zero hardship it would be for James. With a smirk, he added that the total cost including two extra spare tyres was just over 400 000 Aussie dollars. AP's lawyer would henceforth serve the community in luxurious safety.

Time to leave. I shook hands all round. Jilpie Len gave me a three-metre spear "to protek you in Africa, my loyya!" Last stop was my former office. Brand new desk, chairs and laptop proclaimed 'under new management', and prominent wall-pictures showed politician James shaking hands with smiling dignitaries. A framed photograph of his pretty wife gazed adoringly from the wall. Feeling vaguely disorientated, I shook his hand and wished him luck with all the sincerity I could muster, my parting words, "Happy driving in that Nissan, James." He smiled broadly as if to acknowledge that some are destined for superior journeys. I left with steps that quickened as I headed for the door.

Two months later I contacted my friend Trev to ask how things were going, and of course how my replacement was doing. "Haven't you heard?" he asked with that tone that promises a whopper. "James has resigned. He had a bad accident in his second week, and wrote off that fancy Nissan." I was intrigued, and demanded details.

James had taken the silver Nissan to Mimili, one of the furthest outposts on the eastern AP lands. Why he chose such a dangerous trip for his maiden voyage and did not take Trev as a guide, remains a mystery. One stretch of that road was 145 kilometres with no break, and the confusing landscapes plus heat had previously claimed many victims. I imagined James setting forth confidently, kitted out with wide-brimmed hat, colourful cravat, expensive cologne mingling sweetly with the new-car aroma. As Murphy's law would have it, deep into his journey the massive Nissan Patrol sputtered to a standstill. With the hope of being rescued by a passerby close to zero. But wait. No need for anxiety, as this baby was kitted for any type of emergency. Flares, food, and drink for a week and, of course, that expensive satellite phone.

As Trev related the drama that unfolded, my imagination painted in an increasingly dishevelled James, living his worst nightmare. First, he tried the starter again and again with no success, until the battery went flat. Cursing and sweating by now in the rapidly heating vehicle, he took the brand-new satellite phone out of its box to call for help. Horror of horrors, he had not recorded or had lost the pin number, rendering it useless. Breaking bushcraft rule 101, panic set in. The midmorning heat now baking around 40 degrees. Plan A had failed. Instead of first taking his water and food to a shady spot to await help, or lighting his flares, he decided that the best way to call for help was to make a big fire.

About thirty yards from the Nissan he gathered dry branches, and soon a plume of brown smoke rose into the sky. So far, so good. For a short while he might have surveyed the growing blaze and congratulated himself on his creative bushcraft. This would have been short lived. The wind changed, without warning, and the now-roaring fire suddenly gusted towards the nearby Nissan. James tried desperately to stop it, but finally had to give up and run upwind for his life. Within minutes the blaze had engulfed the Nissan which burned furiously and then exploded, pumping a massive plume into the sky. A composite of Japanese engineering, safety equipment, tyres, precious water and food, all contributing to the column of angry black smoke.

James witnessed his pride and joy burning rapidly to a cinder. Without water, he would have died within a day. Luckily, the dense column of smoke was visible for hundreds of miles and a rescue vehicle was soon dispatched, finding him dishevelled and incoherent nearby the charred carcass of his Nissan Patrol. After medical treatment for trauma in Alice Springs, he handed in his resignation, and AP Pitantjatjara saw the retreating peacock's backside.

I still wonder how James tells this story, and if the funny side of it ever dawned. I suspect not.

PARENTS

38

Mad About Bees: Francis Guy Chennells

January 2006. My aged mother and six middle-aged siblings stand around a plain beechwood coffin. A hot summer's afternoon in the brick-paved courtyard of our family home, Navarre. The English plane trees are in full canopy, their seeds starting to swell and emit fine pollen. We are gathered to take leave from our once indestructible father. In the open coffin he lies, looking younger than his eighty-seven years, his face set in a knowing smirk as if amused at the array of creams and powders applied to brighten his demeanour.

I half expect a cheeky wink and thumbs-up to say it is all a joke. Mimi, his beloved Rottweiler and walking companion, lies on guard under the coffin. A few steps behind the family circle three senior farm workers stand in threadbare suits, hats in hand, shifting from one leg to the other. The gathering feels more uncomfortable than sad, the unusual onset of grief at odds with our family tendency to suppress messy emotions.

My father died from injuries sustained in a car accident. He was a dreadful driver, and we should have long banned this advanced octogenarian from the roads. On the fateful day he had loaded two hives of bees onto his Ford 1200 bakkie, so his attention was on his precious cargo, probably glancing backwards over his shoulder as he drove onto the busy R44 at the Klein Helderberg turnoff. The accident left him with multiple broken bones, and killed him after three agonising months in ICU. Even at that advanced age, his death seemed premature.

Oldest brother Jonathan is serious and drawn, a heavy mantle now settling on his shoulders. Younger brother Mark clenches his fists, seemingly in anger, and youngest brother Miah has grown so pale I worry he might faint. Sister Biddy stands protectively by my mother who remains serenely contained, in contrast to youngest sister Jilly, whose tears flow freely. I remain strangely calm. But I have no clue how to take leave of Francis Guy Chennells who will shortly be loaded onto the cremation hearse standing in the yard.

Dad was a celebrity in Eshowe, our hometown. During WWII he was awarded a Military Cross for bravery as a tank captain who fearlessly saved three of his men whilst under fire in the Battle of Monte Casino, Italy. Mum owns a yellowed copy of an article published in the local *Zululand Times* during the war reporting on his deeds, stating that he shot a German soldier at close range, and displayed supreme courage by 'dashing and darting' between burning tanks to save wounded comrades. A coy and pretty Eshowe teenager of fifteen, she could not have imagined that she would one day marry him. Ten years her senior, he was sternly handsome, not given to display of emotion, and their courtship after the war turned into a feel-good fairy story for our village.

After their marriage (the entire community had been invited to the wedding) six children were born in quick succession. Dad became the stern patriarch enforcing austere English values on the boys with his army cane. The two girls were spared beatings; our gentle mother softening the Victorian parenting unit with boundless love and imagination. At bedtime she made up and told Fellican stories to six kids sleeping in a row, about a family of tree goblins who were hunted by the Black Witch. These were as exciting to Jeremy, the youngest at three, as to Jonathan, the oldest at eleven. Then bedtime prayers murmured together. "God bless Mum and Dad, Vi and Maurice, and all my brothers and sisters and all those we love. Help me to be a good boy/girl, and keep us all safe from harm. Amen." Then hugs and kisses all round and goodnight.

An early memory lands like a bird on a bough as I shift in the afternoon heat. I am ten. Mance, the dignified old farm nduna (foreman) has just died, and Dad suggests that I go with him to the traditional Zulu funeral. I feel honoured but am also anxious. The burial site is about a mile from home, and we walk there in silence.

A hole about four foot deep has been dug below some tall mdoni trees, near the old railway siding, where a group of keening Zulu women sway and support each other, wailing in the direction of a blanket-wrapped bundle. Mance's earthly remains. A dozen or so Zulu men wearing suits and ties welcome our arrival and open a space for us to join them, the only whites at the ceremony. Some take pains to nod at and acknowledge me, which makes me feel grown up and special. The men carry fighting sticks, some with spear and shield as well, which to me uniquely dignifies their formal Western attire. Two bare-chested men lean on spades behind a clump of rhus and tecomaria shrubs, towelling off sweat. Their grave-digging duties over, they change into dark suits.

I resist an urge to hold Dad's hand. I have never done this before and sense this will not be welcome. I am queasy in the presence of death, but also buoyed up with a morbid curiosity. Gazing at the blanket bundle down in the grave, I try to imagine old Mance's craggy face frozen in final expression. No other children are present, and I am mesmerised by the drama.

A Zulu priest dressed in white Zionist robes supervises the laying of a grass mat at the bottom of the hole, then carefully manhandles the blanketed corpse into a sitting position, facing east. He then climbs out the grave, with difficulty; he has a paunch and his pants are too tight. Then he reads a passage from a Zulu Bible. The women's keening from behind the circle of men grows louder.

To my surprise, I notice Dad is wiping tears from his cheeks. The men respond to a series of prompts with muttered Amens, then the priest respectfully invites Dad to speak. The keening drops to a faint moaning, and Dad speaks in fluent Zulu, his voice firm and low. I understand his simple message. Mance was a fine, honourable and proud man. I also recognise the words *inhlonipo* and *udumo* repeated many times, meaning respect and honour. The sombre gathering responds during Dad's eulogy with murmured affirmations of *kunjalo* (it is so) and Amen.

No tears or emotions are visible amongst the men, whilst the wailing and sobbing of the women waxes and wanes. Dad reaches into his pocket, pulls out a half-jack bottle of vodka and climbs into the grave. He places the bottle, together with an opened bag of Boxer tobacco, close to Mance's blanketed feet, and then leaps nimbly out of the hole. Others follow suit, placing gifts such as a walking stick, a bag, cigarettes, tobacco and matches alongside the body; all useful items for the long journey ahead. As if in an afterthought, Dad returns and places a further gift on the blanketed body – a round tin of snuff. Zulu men love clearing their heads with massive sneezes from snuff-taking, and I snigger inwardly at the thought of old Mance sneezing luxuriantly whilst journeying to the hereafter, bolstered by vodka, walking sticks and assorted tobacco treats. After the gift-laying the men take turns to shovel black soil into the grave with two spades. The rising earth swallows the upright corpse plus gifts. As we walk home, Dad puts his arm around my shoulders and explains the Zulu custom of providing final comforts for the journey to the hereafter. We share a laugh at the idea of a tipsy Mance enjoying those final pleasures. Dad's hand heavy on my shoulder leaves a lifelong impression.

Back to Dad's final journey. Awkwardly we stand around the open coffin. Jono, as the eldest, begins with clipped words about our dad being a fine man, an example and an inspiration to us all. Others are invited to speak and do, but our mumbled words are not memorable and have dissolved with time. One by one we file up to the open coffin, dropping rose petals from a bowl onto his chest. Mimi, the dog, watches each person's walk to the coffin intently, as if checking for bona fides. Last of all, his wife (of close to sixty years) steps up and drops petals with pained and contained dignity. Mum's triumph of understatement.

It is now the turn of the farm workers to pay respects. Ou Jan 'Toontjies,' the tractor driver, first walks up to the coffin and repeats the word *oubaas* a few times during his mumbled prayer. He places three loose cigarettes on Dad's chest. Dad had given up smoking for decades, but why not now? Jannie, the junior tractor driver, then shuffles forward. His prematurely wrinkled features contort as he carefully places a walking stick at Dad's elbow. Finally, Sydney, the stocky foreman, walks up to the coffin, his oval and muscular face sombre. After mumbling words at the reclining figure, he hauls a bulky object out from under his coat and places it deep in the coffin and out of sight.

Soon afterwards the lid closes, and our dad is delivered to the ovens.

Decades pass. I have by now practised law in Stellenbosch for thirty years. Sydney has grown old. Once beefy and imposing, he was Dad's right-hand man, and the two had grown unusually close. Diabetes has now claimed both his vigour and his eyesight, and he presents a pathetic figure sitting hunched in the sun at Miah's house. His once-powerful shoulders become bony, cherubic face now drawn and grey.

As I sit beside him, my mind returns to those moments at my dad's coffin. "Sydney," I ask, after reminding him of that afternoon, "wat presies het jy in Oubaas se doodkis daardie middag gesit?"(Sydney, what exactly did you put in Oubaas's coffin that afternoon?)

He thinks for a while. "Ja, ou Rog," a sweet smile slowly stretching his face. "Ek het eers vir Oubaas mooi dankie gesê, en dat ek hom so baie gaan mis. En toe sit ek langs hom in die doodkis 'n glas bottel met 'n klomp mooi heuningbye in. En ek sê vir hom, 'Oubaas, hierdie bye gan sam met Oubaas die hele pad na die hemel trêvel'" (I first thanked Oubaas nicely and told him I will miss him. Then I placed a glass bottle full of honeybees next to him in the coffin. And I told him, 'Oubaas these bees will travel with you all the way to heaven.')

"Oubaas was so lief vir sy bytjies," (Oubaas so loved his bees) Sydney murmured, his sightless eyes growing misty. "Ja, Sydney," I replied, "en dankie vir alles wat jy vir hom gedoen het. Hy was so mal oor sy bye." (Yes, Sydney. And thanks for everything you did for him. He was so mad about his bees). Like old Mance with his snuff and vodka, Dad had been well provided for in his final journey.

The sun sets, and Sydney and I clasp hands. I wonder what items will accompany our final journeys.

39

Don't Fence Me In: Winifred Gray

Eyes twinkle, wrinkled hands wave and tap as we sing that favourite old ballad, "Don't Fence Me In", exaggerating the American drawl in words like 'lookin' mighty pale', 'a-puttin' you in jail' and 'cottonwood trees'. At ninety-four years, my mother is demented, close to bedridden, and living with brother Jono and his Janey in the old farmhouse where she raised six children. She lives in one room, with photos of children and grandchildren against the walls – a far cry from the unfenced freedom glorified in our singing. "Gosh, Rog, isn't life amazing," she says, and repeats often, "You know, it all goes so fast." I marvel at the white hair, still an adornment on her once-striking face, eyes still bright as a fox. I hold the shrunken hands that used to serve aces on the Eshowe tennis courts, cooked countless meals, played timeless tunes on the piano, sewed name tags onto six sets of boarding school clothes. How to make sense of such a life as it nears closure?

Born Winifred Gray, Mum was a gifted athlete and student at Wykeham College in Pietermaritzburg, losing her father to a heart attack at age fifteen. In the same year, 1943, her mother sent her a tiny newspaper cutting from the *Zululand Times*, describing how a local Eshowe man, Guy Chennells, had won the Military Cross for outstanding bravery in the field. This Mum placed in her Bible, only to discover it many years later after she and the war hero were married.

In 1945, at an innocent seventeen years, she attended a party held at the Eshowe Royal Hotel to welcome home the town's returning servicemen, the 'boys'. No doubt the local lasses were a-twitter and dolled up at the prospect of meeting the town's own war heroes, handsome in their battledress. Soon after the party began the electricity failed, throwing the hotel and town into darkness, bringing an end to the music and thus to the dance.

As desperate organisers lit candles and lamps, word went out asking if anybody in the room could play the piano. Without hesitation young Winifred Gray stepped up, and within minutes was belting out a succession of wartime and sing-along ditties. "In the Mood", "The White Cliffs of Dover", "It's a Long Way to Tipperary", "She'll be Coming Round the Mountain" and suchlike. The room rocked all night. We can only imagine our fearless redhead mother saving the occasion, whilst my father leaned against a door getting quietly drunk, and feasting his eyes on the one he had chosen as his future wife. Ten years older than her, matured by five years of warfare, my dad was not only Victorian but also a formidable combination of shy and determined. Soon after introducing himself to Mum that first evening, he asked her for a dance and their old-fashioned courtship began. According to Mum when the music stopped after a few dances, his opening line of conversation was, "So, Winifred, what do you think about post-war reconstruction?"

He must have loosened up after that because soon they were engaged and what was to be a rare partnership was under way. In Eshowe, weddings were public events, and after an open advertisement in the *Zululand Times* virtually the entire town (over three hundred folk) showed up for an Anglican wedding and celebrations in a rugby-field-sized tent. Early pictures show them to be much in love, he serious and protective, she light and lively.

Dad ran the Chase Farm for his aged father Frank, whilst Mum produced child after child at intervals of eighteen months. Farmers place great value on productivity, be it of cows or crops, and when nine months were up Dad would take his wife on bumpy bakkie rides over ploughed fields, which always seemed to hasten the onset of labour. Six children were born in quick time, me coming in second.

Typhoid struck the rapidly growing family in 1957, and the four oldest, namely Jono, me, Sparks and Biddy, were rushed to Eshowe Hospital running raging fevers and hallucinating. Our condition worsened rapidly, and after ten days our doctor had no clue how to avert the inevitable. Our school prayed for us each day in assembly, though we were expected to die soon.

Despite the GP's protestations, Dad urgently obtained a second opinion from a Durban doctor named Adnams, who prescribed a new medication. Within a day the danger was over, and we returned to our active home life. Why some families are blessed as we were and others suffer with less lucky outcomes remains a mystery and cause for abiding gratitude. We proceeded with an intensely collective and boisterous childhood, where six children contended for space and attention, fighting with each other like primates whilst developing sibling bonds. One bedtime story would be told to six children in adjoining beds, all baths and meals shared, and a queue jostled every day outside the only toilet in the house. We often had friends around, when games like 'open gates, banana-ha' and 'kick tin trot' played until the light ran out.

"Rog, you and your creatures. Never a dull moment!" Mum smiles indulgently at me, eyes half closed. "What you put me through, looking after all your animals and snakes." I hold her minute hands and murmur thanks. The young seldom appreciate parents' implied sacrifice, and no doubt I had added greatly to their burden.

I was drawn in youth to an alternative drum beat, irresistibly fascinated by the natural world; by everything that flew, crawled or slithered. I wanted to keep them, know and study them, even skin and stuff them. What began as an interest evolved rapidly into an obsession, and by age ten, I was regarded in our family as being 'unusual' if not distinctly 'odd'. Disappearing for hours on end exploring wild places on the farm, I would return at day's end with birds' eggs, snakes or other creatures in a sack. In the room I shared with sports-mad Jono I housed assorted skulls, a stuffed leguaan, and sometimes a live creature. I enticed Zulu kids to bring in live frogs, snakes or birds, in exchange for peanut butter sandwiches. We went through jar by jar of peanut butter, to be sure, and soon there were boxes of snakes as well as cages with birds (wood owl, dikkop, Wahlberg's eagle, purple Loerie, hamerkop). These, as well as other animals (a bushpig, a bushbaby and Monty the monkey) all required daily care.

When we returned to school for two months at a time, I left strict instructions for Mum to feed the snakes, birds and animals which she did without complaint, paying the Zulu boys in peanut butter sandwiches for their daily supply. The frogs were first fed to the snakes, and then gruesome dishes of minced chickens and mice for the birds of prey. Mum's letters contained reports such as *"Today Rinky (the rinkhals spitting cobra) spat at me twice despite my giving him a fat frog, which looked most depressed as I tossed him into the box. The large grass snake is looking very fat, Rog, I am afraid he seems to have eaten at least five of the house snakes. Monty comes into the house every day to play the piano and make a nuisance of himself. The other pets are all fine and are looking forward to seeing you soon."*

Monty the monkey. Mum giggles when I remind her. "How could I forget Monty, Rog. What a handful!" she muses, smiling indulgently. Two Zulu boys who had kept him on a chain brought him in, tiny and bedraggled. After paying them off in the agreed peanut butter currency, I kept him in a warm box, fed him mainly fruit, and soon he became a playful part of family life, pure embodiment of the expression 'as cheeky as a monkey'. If we were playing cricket on the lawn, he stole the ball to get us to chase him; in the farmyard he jumped onto turkeys who charged around with him clinging on their backs and whooping like a cowboy, always checking that his audience was enjoying the sight. When we swam in the pool on hot days, Monty dived in dramatically and swam lengths underwater, or mimicked the girls sunbathing to score a laugh. He tormented our bullmastiff farm dogs mercilessly by tweaking their ears as they slept, and when they finally attacked him, snarling, he leaped lithely out of reach with hoots of glee.

Endlessly entertaining, a darker side emerged as Monty got older. His riding of the turkeys took on a distinctly sexual flavour, which Dad was the first to notice, with alarm. Clearly hormones were kicking in. Soon after that he swung by to visit Mum and a group of friends having tea on the porch. While Mum offered him a biscuit and told the story of how we had got Monty, he began doing something unusual whilst grimacing happily, showing his teeth.

"What IS the monkey doing, Win?" one of the friends asked, innocently. To their horror, he was energetically masturbating. This was embarrassing for my parents, in whose presence all mention of sex was taboo, and so the discussions about the misdemeanour took place without actually *naming* the deed. Monty's shares were dropping fast.

The last straw for my dad was when the monkey stole a box of Cuban cigars from the front seat of his friend Cecil Bircher's Mercedes, and carried it proudly to the top of the large fir tree. When Cecil and my dad discovered the theft, they first cursed and then begged the by-now excited Monty to descend with the prized delicacies. Spurred on by their frantic pleadings, he took each cigar out of its casing, then took great bites, spitting out chunks of prime tobacco which fluttered to the ground. The more the men below popped with anger, the more he chattered with glee and munched until the Cubans were history. Things were surely coming to a head.

"Gosh, I have never seen Cecil so cross," Mum chuckles. "And do you remember the garden club party, Rog?" She is alert again, her recollection is firing, initiating old memories. Which happens less and less. Back to Monty we go, and to the infamous 1964 Annual General Meeting of the Eshowe Garden Club.

My gran was proud Life President of this noble institution, and Mum the provider of tea, cakes and venue. Us kids were at school, far away. Twenty or more metal chairs had been arranged on the lawn for the annual event, each one close to the five festive tables laden with scones, cakes and tea. As the elderly and primly dressed members arrived, my gran in the lead, Mum gazed anxiously around the garden, hoping that Monty was otherwise engaged. He was nowhere in sight, so far, so good. After a tour of the garden to work up an appetite, the members then all sat on the chairs to await the highly anticipated highlight namely tea, cakes and a few speeches.

All wore colourful dresses, many adorned by the coiffured 'blue-rinse' hairdos of the day. As they settled down, chatting happily, Monty swung down from a tree and sidled by, ever inquisitive, immediately spotting potential for mischief. There was no warning for what was to follow. Leaping onto the shoulder of the closest portly matron, he first grabbed a handful of blue-grey hair, and gave a sharp tug. The result was spectacular. With a loud shriek, teacup and hot tea went flying, and she fell backwards in a tumble of skirts and stockinged shoes.

Energised by this response, Monty now sprinted between tables, a grey flash, leaping onto shoulders and wildly ruffling the hair of every person he could reach. Pandemonium erupted and soon half the ladies were on their backs screaming, some scalded by tea, most with hairdos messed up, all trying to escape the mayhem. Mum tried to lure Monty into the house with a bag of nuts, in vain. Only after the clamour became too much did Monty finally grab a biscuit and leap into the fig tree. Traumatised ladies were given smelling salts as they were helped to their cars, whilst others tottered towards the safety of the house. The aborted meeting is still discussed in Eshowe Garden Club folklore as the most exciting fiasco in their history.

"That party was the last straw," Mum adds. "Dad said finally that he simply *had* to go."

I start to remind her about how I let Monty join a wild troop of monkeys the very next holiday, but I can see that her mind is elsewhere. A cloud settles over her features at the mention of my dad, and she is processing something. After a long pause, she looks up and seems to see me as if for the first time. With a deep sigh, she then asks in a small voice. "Please tell me again, Rog, what happened to Guy"?

My dad, her husband of close to fifty years, died fifteen years ago, but latterly she calls on the memory of him more and more often. "Please remind me, how did Guy die?" Her face seems smaller and more crumpled. She knows that she *should* know what happened, but somehow her brain has become 'fuzzy', and clarity eludes her. Interesting that she now calls him Guy to me, and not Dad.

"Mum, as you know he died after a car accident. Remember, he was driving his bakkie and taking a hive of bees to a friend?"

"Really? How sad," she replies, tears forming in both eyes. She is still racking her brain, but recalls nothing of the death of her husband and life mate of half a century. None of the public and private funerals, the outpourings of support, or the weeks of family mourning and processing seem to be available in her memory.

"Remember, Mum. He was so badly injured by the accident. We visited him in hospital for three months, and at the end he just slipped away."

"How sad. I *do* miss him so. He was such a *brave* man, you know."

She slips deeper and deeper into her own thoughts, eyes half closed, her breathing laboured as she processes inner matters. I wonder what is going on in there, and if she might need help? How special though that she singles out bravery, amongst Dad's many other qualities, as his most memorable attribute.

As I am about to rise and leave her, she opens her eyes and starts to hum the words of her favourite song that we sang together the day before; "Do Not Forsake Me, Oh My Darling", in which Cary Grant announces the impending agony of parting to his sweetheart in the movie *High Noon*. And I know that I too must be gone. I join her in the song as she sings the words with perfect recall. Perhaps they will meet again, where there are no fences.

As I leave the room, my mother has returned to a world that I cannot access. Her eyes are closed, and a sad smile lingers.

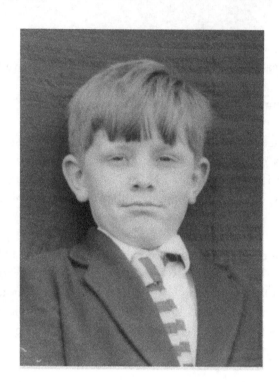

Left: The author, aged 8, Eshowe Primary School uniform.

Right: The author, aged 18, during first month of basic training at Valhalla Air Force Base, Pretoria.
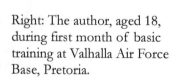

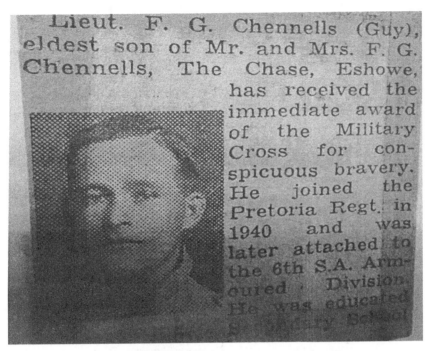

Lieut. F. G. Chennells (Guy), eldest son of Mr. and Mrs. F. G. Chennells, The Chase, Eshowe, has received the immediate award of the Military Cross for conspicuous bravery. He joined the Pretoria Regt. in 1940 and was later attached to the 6th S.A. Armoured Division. He was educated at Military School

Faded extract from the Zululand Times (1943). Winifred Gray (15) placed this in her Bible before she met Guy Chennells in 1945.

Chennnells family, 1966
Back L to R: Jeremy, Mark, Johnathan, Bridget.
Seated: Winifred, Guy, Jilly and Roger.

SWAZI FLAG INCIDENT 'REPRIMAND'

Mercury Reporter

Below: The Law Clerks Rugby team, 1976

PIETERMARITZBURG THREE local articled clerks who spent several days in a Swaziland gaol for stealing a Swazi flag at Mbabane last week will be reprimanded for their behaviour, the Natal Law Society decided yesterday.

Mr. Olivier Hart, president of the society, said the matter was now considered closed.

The three men are due to qualify as attorneys later this week.

"PORKY" HARTLEY, "JINKS" BLANKENBERG
"PINETREE" SCOTT, SPENCE TARR, "GASPER" GEMMELL
RICH FINDLAY, "MURMER" MICHAU, TREV PERRY, "IRISH" O'CONOR,
HARRY BROWN, "THEORY" REID, "CLINT" SEYMOUR, "STROPPY" BOYES
"DUP" DU PLESSIS, ROG CHENNELLS

Roger, an Aboriginal leader from Fregon, Pitantjatjara lands, Central Australia.

San leader Dawid Kruiper entertaining around the camp fire with a story about a Brontosaurus.

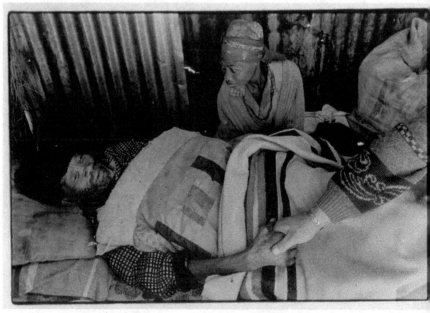

Patriarch Regopstaan Kruiper, during the author's last visit.
Photo by Paul Weinberg.

Left:
Buks Kruiper, the hunter.

ight: The author and
awid Kruiper discussing
e San land claim.

Dawid Kruiper finally meeting with Minister Derek Hanekom at the village of Welkom, Kalahari, 1998.

Deputy President Thabo Mbeki with San leaders Dawid Kruiper and Petrus Vaalbooi after the land claim ceremony at Molopo, Kalahari, 21 March 1999.

Above and below: Some leaders of the Jamaican Rastafari Temples who invited the author to Jamaica, 2007.

"Professor" Nemarude, wise woman elder
of the Ramunangi Venda clan.

The author doing an impromptu version of the *Stulumazambane* (potato stew) war dance, 2010.

LAST WORD

40

The Ingwavuma/Swaziland Case

In May 1982, the tiny Durban law firm Chennells Albertyn, founded earlier that year, comprising Chris Albertyn and me as lawyers, plus a secretary and messenger, received urgent instructions from the chief ministers of the KwaZulu and Kangwane governments to stop a government backroom deal, namely the ceding to Swaziland of a massive portion of South Africa, including beautiful Kosi Bay in the northern part of KwaZulu known as Ingwavuma.

President PW Botha was the iron-fisted ruler of the beleaguered apartheid government at the time, with Pik Botha as his long-standing foreign minister and MC Botha as Minister of Cooperation and Development. A true Bothastan! Plus, the famous Piet 'promises' Koornhof, Minister of Black Affairs, was deeply involved. After plotting in secret with emissaries of King Sobhuza II, the government hatched a plan to unilaterally cede to Swaziland the Ingwavuma region of KwaZulu and the whole of Kangwane homeland, thereby providing that landlocked country with a broad corridor to the sea and to the natural harbour of Kosi Bay. In exchange, a grateful Swaziland would commit to supporting South Africa at the United Nations, where friends were few.

No consultation took place with the many thousands of South Africans that were, with the stroke of a pen, destined to become Swazi citizens, nor with the purportedly independent governments of the two affected homelands. Chiefs Gatsha Buthelezi and Enos Mabuza of the KwaZulu and Kangwane homeland governments instructed us with great urgency. Chris Albertyn had been referred to Chief Buthelezi as a lawyer who could be trusted, and he knew me through his long-term friendship with my father.

Government Gazette proclamations R108 and 109/82 had in classic apartheid-style been unilaterally issued the previous week in order to give effect to the secret deal; the first abolishing the Kangwane general assembly, and the second, ceding the entire KwaZulu region of Ingwavuma to Swaziland. Issuing these proclamations without knowledge or approval from the governments of the purportedly 'sovereign nations' they affected was not only an insult to these homelands, but would have the effect of literally transferring thousands of citizens to the Kingdom of Swaziland – typical bullying behaviour from the formidable apartheid government. (I am reminded of the two powerful opponents in Malcolm Gladwell's book *David and Goliath;* that the very same qualities that appear to give them strength are often the source of great weakness.)

Our modest task was to stop the entire deal.

Chris took the lead, assembling a formidable team consisting primarily of advocates Doug Shaw QC, David Gordon SC and Malcolm Wallis. Central to our fighting the case was the fact that the eleven apartheid homelands fell under the National States Constitution Act[19] (1971) (NSCA), the cornerstone of apartheid homelands and the policy of separate development. The NSCA provided for three stages of development: 1. legislative assembly (Kangwane), 2. self-government status (KwaZulu) and 3. independence (Transkei, Bophuthatswana, Venda and Ciskei). Each stage entailed certain rights and duties from the government, which, in our opposition to the deal, we would prove had been fatally breached.

On the first Friday afternoon after the proclamations, we launched our first urgent application in front of three judges (Shearer, Didcott and another) arguing that the SA government was obliged to consult the legislative assembly of KwaZulu, which they had not done. It was decided in our favour by the Durban and Coast Local Division firstly, that the KwaZulu Legislative Assembly had *locus standi* to make the application, and secondly that proclamation 109 was *ultra vires,* ie null and void.[20] The proclamation was duly set aside with the result that Ingwavuma was reinstated as part of KwaZulu for the weekend. Our relief was short-lived.

On the following Monday morning, and with alacrity that showed the urgency from government side, the State President issued a fresh proclamation R121. This one was however issued in terms of the Black Administration Act (1924) (BAA), again purporting to remove

Ingwavuma from KwaZulu. In terms of the BAA, the State President had absolute powers to do whatever he wanted for the administration of the black population, including the government bypassing the NSCA. We brought a second urgent application.

Our team put forward a creative argument devised by Malcolm Wallis, namely that the BAA had been *pro tanto* (ie to the degree shown) repealed by the 1971 legislation, the NSCA, to the extent there was any conflict between the two. The Law, we argued, is deemed to intend the necessary impact of any subsequent legislation upon earlier legislation when there is a conflict between them. So, notionally the SA Parliament, when passing the later NSCA, was deemed to know and intend that the effect of that legislation was to effectively repeal the absolute powers of the State President under the BAA, to the extent that different provisions were created in the NSCA. This novel argument succeeded, and we won again in front of a three-judge bench.

Round two to us![21] Again, the relief was of very short duration.

The government immediately took the case on appeal directly to the Appellate Division, and we applied for an interim injunction in order to restore the status quo of Ingwavuma and its citizens, pending the outcome of the appeal. To the best of our knowledge, precious few residents of Ingwavuma or Kangwane knew what was at stake, or of the desperate legal sparring taking place in the distant lofty heights of the Supreme Court.

Due to the urgency of the case, from the government's perspective, the Appellate Division (the then ultimate court of appeal) agreed to hear the case in the record time of three months. We travelled to Bloemfontein to hear the case, knowing the government would throw everything at us in its determination to succeed. Chief Justice JP Rumpff presided with a full Appellate Division bench.

After an entire day of argument, during which it became increasingly apparent that the judges were concerned about a large chunk of South Africa being unilaterally ceded to Swaziland, the government's appeal was dismissed, and our case conclusively won, with costs. Ingwavuma was fully restored to South Africa, which should have put the entire matter to bed.

PW Botha was however not one to accept legal defeat.

After its resounding defeat in the Appellate Division, the government appointed Chief Justice FLR Rumpff[22] as chair of a commission in order to deflect further fall-out from their failed attempts, and to further investigate the issue. Several articles appeared in the press about the government's misguided dalliance with Swaziland, but in my view daily newspapers underreported the case. As a result, the entire drama that had taken place in the courts was relatively unknown to ordinary citizens. Altruistic reasons were now proffered by the government as motivations for the deal, including reference to the injustice of the fixing of the Swaziland border in the late 19th century, and the longed-for repatriation of tribes who showed more allegiance to Swaziland than to South Africa. Pik Botha persuasively motivated the inherent justice of the deal based upon correcting historical wrongs, namely the drawing of the Swaziland boundary to exclude the Swazi-speaking people in the south.

Our research showed that the presence of Swazi-aligned citizens in South Africa had indeed simmered throughout the 19th Century, and in 1880 a government commission had been set up to investigate. A magistrate from Eshowe had travelled to the Ingwavuma area and had pronounced that from his investigations the tribes in the area indeed owed allegiance to Swaziland. In 1884 Swaziland was then pronounced a 'protected dependency' of the Transvaal republic, but in 1903 after the Anglo-Boer War, was taken over again by Britain as a Protectorate.[23] Modern apartheid reasoning, which insisted on altruistically imposing self-determination on ethnic groupings without first obtaining their approval, continued to pervade the entire exercise.

Finally, the government accepted defeat. On 19 June 1984 Minister MC Botha formally announced that Ingwavuma and Kangwane would not be unilaterally incorporated into Swaziland, thereby closing the door on the sorry saga. The Rumpff Commission ceased to function, and the entire Swaziland project fizzled to an end.

This was the first major case for our small firm, as a result of which the government treated us with much more respect, and we were placed more firmly 'on the map'. The credit for this David vs Goliath saga belonged entirely to my partner, Chris Albertyn, who was the leader of the case and of the strong team that put the senior advocates of the

269

government to the sword. For some years afterwards, our firm continued to do work for the KwaZulu and KaNgwane governments until this began to clash with our primary loyalty to COSATU unions and the African National Congress, and so we amicably parted ways.

Times have changed regarding litigation costs. Our entire fee, for two years of arduous work for two homeland governments, harrowing conditions, countless hours, forests of paperwork and repeated court challenges involved in successfully defeating the South African government, was the sum of R60 000.

For a short while, we felt rich.

41

The !Khomani San Land Claim

On 21 March 1999, Thabo Mbeki, sharing a stage with Dawid Kruiper and Petrus Vaalbooi at the Molopo Lodge in the Kalahari, announced the transfer of 40 000 hectares of land to the !Khomani San.[24] Sitting in the sun on plastic chairs, more than three hundred members of the San community listened attentively. Nearby, stood the black helicopter which had brought the (then) Deputy President of the country to the ceremony to mark the conclusion of the San land claim – the end of the journey that had commenced with Ou Regopstaan at Kagga Kamma in 1992. I had a lump in my throat throughout the ceremony, whilst community members expressed their joy with singing and dancing. If only Regopstaan, original clan leader and Dawid Kruiper's father, could have witnessed this day.

In 1990 when the Kruiper family moved to Kagga Kamma farm as part of a tourism venture, the San were generally regarded as all but 'extinct' in South Africa. While their rock art in the Drakensberg and Cederberg mountain ranges was acknowledged, the hunter-gatherer nation that had predated all other people on the continent was little known in South Africa. History lessons in schools described the San as noble hunter-gatherers living close to nature in skins, little knowing that they still existed in pockets and on the fringes of society. The stories in this collection offer some personal accounts of the San and their land claim. What follows is a brief overview covering the people, the process, the law, the land claimed, the negotiations, and the outcome of the formal claim lodged with the Department of Land Affairs in January 1995, and concluded on 21 March 1999.

The people

The San people, also referred to generally as well as by themselves as Bushmen, are the most iconic and well researched of all hunter-gatherers. Popular accounts focus on their near supernatural hunting and tracking skills, complex rock art and peaceful, non-materialistic cultures. They number about 100 000 in Southern Africa, speak at least seven entirely distinct languages, and live mostly in far-flung rural communities across Namibia, Botswana, South Africa, Angola and Zimbabwe.[25] The development of San organisations in Southern Africa during the 1990s took place during a period of renewed interest in and respect for indigenous peoples internationally, reflected in the United Nations Decade of Indigenous Peoples (1995 to 2004.)

After I'd met the Kruiper family at Kagga Kamma, I contacted an anthropologist Professor HP Steyn who, together with his student LJ Botha, had assembled unpublished research on the Kruiper clan, which they described as a combination of the N/amani and !Khomani language groups (the Southern Kalahari San). This valuable research enabled me to better understand the origins and make-up of the San community.

One of our first tasks was to track the diaspora so that as many San as possible could participate in their historic and once-only South African land claim. With the help of anthropologists Nigel Crawhall, Hugh Brody and Bill Kemp, family trees were charted, tracing the names and details of San scattered far and wide. Hugh Brody filmed many of the interviews, now recorded in a massive body of work, "Tracks Across Sand." This contains 16 films and 4.5 hours of interviews tracking fifteen years from commencement of the case.

Among the countless highlights of this rare documentation of a hunter-gatherer community's struggle and progress towards owning their traditional land was an interview with Ouma Elsie Vaalbooi. This 95-year-old matriarch (and mother of Petrus Vaalbooi) was discovered to still speak the N/uu language fluently, officially declared extinct fifteen years earlier. This led to the discovery of Ouma /Una Rooi and at least twenty other San who still spoke the ancient language, providing poignancy and energy to the cultural revival. At the time of writing, there is a thriving N/uu language school in Upington run by Ouma Katrina, which teaches the language to San youngsters.

The process
As a lawyer my first instincts were to understand the nature and size of my client community. This required us to hold meetings, elect committees, ask questions, reduce everything to writing. Budgets,

targets, names and addresses of applicants were recorded and logged in my file which rapidly grew as high as a sand dune.

In reality, things were far less linear. One of the stories in this collection – Rotman, a Minister and an Arrow – recounts my first meeting with the San in a Kagga Kamma cave under the influence of marijuana. This encounter included a large rat and lists many people as 'present' who were no longer on earth. The views of the ancestors needed to be taken into account; something I did not learn at law school. Not one of my clients had email, let alone a cellphone, and many of their addresses simply listed a rural region. Punctuality was a non-starter, and many important meetings were accompanied by the powerful whiff of the dagga-Boxer-tobacco combination.

In the words of Hugh Brody, "Such people don't like schedules and decide what they are going to do while they are doing it, and are in some sense disorganised whilst being highly organised underneath." The boundaries that segment the Northern Kalahari had been drawn millennia after the San had roamed the vast region; the San communities ignored these national borders as many lived in Namibia and Botswana.

And a final challenge to the legal team – the San leader Oom Dawid Kruiper was a classic trickster, which meant that he followed spirit over reason, could only be relied upon to do the unexpected, and ensured that the words 'a San plan' became a frustrating oxymoron. Wise yet unpredictable. Intelligent behind a childlike innocence, a storyteller and poet. He would have giggled to find out that the Upington municipality is now named after him.

Once every month a trip was made from Kagga Kamma to the Kalahari, where meetings were held under trees and in shacks to process the enormous transformation being envisaged. After millennia of living lightly on the earth, discriminated against for their lack of ambition or success, and owning nothing, the San were preparing to become one of the largest landowners of the Kalahari where they would be masters of their own destiny.

The implications were hard to process. No more being endlessly displaced or chased off land by powerful owners, or being harassed for having nowhere to stay. In preparation for collective management of their farms, committees needed to be elected to represent families and communities, and office bearers needed to fulfil new roles such as chairperson, secretary, treasurer and spokesperson.

I became aware of the distinction drawn by anthropologists between societies on the basis of how they exercise power in their daily lives. For example, in agricultural or pastoral societies, such as most African tribes, a steep hierarchy is accepted. The chiefs wield enormous power over various rungs of status below them, according to ancient rules. These members become accustomed to strong leadership, where known chiefs give orders and expect compliance.

Hunter-gatherer societies, such as the San, operate differently. In small extended family groupings, leadership is usually related to one or other area of excellence (hunting, dancing, gathering, medicinal knowledge) and everyone is regarded as pretty much equal. Every single person's opinion counts. Sometimes after chaotic meetings, where each voice needed to be heard and nobody would take orders from anybody else, I pondered the term 'zen anarchists' to describe my independently minded San clients. After much debate, consensus was usually reached on important issues, and we moved forwards.

The law

In countries such as Canada, Australia and the USA, court cases claiming land on behalf of First Nations sought to establish 'aboriginal title' to the land, in other words the acknowledged ownership of ancestral territories which pre-dated the arrival of colonial powers. In a succession of cases, (the Mabo[26] case in Australia is one of the best known), indigenous peoples were required to prove prior occupation of their territories as well as an unbroken connection to the land via their laws, traditions and customs. The Mabo case finally overturned and discredited the colonial doctrine of *terra nullius*, which conveniently claimed that land occupied by tribal peoples was 'empty', belonging to nobody, and therefore ripe for annexation.

Proving aboriginal title in South Africa would have been difficult for technical reasons but the Restitution of Land Rights Act (1994), the same year as the first democratic election and Mandela becoming the first president, provided an effective framework for the !Khomani San claim.

In terms of this Act we were required to prove firstly that the land claimed was occupied and owned by the !Khomani, and secondly that they had been dispossessed as a result of a racially based or discriminatory law. On the latter aspect, the claim stated:

> In 1931 the Kalahari Gemsbok National Park was proclaimed, which had enormous implication for the Bushmen then living within the park boundaries. A process of evictions took place which continued until they had all been moved to Welkom outside the park.

One legal difficulty I faced was that the !Khomani San, along with First Nations and indigenous peoples worldwide, frame their relationship with ancestral land as one of 'belonging to', rather than 'ownership of'. As described earlier in this book, they would run the red sand through their fingers, describing how the sand represented their forefathers, and to which they would one day return. The word ownership implying strict boundaries and exclusion, made no sense as their culture simply recognises the land as their source of life and metaphorical 'mother.' In the formal land claim document, we described the San rights to land ownership in this way:

> The San claim rights to the land in terms of 'aboriginal title', being "land occupied in terms of a received system of law", in addition to the principles of the Restitution Act as well as the South African Constitution.

Acknowledging the unique nature of the San claim, as well as the competing interests of other landowners including the South African National Parks, we proposed an *extra-curial* or non-court process to balance the equities, rights and interests involved. Minister Derek Hanekom, who headed the Department of Land Affairs, committed himself to address the claim of the San. After a process of evaluation, he formally acknowledged the validity of the claim in January 1997, and instructed negotiations to commence.

The land claimed

The task was to claim, clearly and assertively, rights over land that the San 'belonged to' and had roamed over and utilised for millennia. Whilst Bushman groups traditionally identify themselves with specific territories, unlike Western owners, they never excluded other groups from sharing the resources. In addition, they migrated freely within their territories depending upon herd migrations, rains, availability of seasonal food, water supplies. In the words of the patriarch Regopstaan Kruiper, "us Bushmen cannot stay in one place. If we live with the tsamma melons, we eat them up, and then must move. If we live with the gemsbok, we eat them up, and then must move."

After referring to and comparing many theories and analyses of territories San peoples occupied and used, we finally arrived at this formula:

> In summary, the territory of the Bushmen of the Southern Kalahari, estimated from not only historical data but also from the empirical research referred to above, probably covered an area of approximately 4000 square kilometres, centering on the southern area of the Kalahari Gemsbok National Park and extending into the dune-land to the west which is presently part of the Mier reserve.

The San claimed farmland outside the park to settle the community as well as permanent cultural rights in the massive Kalahari Gemsbok National Park. We aimed to secure the massive area of land as described on the claim, so the next task was to negotiate with the Mier, SAN Parks and the government.

Negotiations

The unschooled and regularly overwhelmed San committee engaged with the often antagonistic representatives of government, SAN Parks and Mier, in order to secure an acceptable outcome. In about 1997 the residents of the Mier 'Coloured' reserve, largely descendants of the Baster leader, Vilander, who had settled south-west of the park, had also lodged a land claim. This to an extent clashed with the San and was to be negotiated simultaneously.

Kobus Pienaar from Legal Resources Centre, a trusted and passionate ally, was the lawyer for the Mier. The stakes and therefore tensions often ran high, whilst in meeting after meeting the San were required to respond to positions, views and arguments presented by others to limit their claim. SAN Parks, referred to metaphorically as the 'Lion' in our private meetings, was opposed to our claim for a share of the KGN Park, and remained more committed to its mission of animal conservation rather than an arrangement that included the San as part of the park. Elna Hirshfield was a passionate representative of the then Department of Land Affairs, and Bertus du Plessis represented the South African National Parks. In order to assist parties with the process, experienced mediators, firstly, Chris Spies and then later Dawie Bosch, were appointed, providing essential and skilled assistance to the parties. The South African San Institute (SASI) headed by MJ Wildschut supported the entire San team throughout the case.

In our meetings the San became steadily more confident and persuasive, Dawid Kruiper's trickster leadership combining well with the passionate activism of the chairperson Petrus Vaalbooi and his assistant Andries Steenkamp. Four years after lodging the San claim, and an exhausting process of often antagonistic negotiations, agreement was finally reached which awarded the San six large farms near Molopo, 28 000 hectares in the south of the park subject to conservation rules, and heritage rights over 4000 square kilometres of the Kalahari Gemsbok National Park (later renamed as the Kgalagadi Transfrontier Park).

Conclusion
At the 1999 Molopo Lodge ceremony, Thabo Mbeki, Petrus Vaalbooi and Dawid Kruiper made passionate speeches, all emphasising the historic nature of the event. Ouma /Una, at eighty-five years still the most eloquent of the rediscovered N/u speakers, was given the mic and spoke passionately of how their culture and language had remained buried, for so many decades, under the red sand. The San, victims of centuries of dispossession, had now become the largest communal landowners in the Kalahari, and Regopstaan's dream was to be finally realised. The rains would come, and they did. When the dust of the celebrations died down, the !Khomani San would start the process of learning to manage and enjoy the fruits of their very own land.[27]

Oupa Regopstaan, wherever he was, would surely have smiled.

42

Rooibos, Traditional Knowledge & the San

"Shops? We had no shops. Nature was our shop. And the old people knew what plant to use for every sickness." This was the San's explanation of traditional knowledge (TK) which over the last three decades has become the focal point of appreciation of indigenous peoples and their value to humankind.

In 1992 the Convention for Biological Diversity (CBD) was approved by 196 State parties, an overwhelming consensus of Nations, establishing a global pact for protecting Life on earth and its value for humans. The third of its three objectives[28] (to share the benefits of Biodiversity more fairly) proposed measures to protect traditional knowledge, and to compensate the indigenous owners of TK where such knowledge was commercially used. This provision required benefit-sharing and brought about a global revolution which exploded amongst the San people of the remote Kalahari.

In March 2001, I received a phone call late one night. It was Anthony Barnett from *The Observer* newspaper in the UK. "Mr Chennells," he began, plummy voice over a bad line, "I believe you are the lawyer for the San people?" I assured him that was correct. "How can that be, as I gather from reliable sources that the San tribe is extinct?" I suggested that his sources were flawed and invited him to kindly explain further. Pfizer, the pharmaceutical giant, had that day announced their new weight-reduction Hoodia Project in a press release. In the article, Pfizer had stated that the San people, from whom the original knowledge of hoodia was obtained, were extinct. I thanked Barnett for this information and made two late-night phone calls to the Kalahari. The San challenge of the Pfizer Hoodia deal had begun.

Pfizer had purchased a weight-loss patent from the South African Council for Scientific and Industrial Research (CSIR) code named P57, based upon the active ingredient of a strange plant named *Hoodia gordonii*, a thorny cucumber-like succulent of the Kalahari. The San had used hoodia for centuries to reduce their appetite while on long hunting trips. This was going to be Pfizer's next blockbuster drug (their most recent had been Viagra). Part of their objective was to make untold wealth from their new drug, aimed at fighting the obesity epidemic in the Western world, with no intention of acknowledging let alone sharing benefits with the original providers of the TK. The San's knowledge had clearly been the source of the patent, even if it had not been physically 'stolen', making the CBD principles relating to fair sharing of benefits directly applicable. The Pfizer/CSIR[29] deal was at loggerheads with the CBD, and we needed to stop it.

San leaders from South Africa, Namibia and Botswana were divided on many issues, but united on the need to protect their heritage rights. They disliked meetings and normally I had difficulty holding their attention for more than an hour or two. But when heritage was discussed, every eye in the room sparkled. It was and became personal. And so in March 2001 the South African San Council was formally constituted, with a mandate from their Namibia and Botswana colleagues to challenge the P57 patent. This meant fighting the largest pharma company in the world, including the CSIR.

Fortuitously, I had studied Intellectual Property Law for an LLM at the London School of Economics twenty years earlier, never dreaming that this knowledge would become crucial in enabling our tiny team to challenge the giants. The San leaders, wise in the ways of Nature, were babes in the wood when it came to matters such as intellectual property law, contracts and international law (such as the CBD). So, my first task was to put them on a crash course of all the relevant knowledge stated above, whilst also consolidating our own knowledge of hoodia. My ambition was that the San, rather than their lawyer Rotman, should be able to confidently articulate all the issues. It was fascinating during this process to discover from San elders that *gaap* (as hoodia was called) was not only used as a hunger suppressant, but was also a prized aphrodisiac. Many informants giggled as they provided this information, whilst confirming its veracity. We decided to keep this surprising fact to ourselves however, not wanting Pfizer nor the public to confuse issues of obesity with the cure for a fading libido.

From my desk, the San objected by letter to the CSIR's P57 patent on the grounds that there had been no 'prior informed consent' from the holders of the TK. Note that if we could show in court that the San knowledge pre-dated the patent, (which it clearly did), in other words that the P57 patent was therefore not an 'invention' or 'a novel step', then the CSIR patent would be rejected, and the entire deal thus invalidated. South Africa had at the time not yet enacted legislation to put the CBD into law, so we had to proceed in a legal vacuum, whilst guided by the benefit-sharing principles of the CBD.

The CSIR responded to my letter with surprising humility, apologising for the oversight in keeping their patent from the San, and suggesting (in a manner close to pleading) that the San should negotiate with them rather than challenge the P57 in court. Encouraged by my belief that alternative dispute resolution is always preferable to litigation, the San agreed to forego litigation, and to enter negotiations. Relief! I did not relish facing up against the huge legal department and deep pockets of Pfizer and the CSIR. We agreed to meet the CSIR in Pretoria. The San's earlier training would now be tested. The San leaders' natural ability, enhanced by the crash course, contributed to their engaging with business managers, scientists, doctors and other learned types; the process being guided by the question, "What would be a fair share to compensate the San peoples for their traditional knowledge of hoodia?"

In March 2003, after a roller-coaster process of negotiations, the historic hoodia deal was finally struck, providing the San with a percentage of the royalty proceeds as agreed to in the contract. Petrus Vaalbooi, the then leader of the San Council, signed the final benefit-sharing agreement along with the Minister of Science and Technology at Molopo Lodge (scene of the 1999 land claim celebrations as well as of the angry lion incident years before). The hoodia agreement was announced and celebrated as an internationally important pioneering benefit-sharing case under the CBD.

Over the next decade hundreds of articles, books and PhDs were published on the agreement, regarding it as the benchmark for a 'partnership' between indigenous people and modern science. Sadly, over the next decade the hoodia trajectory faltered and the dream faded. Pfizer withdrew, for unknown reasons, with Unilever taking over the worldwide patent rights. Soon thereafter scientific tests indicated health problems with the weight-loss formulations, leading to a decision by Unilever to shelve their advanced plans to use hoodia in a slimming snack bar. Depressingly, for those willing it on, by 2010 the entire hoodia industry collapsed, underscoring the difficulty of making a commercial success from a natural medicine. Nevertheless, the hoodia saga taught the San team so much.

Over the years that followed the San were contacted by companies wishing to trade in medicines made by means of their traditional knowledge, using indigenous plants such as Buchu, Aloe, Pelargonium, Sceletium, Devil's claw, Honeybush and Rooibos. South Africa had promulgated the Biodiversity Act in 2004, which set out requirements for benefit-sharing agreements, and the Environmental Affairs Department oversaw matters with increasing efficiency. With my ongoing support, the San leaders became increasingly competent in the field, negotiating agreements in relation to several of the above indigenous plants.

During all this time however, the mother and father of all indigenous plant-based industries, the burgeoning *Rooibos Industry*, hovered over our heads untouched and untouchable, like a dark aromatic cloud. About three hundred and fifty farmers grow the rooibos plant, employing five thousand people, producing fifteen thousand tons per year, which is processed and largely exported around the world as the iconic health tea, together with other health products. Annual turnover of rooibos products is estimated at fifty million USD.

It was never disputed that traditional knowledge identifying rooibos as a healing plant and tea had been obtained from San people, but this had taken place well over a century back. More recently, Tryntjie Swarts, for example, was a local Khoi woman from the Cederberg, who in the 1920s had shared her knowledge about rooibos seed being stored in ant nests. Local academic, Rachel Wynberg, supported us with information and shared her considerable knowledge of the industry. Many international 'experts' however believed that like tobacco, coffee, potatoes and other natural products too much time had elapsed since the transfer of knowledge, placing rooibos traditional knowlege squarely in the 'public domain' which meant the intellectual property rights belonged to all. According to the experts, rooibos did not fall under the CBD and its implementing framework, the Nagoya Protocol. The criticism of my advising the San on their rooibos claim hinted at a serious lack of intelligence and/or integrity, which of course stung me personally.

I pondered long on this issue, spurred on by the wise words of my law principal and first boss, Oliver James. "Remember, boy. Law is meant to be *logical*. If something feels wrong, there should be a logical, legal remedy." (I called him Betjane, meaning Black Rhino, due to a prickly disposition and a reluctance to give praise.) Even local friends and colleagues poured cold water on my idea of claiming San rights to rooibos, quoting the reasoning listed above. Mining a stubborn vein of self-belief that has flourished all too seldom in my career, and with the full backing of the San Council, I drafted a letter to the Minister of Environment Affairs in August 2010 setting out the San claim to a share of the Rooibos industry in terms of the Biodiversity Act 2008. The legal argument that I submitted, in contradiction of the experts and following the logical approach, was that in the law of Equity there is no time limit for wrong doing. If valuable knowledge was taken, without permission, it matters not whether the unfair transaction happened one year or one century earlier. The wrongfulness has no expiry date. In addition, whether the rooibos was turned into soap, tea or complex healing compounds, the traditional knowledge was the proximate cause of its discovery, and the enrichment of the rooibos industry, without compensation for that knowledge, was unfair. A legal remedy was therefore required to mitigate the unfairness. My old boss would have smiled wryly, and perhaps have even squeezed out a 'Well done, boy!'

For three years little progress was made. The powerful rooibos leaders refused to engage, denying that the San and Khoi had any legitimate TK rights under the Act, and the government dilly-dallied and fretted over this new hot potato. In 2013 the San invited the Khoi peoples,[30] who are genetically related to the San and similarly holders of rooibos traditional knowledge, to join the San claim for restitution of their TK rights.

In order to avoid the splitting and disunity experienced by indigenous peoples in other countries, a negotiating pact was reached, confirming equal representation, and equal splitting of any proceeds between San and Khoi. Lesley Jansen from Natural Justice provided legal support to the National Khoisan Council, which was chaired by Cecil le Fleur. The San Council was legally supported by me, with Collin Louw the chairperson. The government appointed a panel of experts to investigate the validity of the San claim, and the government-appointed technical report headed "Traditional Knowledge associated with rooibos and honeybush species in South Africa" came out in 2014, confirming that the San and the Khoi were sole holders of traditional knowledge about rooibos. The scene was finally set for negotiations.

The rooibos bosses finally came to meet us, sullen and defensive. With a pin-striped lawyer in tow from the largest law firm in the country, they made no secret of their frustration at being forced to the table. No doubt our own teams were equally annoying, being assertive, bordering on aggressive, plus claiming moral high ground in the matter. The Department as facilitator tried hard not to show bias towards either side, and mostly succeeded. The worst and the best of negotiations commenced. Some called on higher powers via rousing opening prayers, and then would bully, bluff, lose tempers, make rash statements, cry foul or claim moral high ground as required. Both sides used these tricks and more. In addition, during breaks over tea, jokes were inevitably shared, common ground emerged and relationships were forged with individuals from opposing teams, which were to prove crucial when, years later, we finally got closer to the nitty gritty of an agreement. Primary topics of debates were, "Why did the San and Khoi deserve a levy from the suffering rooibos farmers? If they did, where exactly in the economic chain (from farmer to retailer) should such a 'tax' be levied on rooibos? How much would be fair? How could any fund be protected from corruption?" As the relationships bore fruit more positive questions came onto the agenda such as, "Could the agreement be of benefit to rooibos?" and "How can the parties better collaborate into the future?"

Year after year we negotiated, meeting every one or three months. Highs, lows, disappointments, ugly fights, relieved make-ups followed like erratic seasons. Books could be filled. Some of the key role players are acknowledged here.[31] Eventually, sneaking up on us, almost unexpectedly, we were suddenly ripe and ready. On 25th March 2019[32] the Rooibos Agreement was struck. Noted globally as a breakthrough and iconic agreement, much like the hoodia one fifteen years earlier, this had a solid economic basis. Not a peep was heard from all those who had initially and so loudly denounced the validity of the claim. The agreement was formally celebrated at !Khwa ttu on 15 September 2019 with a huge celebration where the Minister of Environment, Forestry and Fisheries, Barbara Creecy, proudly announced it to the world. Grateful speeches were made by all parties. Feasting and dancing followed. I hugged the pin-striped lawyer as well as rooibos leaders with whom swords had been crossed, and, of course, my own client/friends. It was going to bring an estimated fifteen million rand to the San and Khoi in the first year, which would surely raise serious challenges going forward. But these problems lay in the future, for other persons and another day. Right now, it was glorious to look back at a flavourful nine-year brew, resulting in an agreement that would produce fruits into the unknown future.

The Rooibos Agreement was fittingly my swan song, my final legal challenge on behalf of the San. And every sip of Rooibos tea makes me smile, as a few more cents plop into that deserved and aromatic pot!

What more could I ask for?

Endnotes

1

Convention for a Democratic South Africa.

2

Slang for magistrate.

3

The refrain from Asimbonanga by Savuka:
Asimbonanga--------------------(we have not seen him)
Asimbonang' uMandela thina-----(we have not seen Mandela)
Laph'ekhona--------------------(in the place where he is)
Laph'ehleli khona--------------(in the place where he is kept)

4

Name changed to preserve privacy.

5

The process was called CODESA.

6

Myalgic Encephalomyelitis.

7

Scotty's Fort is a 4000-hectare farm named after one of its early owners Scottish-born Kalahari bandit Scotty Smith, a local 'Robin Hood' who tormented local government officials at the turn of the century.

8

The linguist Professor Tony Traill had declared the language to be extinct, meaning there were no known speakers, more than twenty years previously.

9 Name changed to preserve privacy.

10

!Ngate Xgamxebe, the Bushman tracker, in the documentary *The Great Dance*.

11

Bushman prisoner in *A Story Like the Wind* by Laurens van der Post.

12

The UN Declaration on the Rights of Indigenous Peoples was concluded in 2008, and remains a cornerstone of Indigenous rights in the world. Reference. www.undrip.un.gov

13

The World Intellectual Property Organization is one of the 15 specialised agencies of the United Nations.

14

Australian Aboriginals use the word 'mob' broadly to mean family or community group.

15

Aboriginal slang for friend or 'mate'.

16

Genesis 1: 26. St James Bible.

17

Peter Yates (2001). Anangu Pitjantjatjara Lands, Social Economic and Impact Study (unpublished).

18

Community, family.

19

This Act was renamed many times, first being the Black States Constitution Act 1971, then the National States Constitution Act 1971, and finally the Self-Governing Territories Constitution Act 1971.

20

Government of the Republic of South Africa and another vs Government of KwaZulu and another, 1982(4)SA 387(A).

21

Government of the Republic of South Africa and another vs Government of KwaZulu and another 1983 (1) SA 164 (A).

22

The Rumpff Commission was appointed on 10 December 1982 by Government Notice 901.

23

The Ingwavuma Land Deal: A Case Study in Self-Determination. By TW Bennet and NS Pearl. Boston College Third World Journal, Vol 6, issue 1, (January 1986). One of the conclusions of this paper was that there were indeed historical reasons why the colonial boundaries might have been challenged, by excising Ingwavuma from South Africa. What made the entire exercise invalid was, like the apartheid government's imposition of homelands under the guise of 'self-determination', the lack of an authentic process to consult with and ascertain the will of the affected people.

24

The land that was returned to the San comprised six Kalahari farms totalling 40 000 hectares, in addition to ownership of 28 000 hectares South of the Auob river in the Kgalagadi Transfrontier Park, plus specified 'heritage rights' to the entire remainder of the Park. These details were to be finalised together with transfer of two more farms and the signature of the Ae!Hai Kalahari Heritage Park Agreement at a later ceremony in May 2002.

25

In the 1990s San Councils were elected in Namibia, Botswana and South Africa, being joined in the regional San network known as WIMSA (Working group of Indigenous Minorities in Southern Africa) to represent the San on human rights and other issues. In addition NGOs were formed, such as South African San Council in South Africa, and Kuru plus Letloa in Botswana, each playing important roles.

Mabo vs Queensland (HCA 23, (1992)175 CLR) was the landmark case that recognised the pre-colonial land rights of First Nations people within Australia's common law, and confirmed the overturning of the *terra nullius* doctrine. This led the way to "native title" as the form of ownership exercised by First Nations, and to a succession of further claims for land restitution by Aboriginal peoples in Australia.

27

In August 2002 the second stage of the land claim was celebrated, with the formal signing at the Kgalagadi Transfrontier Park of the Ae!Hai Kalahari Heritage Park Agreement.

28

The CBD objectives are 1. to Conserve biodiversity, 2. to use it sustainably and 3. to share its benefits fairly and equitably.

29

CSIR in fact licensed the P57 patent rights to a British company, Phytopharm PLC, who had in turn sub-licensed the patent to Pfizer. If Pfizer was successful, as per a number of milestones towards commercial release of the drug, a share of the profits would go to Phytopharm, and eventually to CSIR. The complexity of this licencing agreement is regardd as unnecessary for this summary account.

30

The Khoi peoples were represented by the National Khoisan Council, (NKC) which was created by President Mandela in 1999 to represent the Khoi and San peoples and to negotiate their rights under the new constitution. The NKC was made up primarily of representatives from Cape Khoi, Griqua, Nama, Koranna and San communities.

31

Rooibos primary negotiators: The San leaders were Collin Louw, Chrisjan Tieties, Zeka Shiwarra and Leana Snyders, legally supported by Roger Chennells of Chennells Albertyn. The Khoi were represented by Cecil le Fleur, Stanley Pietersen, Poem Mooney, Barend Salomo, Alida Afrika, Kennett Maarman, legally supported by Lesle Jansen of Natural Justice. The Rooibos Council was represented by Martin Bergh, Dawie de Villiers, Ernest du Toit, legally supported by Marius Diemont of Webber Wentzel. Process secretariat ably run by Marthane Swart and Margo Slabbert. Department of Forestry, Fisheries and Environment represented by Natalie Feltman, Lactitia Tshitwamulomoni and Ntambudzeni Nepfumembe. Agreement signed by DFFE Minister Barbara Creecy.

32

Two excellent articles that explain the Rooibos saga are: 1. How Justice can be Brought to South Africa's Rooibos Industry, by Rachel Wynberg (2016) https://bio-economy.org.za/rooibos-industry and 2. The Rooibos Benefit-Sharing Agreement: Breaking New Ground with Respect, Honesty, Fairness and Care

by Doris Schroeder, Roger Chennells, Collin Louw, Leana Snyders, Timothy Hodges at:
https://www.cambridge.org/core/journals/cambridge-quarterly-of-healthcare-ethics/article/rooibos-benefit-sharing-agreementbreaking-new-ground-with-respect-honesty-fairness-and-care/

Printed in the USA
CPSIA information can be obtained
at www.ICGtesting.com
LVHW081745031123
762986LV00046B/1032